OTHER BOOKS BY J. N. HOOK

The Grand Panjandrum, and 1,999 Other Rare, Useful, and Delightful Words and Expressions

People Say Things Different Ways

History of the English Language

The Story of American English

The Story of British English

English Today

The Teaching of High School English

FAMILY NAMES

FAMILY NAMES

How Our Surnames Came to America

J. N. Hook, Ph.D.

MACMILLAN PUBLISHING CO., INC. New York
COLLIER MACMILLAN PUBLISHERS London

Acknowledgment is made to the following: To Brandt & Brandt, Literary Agents, for permission to quote from Stephen Vincent Benét's *Western Star,* copyright 1943 by Farrar & Rinehart, Inc.

To G. K. Hall & Co., Publishers, for permission to quote from *Black Names in America,* collected by Newbell Niles Puckett and edited by Murray Heller, copyright 1975 by John G. White Department, Cleveland Public Library.

To Harper & Row, Publishers, for two selections: (1) From *What's Your Name?* by Louis Adamic, copyright 1942 by Louis Adamic, renewed 1970 by Stan Adamic. Reprinted by permission of Harper & Row, Publishers, Inc. (2) From "The Enemy," in *Far and Near: Stories of China, Japan, and America* by Pearl S. Buck (John Day Company), copyright 1942 by Pearl S. Buck. Reprinted by permission of Harper & Row, Publishers, Inc.

To Robert M. Sutton, professor of American History, University of Illinois at Urbana-Champaign, for reading the manuscript critically and making helpful suggestions.

To the following consultants: Dr. Lillian Lahti, Wisconsin State University, Whitewater (Finnish); Dr. Daniel Paik, Los Angeles (Korean); Professor Ryoji Inoue of Nagoya and Professor Kazuo Hoshino of Oyama (Japanese).

To Rachel G. Hook, for her help with the research and for changing her name from Gerhart.

Macmillan Publishing Co., Inc.
866 Third Avenue, New York, N.Y. 10022
Collier Macmillan Canada, Inc.

Library of Congress Cataloging in Publication Data
Hook, J. N. (Julius Nicholas), 1913–
Family names.
Bibliography: p.
Includes index.
1. Names, Personal—United States. 2. Ethnology
—United States. I. Title.
CS2487.H66 1982 929.4'0973 81-18646
ISBN 0-02-552100-4 AACR2

10 9 8 7 6 5 4 3 2 1

Designed by Jack Meserole

Printed in the United States of America

CONTENTS

Part II
THE BRITISH AND THE NORTHERN EUROPEANS

Part IV
FROM THE REST OF THE WORLD

Part V
CHANGING NAMES IN AMERICA

We [Americans] are literally the world in miniature.

—*Louis Adamic*

The true American, in the existential sense of the man who makes himself, is the immigrant, for he is American by choice. His nationality was not handed to him with his birth certificate. It came as the result of a deliberate effort. He *wanted* to *become* American. He gave up another life, and often another language, to be American. He made the leap of faith, from the web of Old-World associations to a new infancy. The true American is the one just off the boat, with a tag pinned to his coat (as in the Ellis Island days) announcing his destination, which he mispronounces.

—*Ted Morgan*
(formerly Sanche de Gramont)

Part I

THE WORLD IN MINIATURE

1

In Love with a Million Names

THIS BOOK is the history of the United States as reflected in our surnames.

I opened the Chicago telephone directory at random and faced two solid pages of people named Williams, from twenty-nine Freds and Freddies through a dozen Joyces; the rest of the Williamses occupied eight more pages. I tried again and hit some of the Browns; the left page started with thirty-three Jos Browns and the right ended with ten Robt J Browns.

Some pages back I encountered variety, 141 different surnames on a single page. Here I saw the Jewish-German Baruch, English Barwick, Polish Barwacz, Italian Basco, Russian Baskov, Armenian Basmajian, and someone named Mohammed Bashir who probably derives from another Mideastern heritage but may be a renamed black. I noted names as similar as Baskett and Baskette, others as unlike as Bill Baskerville and Anna Basladynski.

How, I used to wonder, does an assortment of names like that find its way to one page? What accidents, what developments across the seas, what dreams brought Haralenne Basaravaj and John Base or their ancestors from somewhere else to the same column of my Chicago telephone book with only a few people like Paul Basbagill, Michael Basch, Mary Baschieri, and Edward Baschleben separating them?

Why are there so many Polish names in Hamtramck, Michigan, while Grand Rapids and Holland in the same state have more than their share of Dutch names, and other Michigan communities are preponderantly Finnish, Swedish, or German? Why did so many Germans settle in Pennsylvania, so many Jewish people in New York City? Are the Latinos who are flooding in today at all similar in aspiration and promise to the Irish and the Germans of a century and a half ago, or to the Italians and central and eastern Europeans of 1880 to 1910? How, in the apartment house where I once lived in Washington, D.C., did names from about twenty national backgrounds get together in the list of residents?

And how, I also wondered, did so many different surnames originate? I checked with the Social Security Administration and found that its rolls list in the latest compilation (1974) 1,286,556 *different* surnames of Americans. Among these names more than a third are unique: there are 448,663 single occurrences of a name. Where did so many names come from—the common Smith and Jones and the unique or unusual Mr. Lz or the Jaspper that may follow a whole column of Jasper? I learn from the SSA that two Americans have the surname Q—nothing else, just Q—and that there are two X's, four Z's, twenty-four A's. In fact, every letter of the alphabet occurs singly at least twice. Who knows what the story of O is—to be exact, sixteen O's with sixteen stories?

My curiosity expanded. Do all these names, or many of them, have any common sources, any common meanings? I knew or quickly discovered that English Smith or Smythe, German Schmidt, Czech Kovar, Finnish Seppanen, Italian Farrari, Polish Kowalski, Spanish Herrera, and Syrian Haddad all mean ‹smith›, a worker with metal, as do several dozen other names and variants. And the ubiquitous "son of John" occurs as English Johnson or Jennings or Hancock,

Welsh Jones or Evans, Irish Shane, Lithuanian Jonaitis or Jonynas, Dutch Jansen or Janke (probably the source of our *Yankee*), Scandinavian Johanson or Jonsson, Yugoslavian Jovanovic(h), Hungarian Janosfi, Greek Gianakakis, Italian Di Giovanni, and Spanish Ibañez, again along with dozens of other forms. Russian Ivan Ivanoff, I found, has a name identical with John Johnson's.

For about ten years now, questions like these have absorbed part of my recreational time. I found that I was not alone. Several books had been written about surnames, including two very useful ones by a Chicago lawyer named Elsdon C. Smith, to whom my own book is much indebted. There's a magazine called *Names*. Onomastics, the study of names, is a recognized specialty among professional linguists. Over thirty years ago a book on American placenames was a Book of the Month Club main selection. And the growth of interest in genealogy, spurred in part by the tremendous success of Alex Haley's *Roots*—which sold 5 million copies in hardcover alone, was translated into 26 languages, and was seen by 130 million viewers in its televised form—has given millions of Americans an interest in names.

Many in their genealogical search have found, for instance, that different branches of their family have come to spell their name differently, or that some members have changed the name entirely, or perhaps that an immigration officer or some other public official a century ago wrote down a wrong form which now has become the accepted one. Others have learned for the first time the original, literal meaning of their name, for instance, that the first Frenchman to have the name Lesueur was named for his job, making shoes, or that Ramsbottom has nothing to do with ovine anatomy: the ancestral Ramsbottom came from the village of that name in Lancashire, and *ram* means ‹wild garlic› and *bottom* was the lowland where it grew.

In the past decade of pleasure reading I've come to love American surnames. I love their almost infinite variety. I like to find—or to imagine, if facts aren't available—the story behind each. I've spent weeks in the large genealogy room of the New York Public Library browsing through some of the endless volumes depicting or bragging about the doings and the accomplishments of dozens of the families that make up America. I've read and read about the Swiss in America, the Italian Americans and their early subservience to their *padroni*, and the hardships of nineteenth-century Pat and Mike. I've discovered the varied reasons why so many people have found their ways across the seas to our shores, and why the early settlers of each nationality settled where they did.

I've learned the fascinating story of how black men and women, once slaves, chose their own names when the shackles were cut, and I've noted the well-known change of Cassius Clay into Muhammad Ali. I've traced the transformation of Sczymczak into Simon or Simpson, and the somewhat different evolution of an occasional Rosenheimer through Rosenheim, Rosen, and Rose to an "American" Ross.

This book is a distillate of what I have learned about surnames and their role in America's development. It's a love story, really, and it's unabashedly sentimental at times. My love affair with surnames has intensified my affection for America. Those names represent what America was and is, hint what it can be.

In my church one family is named Thetphasone. They've not been here long. They're Laotians caught up in the troubles in Indochina, forced to flee their country, found somehow and adopted by our small-town church. Except for the teenage girl, they speak almost no English. The father has a job as a laborer, the mother knits beautifully and sells the results, the three children are in school.

No one, of course, can specifically predict what will happen to the Thetphasones. But the probabilities, in light of our national experience, are that they will stay in this country; they will eventually shorten and simplify their name; their children and *their* children will all read and write English; most of them will vote; they will continue to earn honest livings; Laos will become for them only the name of a place dimly connected with the family's past; they will learn the latest slang and the latest dances and the names of the latest star entertainers; some will marry Americans who are not of Laotian descent; some will live in *your* state and perhaps your city (for Americans are mobile); and some of them will make a recognizably positive contribution to society, to American well-being—will reach, if not *Who's Who,* at least a school honor roll or a commendatory note in a factory newsletter. Most of us, in retrospect, are like the Thetphasones. Now and then I despair because we never come close to our potential, but in general I love us, us Thetphasones and our stories.

Woodrow Wilson, addressing a group of newly naturalized citizens in 1915, said,

> Fellow Citizens: . . . You have taken an oath of allegiance to a great ideal, to a great body of principles, to a great hope of the human race. . . . And while you bring all countries with you, you come with a purpose of leaving all other countries behind you—bringing what is best of their spirit, but not looking over your shoulders and seeking to perpetuate what you intended to leave behind in them. I certainly would not be one even to suggest that a man cease to love the home of his birth and the nation of his origin—these things are very sacred and ought not to be put out of our hearts—but it is one thing to love the place where you were born and it is another thing to dedicate yourself to the place to which you go. . . .
>
> We cannot exempt you from work. No man is exempt from work anywhere in the world. We cannot exempt you from the strife and the heartbreaking burden of the struggle of the day—that is common to mankind everywhere; we cannot exempt you from the loads that you must carry. We can only make them light by the spirit in which they are carried. That is the spirit of hope, it is the spirit of liberty, it is the spirit of justice.

2

From a World Without Surnames

WHEN the world's population was small and even a city might hold only a few thousand people, and when most folks never got more than ten or fifteen miles from their birthplace (usually walking), and when messages were sent by personal messenger rather than by impersonal post, there was hardly a necessity for more than one name. Even kings got by with a single name. When someone referred to King David, there was no need to ask David who?

No one knows who first felt the need to apply any name at all to himself or any of his fellows. According to Pliny, some ancient tribes were *anonymi* ‹nameless› and it is barely possible that a few *anonymi* may still exist in remote corners of the world. But for the most part personal names of some sort exist wherever there are human beings. As British onomatist C. L. Ewen has said,

> The most general custom among the savage tribes was to give a child the name of a deceased ancestor, but any descriptive word which might indicate sex, order of birth, race, caste, office, physi-

cal feature, god, historical fact, or a more fanciful concept, served the purpose of a distinguishing label.

"A distinguishing label"—that of course is what a name is. It differentiates one person from another, allowing a mother to single out one child's attention, helping an officer to address a command to an individual, assisting any of us to carry out our daily tasks that depend on distinguishing one person from another.

Customs in naming have varied considerably, and some seem strange to us. Ewen mentioned an African tribe in which young boys had names that were changed to something else at puberty, and another tribe in which a father took a new name when his first child was born, his virility having thus been confirmed. Members of other tribes change their names after serious illness or when they get old. Some American Indians had different names for different seasons. People of Dahomey, in East Africa, once had several names, including some that named guardian spirits and others that were kept secret except from intimates. Some names have been very long: *The Encyclopedia of Religion and Ethics* mentions a Babylonian name that can be translated "O Ashur, the lord of heaven and earth, give him life." To this day, the Balinese have no surnames, and as youngsters many often change their personal names. They do have caste and birth-order designations that stay with them all their lives.

The ancient Greeks generally used only single names (Sophocles and Plato, for example), but occasionally employed additional phrases for further identification. Thus Alexander, whom we describe as "the Great," was Alexandros o Philippon ‹Alexander the son of Phillip›.

During Rome's centuries of greatness, Romans—especially those of the upper classes—were likely to have three names, like Gaius Julius Caesar. The *praenomen* (Gaius) corresponded to our given names. The *nomen* or *nomen gentilium* (Julius) identified the clan or tribe *(gens)*, which usually consisted of a number of families sharing this name. The *cognomen* (Caesar) designated the particular family within the *gens*. There might even be a fourth name, called an *agnomen*, which could be a mark of distinction (like "Africanus" bestowed on Scipio after military victories in Africa), or just an additional mark of identification (for instance, Emperor Octavian, born Gaius Octavius, added the name Julius Caesar after Gaius, but retained Octavianus as an *agnomen*). During the period of Rome's decline, some persons adopted or were given even more names—as many as thirty-six.

In Roman times the *cognomens* were most like our surnames. They were hereditary, and they usually fell into the same classifications as English and Continental names (for more on this see page 13). Some indicated the place from which the family had come or with which it was associated: Gnaeus Marcius Coriolanus, about whom Shakespeare wrote a play, is said to have won the battle of Corioli in 493 B.C. A few names are those of ancestors: Agrippa, the family name of some of the descendants of Herod the Great. Some plebeians bore *cognomens* that named their occupations, as Metellus ‹servant›, Missor ‹archer›. The Romans especially liked descriptive *cognomens,* as Sapiens ‹the wise›, Crassus ‹the fat›, or Marcellus ‹the little hammer›.

After the fall of Rome, multiple names largely disappeared for a few centuries throughout Europe, although compound names were fairly frequent in some places. Thus Irish Faolchadh was a compound of ‹wolf› and ‹warrior›, and the German Gerhard was compounded of ‹spear› and ‹firm›.

In the tenth century Venetian noblemen began to adopt hereditary family names. This custom was to be followed later by the Irish, the French, the English, and then the Germans and other Europeans.

Suppose that you were living in England in the Middle Ages. Suppose further that your name was John. Not John Something—just John. The Somethings did not yet exist in England. King or commoner, you were just John.

Your male ancestors had also been John, or Thomas, Robert, Harold, Richard, William, or more anciently Eadgar or Eadwine or Aelfred, and their wives may have been Alice, Joan, Berthe, Blanche, Beatrice, Margaret, Marie, Inga, or Grette. Most names of your day were Norman French, since the descendants of William the Conqueror and his followers ruled the land. Huntingdon, for instance, had only 1 percent recognizably Anglo-Saxon names in A.D. 1295.

The number of different names was not large. The same Huntingdon list shows that 18 percent of all males in that county were called William, 16 percent John, 10 percent Richard, and 7 percent Robert, and that only 28 other names made up the remainder. So over half of these men shared only 4 names. In Yorkshire in the fourteenth century, in a list of 19,600 mixed male and female names, C. L. Ewen found that John accounted for 17 percent of the total, followed by William, Thomas, and Robert, with Alice (5 percent) and Joan (4 percent in various spellings) the most popular names for women. There were some biblical names other than John—almost 2 percent Adam, for example—but the popularity of Peter, Paul, Abraham, David, and others was still in the future.

England, like other countries in the Middle Ages, was mainly a rural and male-dominated society. There were no large cities. Some groups of people lived within the walls of a castle or nearby; still others clustered in villages from which workers trudged short distances each day to tend the crops or the livestock, or where they remained to do their smithing, wagon making, tailoring, or other tasks. Women often worked beside the men in the fields, and in a family wealthy enough to have its own cow or a few pigs or sheep, the women were likely to be responsible for the animals' care. Women's liberation was centuries away and largely undreamed of—although older England had had some strong queens, and Shakespeare's plays would later reflect some influence of women on medieval national affairs. In general, women were subservient, and their subservience was to be shown in the naming processes getting under way.

Almost all the occupational names, for example, refer to work done mainly or entirely by men in the Middle Ages, and countless fathers but few mothers were memorialized in names that would become family names. Had women's prestige been higher we would today have many persons with names like Milkmaid, Buxom, and Margaretson.

If the Middle Ages had been urbanized, no doubt the use of second names would have accelerated. If a city has three thousand Williams, ways must be found to indicate which William one talks about. A typical medieval village, though, might have had only five or ten Williams, a similar number of Johns, and maybe two or three Roberts or Thomases.

Even so, distinctions often needed to be made. If two villagers were talking about you (John, you remember, is who you are), misunderstandings would arise if each had a different John in mind. So qualifications were added, as in imaginary bits of conversation like these:

"A horse stepped on John's foot."
"John from the hill?"
"No. John of the dale."

"John the son of William?"
"No. John the son of Robert."

"John the smith?"
"No. John the tailor."

"John the long?"
"No. John the bald."

In the rush of conversation the little, unimportant words could drop out or be slurred over so that John from the hill became John hill, and the other persons could be John dale, John William's son, John Robert's son, John smith, John tailor, John long, and John bald (or ballard, which means ‹the bald one›). The capital letters that we now associate with surnames are only scribal conventions introduced later on.

Distinctions like those illustrated in the conversations were a step toward surnames. But the son of John the smith might be Robert the wainwright ‹wagon maker›. That is, he did not inherit the designation *smith* from his father. There were no true English surnames—family names—until Robert the son of John smith became known as Robert smith (or Smith) even though his occupation was a wainwright, a fletcher ‹arrow maker›, a tanner or barker ‹leather worker›, or anything else. Only when the second name was passed down from one generation to the next did it become a surname.

That step did not occur suddenly or uniformly, although throughout most of Europe it was a medieval development. Ewen has described the details of the development in England, basing his scholarly analysis on thousands of entries in tax rolls, court records, and other surviving documents. He has pointed out that before the fourteenth century most of the differentiating adjuncts were prefaced by *filius* ‹son of›, as in Adam fil' Gilberti ‹Adam, son of Gilbert›, by *le* ‹the›, as in Beaudrey le Teuton, by *de* ‹of, from›, as in Rogerius de Molis ‹Roger from the mills›, or by *atta* ‹at the›, as in John atte Water ‹John at the water›, which later might be John Atwater. These particles often dropped out. Thus a fourteenth-century scribe began writing his name as David Tresruf, but other evidence shows that Tresruf was simply a place name and that David de Tresruf was the way the scribe earlier wrote his name.

Almost all English and Continental surnames fall into the four categories I have illustrated:

Place Names	John Hill, John Atwater
Patronyms (or others based on personal names)	John Robertson, John Williams, John Alexander
Occupational Names	John Smith, John Fletcher
Descriptive Names	John Long, John Armstrong

With a few exceptions the million-plus surnames that Americans bear are of these four sorts. If we were mainly an Oriental or an African nation, the patterns would be different. But we are primarily European in our origins, and in Europe it seemed natural to identify each person during the surname-giving period according to location, parentage, occupation, appearance or other characteristics.

It never used to occur to me that my name and almost everyone else's name has a meaning, now often unknown even to its possessors. My own name, I found, is a place name. A *hook* is a sharp bend in a stream or a peninsula or some odd little corner of land. My paternal ancestors, who came from Somerset in southern England, lived on such a hook, probably one of the many irregularly shaped bits of land in Somerset. The numerous Hookers, like General Joseph Hooker in the Civil War, lived in similar places in the name-giving period. Hocking(s), Hoke(r), Horn(e), and Horman(n) are other English or German names that share the meaning of Hook, so they are my cousins, by semantics though not by blood. So are the Dutch Hoekstra, van Hoek, and Haack, who lived in their own odd little corners in the Netherlands.

By coincidence, my mother's father (part Finnish, mostly German) bore a name that also referred to a bend or angle. He was Engel, and his ancestors had lived in Angeln, in Schleswig in northern Germany. The Angles who came in the fifth century to the British Isles with the Saxons, Jutes, and Frisians to help the Celts against the savage Picts (but eventually drove their hosts to the western and northern reaches of the islands) took their name from the same German area, and England—Angle-land historically—is named for them. Angeln got its name because it was shaped somewhat like a fishhook; the word is obviously related to *angle* and the sport of *angling*.

In this book I'll briefly define many surnames. Many more are defined in Elsdon Smith's *New Dictionary of American Family Names* (Harper and Row, 1973).

The fourfold identification of people by place, ancestry, occupation, or description has worked well, and only science fiction writers today ever suggest that our names may or should be replaced by numbers or number-letter combinations. Even an ordinary name like William Miller, George Rivers, or Anne Armstrong can acquire an individuality and a rememberable quality hard to imagine for 27-496-3821 or Li94T8633. I'd probably not enjoy a love affair with American names that looked like mere license plate identifications.

The proportion in each category of names may vary from one European language to another. Thus 70 percent or more of Irish, Welsh, and Scandinavian surnames are patronyms. Spanish families have also preferred patronyms, but place names are not far behind. In France patronyms lead once more, but names of occupations are in second place. In Germany, however, patronyms of the simple English sort are relatively few, although hereditary combinative descriptions like the previously mentioned Gerhard (page 10) are common, occupational names are frequent, and place names not uncommon. In most countries personal descriptive surnames lag behind the others.

Elsdon Smith analyzed seven thousand of our most common American surnames and found these proportions:

	PERCENTAGE
Place names	43.13
Patronyms	32.23
Occupational names	15.16
Nicknames (descriptives)	9.48

In an analysis that I made of several hundred American surnames of English origin, I obtained the following percentages:

	PERCENTAGE
Place names	35.49
Patronyms	32.37
Occupational names	19.66
Personal descriptors	12.47

The fact that large numbers of American surnames are derived from England is reflected in the similarities between Smith's percentages and mine.

Often, superficially different American surnames turn out to be essentially the same name in meaning when translated from the foreign language into English. I've already mentioned some of the foreign equivalents of the occupational name Smith and the patronym Johnson.

Place names, often unique or nearly so, are not likely to be internationally duplicated except when they refer to geographically common features like bodies of water or land masses. We may illustrate the possibilities with the English surname Hill, whose German equivalent may be Buhl, Buehler, Knor(r), or Piehl, paralleled by Dutch Hoger and

Hoogland (literally ‹high land›), French Depew and Dumont, Italian Costa and Colletti, Finnish Maki (one of Finland's most common names), Hungarian Hegi, Scandinavian Berg, Bergen, Bagge, and Haugen, and Slavic Kopec, Kopecky, and Pagorak, all of which mean ‹hill› or ‹small mountain›.

Differences in size or in skin or hair coloration are international, as many of our personal descriptive surnames confirm. English Brown and Black, for instance, may refer to either dark skin or brown or black hair. (*Black,* however, sometimes comes from the Old English *blac,* related to our *bleach* and meaning ‹white› or ‹light›, so Mr. Black's ancestors may have been either fair or dark.) Blake is a variant of Black. The French know the dark person as Le Brun or Moreau, the Germans as Braun, Brun, Mohr, or Schwartz, the Italians as Bruno, the Russians as Chernoff. Pincus refers to a dark-skinned Jew, Mavros to a dark Greek. Dark Irishmen may be named, among other possibilities, Carey, Duff, Dunn(e), Dolan, Dow, or Kearns. Hungarian Fekete has a dark skin. Czechoslovakian Cerny or Czerny ‹black› reveals his linguistic similarity to Polish Czarnik, Czarniak, or Czarnecki and Ukrainian Corney. Spanish Negron is a very dark person.

Many names spelled identically are common to two or more languages, and a considerable number of such names have more than a single meaning. So Gray, although usually an English name meaning ‹gray haired›, in a few instances is French for a person from Gray ‹the estate of Gradus› in France. Gray must therefore be classified both as a personal descriptor and a place name. Hoff is usually German for a farm or an enclosed place, but less often is English for Hoff ‹pagan temple›, a place in Westmoreland. Many Scandinavian names are identical in Denmark, Norway, and Sweden, although spelling variants such as *-sen* and *-son* suggest the likelihood of one country rather than another. In general a person must know at least a little about his or her ancestry before determining with assurance the nationality and most likely meaning of his or her name.

A small percentage of names, few of them common in the

United States, is derived from sources other than the basic four. For example, a few Jewish names are based on acronyms or initials. Thus Baran or Baron sometimes refers to *B*en *Ra*bbi *N*achman, and Brock to *B*en *R*abbi *K*alman. Zak, abbreviating *z*era *k*edoshim ‹the seed of martyrs›, is often respelled Sack, Sacks, or Sachs, although these may also be place names for people from Saxony. Katz is sometimes based on *k*ohen *tz*edek ‹priest of righteousness›, and Segal (in several spellings) can be *seg*an *l*eviyyah ‹member of the tribe of Levi›.

Other Jewish names are somewhat arbitrary German or Yiddish pairings, usually with pleasant connotations, like Lowenthal ‹lions' valley›, Gottlieb ‹God's love›, or Finkelstein ‹little finch stone›. Some modern Swedes have replaced their conventional patronyms (Hanson, Jorgenson, etc.) with nature words or pairings of nature words, like Lind ‹linden›, Lindstrom ‹linden stream›, Asplund ‹aspen grove›, or Ekberg ‹oak mountain›.

Numerous Norwegian surnames are a special variety of place names called farm names. Many Norwegian farms have held the same name for hundreds of years, and people from a given farm have come to be known by its name. So Bjornstad, for instance, means ‹Bjorn's farm›, and Odega(a)rd means ‹dweller on uncultivated land›.

Japanese names are comparable to some of the Jewish and Swedish names mentioned a moment ago, in that they frequently combine two words, one or both of which may refer to nature. So Fujikawa combines two elements meaning ‹wisteria› and ‹river›, Hayakawa is ‹early, river›, Tanaka is ‹ricefield, middle›, Inoue is ‹well (noun), upper›, and Kawasaki is ‹river, headland›.

Chinese surnames are very few—perhaps nine or ten hundred in all—and endlessly repeated. A few dozen of them are especially widely used, like the familiar Wong, which may mean either ‹field› or ‹large body of water›, Chin (the name of the first great dynasty, of more than two thousand years ago), Wang ‹yellow› or ‹prince›, Le ‹pear tree›, and Yee ‹I›.

The names given foundlings could readily provide material for a full chapter. Bastard as an appellation was once freely applied to foundlings or any illegitimate children even among royalty and the nobility, but today the name is opprobrious and there are few if any Bastards listed in American directories. Italian Esposito is the same as Spanish Exposita, for which the Italian spelling is generally substituted. Other Italian names suggest the blessedness or holiness of the foundling: De Benedictis, De Angelis, De Santis, and della Croce ‹one who lives near the cross›.

The English Foundling Hospital authorities once conferred noble or famous names on foundlings, who thus might be named Bedford, Marlborough, Pembroke, or the like, or sometimes Geoffrey Chaucer, John Milton, Francis Bacon, Oliver Cromwell, or even Peter Paul Rubens. Some names were taken from fiction: Tom Jones, Clarissa Harlowe, Sophia Western. Other foundlings were given the names of places where they were found: e.g., Lawrence because the infant was found in St. Lawrence. A little girl in a waiting room of the Southern Railway was named Frances Southern.

Not more than one American surname in twenty, however, can be classified with assurance in any category other than the big four: places, patronyms, occupations, and descriptors.

3

The Beginnings of Our Rivers of Names

THE FIRST IMMIGRANTS to North America were probably those people we call Indians or, more recently but not much more accurately, native Americans. But scientists still argue about just where the Indians came from and when and how. And we know nothing of the names they carried with them in our prehistory. Nor do we yet have much specific information about the pre-Columbian settlers, apparently fairly numerous, who came here not only from Scandinavia but also from Ireland and perhaps other parts of Europe, Asia, and North Africa. The total number of "Indians," including any possibly surviving descendants of these other early settlers, was not large when Columbus came: Some demographers estimate that north of Mexico there were barely a million inhabitants in the fifteenth century.

The first European settlers after Columbus whose settlement has survived were the Spanish founders of Saint Augustine, Florida, in 1565. The English were responsible for the ill-starred Jamestown Colony, starting in 1607. That date is usually given as the beginning of the first of the four major periods of American immigration:

1. The Colonial Period and the New Nation, 1607–1790
2. The Western and Northern Europeans, 1790–1880
3. The Eastern and Southern Europeans, 1880–1914
4. The Years Since World War I

These time boundaries are somewhat artificial. There were Italian and Slavic immigrants before 1880, and many Irish, Germans, and Scandinavians after that date. But the chronological division is useful in describing a fairly well defined pattern.

In coming to the New World, most of the early French and Spanish had different motives from many of the British. The British often came to colonize, to settle permanently, but the motto of the French and the Spaniards, much more often, could have been "Take the money and run." So they captured in their traps the seemingly endless wild animals whose pelts were so valuable to Europeans, and they sought gold or anything else of value that could easily be shipped back home. Had the French or the Spanish been more inclined toward colonization, had they been willing to suffer the hardships of a Jamestown or a Plymouth, the history of this nation might have been very different. It might have been different, too, if the Dutch and the Swedes, who established colonies in the seventeenth century, had been more numerous or more unified in purpose.

As it is, the story of the colonial population and the first years of the new nation is largely a British story—usually English but with an often inseparable admixture of Welsh, Scottish, and Irish. The Jamestown Colony did have a handful of Frenchmen and a few Italians, but it was 99 percent British. So were most of the other colonies that I'll talk about soon.

By 1790, the year of the first American census, the total white population of the infant nation was 3,172,444. Of those, 79 percent were identifiably British, including English, Scottish, Welsh, and Irish.

That proportion changed considerably during the next

ninety years. That's why you perhaps have neighbors named Schultz, Anderson, and a few O'Briens or Ryans, for hundreds of thousands of Germans, Irish, and Scandinavians joined the British already here. Germany sent a million from 1815 to 1860 alone, Ireland two million during the same years, and Norway and Sweden forty thousand who in effect looked over the country before beckoning to their friends and relatives back home. Forty thousand others arrived from Switzerland, twenty thousand from the Netherlands. The discovery of gold in California lured adventurers—and settlers—not only from much of Europe but also from South America and from China, half a world away.

In 1784 and 1785 tribes of Indians had ceded to the government vast stretches of land west of the Niagara River, as well as other areas in the South. Tennessee County, "the region of the big bend of the Tennessee," was formed. An independent state of Franklin (named obviously for Benjamin Franklin, whose name means ‹freeholder›) was set up in the South but survived only from 1784 to 1788. Land fever was raging in areas that earlier pioneers had believed would never be settled.

In 1785 Congress passed a Land Ordinance that provided for surveys in the West and the division of land into townships divisible into square-mile sections that could be sold at a dollar an acre. In 1787 the Northwest Ordinance provided for eventual statehood for areas north of the Ohio River.

Explorers and trappers had returned to the East with sometimes exaggerated stories of the richness of the land and the ease of living farther west. The land abounded in game, they said, and the rivers teemed with fish eager to leap into the frying pan. There were trees for building cabins but endless open land for wheat. A few shrewd traders and speculators were already making fortunes from furs and real estate. Their would-be emulators were numerous: "Let's get our share."

Transportation was becoming easier. The Philadelphia-Lancaster Turnpike, completed in 1794, made that first leg of a westward journey relatively simple. At about the same time the Knoxville Road, the Wilderness Road, and the Old

Walton Road were making parts of Tennessee and Kentucky more accessible. The building of Zane's Trace, the first road through Ohio, was authorized by Congress in 1796; it became a major highway for immigrants. The easiest passes, or "gaps," were found through the mountains. Where nothing more could yet be done, scouts blazed trails through the wilderness. The building of canals began. Larger boats than before were plying inland waters.

Information about the resources of inland America spread through much of Europe. Emigration to the young American nation was retarded for a while, though, by the Napoleonic wars and the British-American War of 1812. Meanwhile, the desire to share in the opportunities of the United States was increasing, but the actual number of immigrants was not very substantial until the 1820s, when there were 151,000 of them.

The 1830s brought about 600,000 to our shores, and that number almost tripled in the 1840s. The 1850s saw yet another climb, to over 2 million. Even in the Civil War years no fewer than 91,000 immigrants arrived in any one year, and in 1866, the war over, the figure jumped to 318,000. The period 1871–80 set a new record of 2,810,000 for a decade.

Of all these immigrants, Germany between 1861 and 1880 sent a million and a half to join those already here, England and Scotland and Wales over a million, Ireland about 875,000, and the Scandinavian countries 368,000—a huge number from those not very thickly populated lands.

In an excellent analysis of immigration, Maldwyn Jones isolated several basic reasons for the flow toward America during much of the nineteenth century. The first is that from 1750 to 1850 Europe's own population doubled, partly because of improved health care and sanitation, and partly because of increasing knowledge of agriculture and the spreading discovery of the potato as a source of nutrition. The larger population resulted in less available land per capita. A second reason was that much cottage industry was replaced by factory work, and in consequence thousands of formerly self-employed persons could no longer sell their products and needed to move in order to survive. Third, small farms were gobbled up by large landholders, and those who had previously eked out a living by tilling the soil lost their livelihood.

Political and religious changes also contributed to the urge to seek a better life somewhere else. Jones explains, "By far the largest group to [emigrate] came with the failure of the revolutions of 1848 in Germany, Italy, and Austria-Hungary and the simultaneous collapse of the Young Ireland movement." Norwegian Quakers, opponents of the Dutch Reformed Church, and German Lutherans who could not endure the members of the United Evangelical Church (and vice versa) contributed to the flow because of the religious differences in their respective countries. Mormons from Scandinavia and Great Britain sought their Zion in the American West.

The Europeans found information about America ever more available. Books and pamphlets about the United States were printed in abundance, and travel agents, shipping lines, and American railroads prepared glowing accounts and sometimes offered great transportation bargains. European newspapers published feature stories on the whys and hows of emigration. Letters from relatives and friends in America often provided the clinching arguments for pulling up one's roots, because even otherwise untrusting folk felt that what these persons wrote must be true.

Each of America's periods of prosperity brought a new influx. Word of a depression stemmed the flow, but it started again with news that the American economy was again moving up. America had "panics," as depressions or recessions were then called, in 1819, 1837, 1857, and 1873, each followed by a year or more of reduced immigration and then followed in turn by a renewed flow. For example, 1857 saw us welcoming a total of 251,000 immigrants, but in 1858 there were only 123,000. Then the trend was upward until the Civil War intervened.

Leaving the "old country" became easier as the nineteenth century advanced. Nations like Great Britain that had formerly put up legal barriers against those who wanted to get out repealed them. Transportation became relatively inexpensive. As many as two thousand ships hauled North American timber to Great Britain, and although they returned westward with various British products, there was generally room for a few passengers. A thousand more vessels carried cotton to British ports, and they too welcomed a few paying passengers on the way back. These passengers would usually not have to travel far to embark, for the small ships used upwards of seventy ports in the British Isles.

On the Continent, railroads were being built, and they carried emigrants to Le Havre, Bremen, Hamburg, or less busy ports. As a result of so much competition, transatlantic fares were reduced by two-thirds in the first half of the century. A steerage berth, although uncomfortable, was available from Liverpool to New York for as little as 3 pounds; from Le Havre to New Orleans for 120 francs. Many Americans sent money or tickets to relatives or close friends still in Europe, and some businessmen paid the fares of workers they especially needed. The consummation of many a marriage awaited receipt of a ticket from the United States.

Sailing vessels still took one, two, even three months for the crossing, and passengers were certainly often uncomfortably crowded. Deaths en route were not infrequent. Cholera and ship fever took their toll. But after the Civil War, sails gradually gave way to steam, and the length of each voyage was cut to a fourth of the previous time.

We Americans have always been of two minds about newcomers to our land, and we still are in the 1980s, as large numbers of people enter, often uninvited, from Mexico, Cuba, the Caribbean, and parts of the Orient. The more generous of us, or perhaps the more historical minded, recall that our own ancestors were given opportunities here that they might not have had elsewhere, and are eager or at least not unwilling to let others have comparable chances. If we are patriotic, we reason that immigrants have made the United States what it is; each fresh group of immigrants has made its special contribution. Still more immigrants will presumably further enhance our country's greatness.

On the other side, some of us fear that the country is growing too fast, that our resources, considerable though they are, will be rapidly depleted by the incoming hordes, that the values we cherish will be supplanted by foreign beliefs which we consider untenable. We argue often that every incoming worker is a potential threat to some American's job. And we ask, "If the shoe were on the other foot, and we needed to escape a tyrannous regime or acute poverty, would those other countries be likely to let us in?"

In the early days of our republic such opposing views were dramatized in long debates over naturalization. A few persons argued that only someone born in America should ever be an American citizen. (If they had won, my ancestors and perhaps yours could not have become citizens.) At the other extreme, some, including Thomas Jefferson, asserted that every newcomer should be accepted as a citizen as soon as the request was made.

In 1790 the Naturalization Act specified a period of residence of two years prior to citizenship. In 1795 this period was increased to five years. In 1797 some members of Congress unsuccessfully demanded a twenty-dollar tax, equivalent to several hundred dollars today, on each certificate of naturalization. In 1798 the probationary period was increased to fourteen years. Then in 1802 it was changed back to five years, as it is today.

Each new group of immigrants has faced hostility. Many Irish workers had trouble in securing employment, sometimes because Americans of English descent recalled old English-Irish conflicts in the British Isles. Many French people were distrusted because they did not speak English, because Englishmen and Frenchmen had fought one another in war after war for centuries, and because the French were Roman Catholics in a mainly Protestant land. Even the Huguenots were not considered "true" Protestants, despite the many who had died for their religion. Germans were believed to be too seclusive, and their loyalty to the United States was questioned as late as World War I, even when thousands of young men of German descent were marching off with other

Americans to fight Kaiser Bill. The Scandinavians fared better than most, for there were fewer of them, and they tended to be out of sight on the farms and in the small towns and cities in places like Wisconsin or Minnesota or the Dakotas that few people in the East knew much about.

4

The Flood

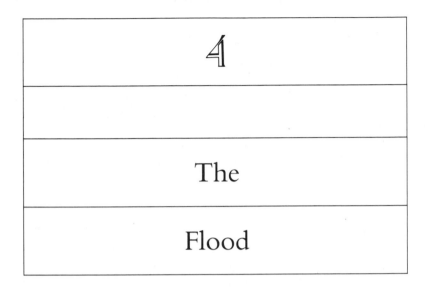

BETWEEN 1880 and 1914 eastern and southern Europeans were by far the most numerous immigrants. Some pertinent figures are in the table on page 28. Perhaps some of your own ancestors or those of some of your friends are hidden among these thousands. The figures for the eastern European countries include large numbers of Jews: immigration authorities kept records on the basis of national boundaries, not religions.

It is true that immigration from the former major contributors did not stop. Yet the United States had a half million *fewer* Irish-born people in 1910 than in 1880; in other words, Irish deaths and out-migration exceeded in-migration by that number. English-born increased by about a fourth in the period, Scottish-born by over a half; the Welsh did not quite hold their own. The Scandinavians, though, came at a much faster pace than before, with Norwegian-born increasing from 182,000 to 404,000, Swedish from 194,000 to 665,000, and Danish and Icelandic from 64,000 to 182,000. The German rate slowed but still resulted in a net gain; in 1880 we

Immigrants from Southern and Eastern Europe

	Number of Foreign-born in America in 1880	Number of Foreign-born in America in 1910	Increase (%)
Poles	49,000	1,140,000	2,227
Czechoslovakians	(unknown)	362,000†	—
Hungarians	12,000	496,000	4,033
Yugoslavians	(unknown)	169,000†	—
Russians*	36,000	1,184,000	3,189
Romanians	(unknown)	66,000	—
Bulgarians	(unknown)	11,000	—
Turks, in Europe	1,000	32,000	3,100
Greeks	1,000	101,000	10,000
Italians	44,000	1,343,000	2,952
Spanish	5,000	22,000	347
Portuguese	8,000	59,000	638

*Including Latvians, Estonians, Lithuanians.
†1920.

had just under 2 million German-born people here, and in the next thirty years the figure reached 2.3 million. In sum, although these groups gained a net total of about a million, the majority of whom were Scandinavians, they contributed only about a seventh of the total increase in the foreign born. Most of the rest came from the groups shown in the list.

There were other, smaller donors. The number of Asian foreign-born in America increased from 108,000 to 191,000, even though the Chinese Exclusion Act of 1882 had resulted in reducing the Chinese-born population by half. The Japanese had taken up the slack, growing from a mere 401 in 1880 to 67,744 in 1910. The number from Armenia, Syria, and other parts of the Middle East (which was then usually called the Near East) had grown from a small but indeterminate number to some 60,000. A few thousand had come here from India, and the numbers born in Africa, Australia, and various Pacific Islands, never large in those times, had doubled from an earlier 13,000. Approximately 18,000 Americans in 1910, mostly of Portuguese descent, had been born in the Azores.

Worried by changes in patterns of immigration in the 1880s, various Americans joined the Immigration Restriction League, the American Protective Association, and similar organizations. Sometimes the worriers became shrill, as did Rena M. Atchison in her book called *Un-American Immigration* (1894), in which she complained about the "rapid deterioration" in the quality of immigrants:

> If foreign immigration continues at the present rate and such immigration continues to come from middle, southern, and northeastern Europe, in 1900 the Anglo-Saxon institutions will no longer be the dominant powers in molding American life and legislation. Will the heir to the heroes of Lexington and Concord, Shiloh and Gettysburg, be still the victorious leader in the battlefield of new ideas? Will the heir to America's Magna Carta, created by the genius of Hamilton and Washington and sealed by the blood of Lincoln, be still the man of destiny—not only preserving in their integrity our free institutions in the spirit and intent of their founders and defenders but also leading a people, absolutely free, toward the solution of the greater issues on the ever widening horizon of progress?

After 1892 the federal government, which previously had left entrance formalities largely in the hands of local authorities, took over the responsibility. It abandoned Castle Garden, the former reception center at the south end of Manhattan, and began using Ellis Island in the harbor. The spacious but drafty halls of this center gave literally millions of immigrants their first view of their new home, and the kind of welcome that federal officials gave them—warm and kindly from some, supercilious and insulting from a few, impersonal from most—offered these people their first impressions of Americans.

In the years from 1915 through 1918 war and the hazards of crossing the ocean in wartime cut immigration to a fraction of what it had been. But the preceding ten-year period, 1905 through 1914, brought us an amazing 10,122,000 immigrants, averaging more than a million a year. Of these, close to a fifth were Italian, and central and eastern Europe sent many more than that, although changing European boundary lines and consequent Immigration Bureau score-keeping make exact nation-by-nation figures sometimes impossible to ascertain.

The lives of many of the immigrants in the period before and after 1900 were perhaps more difficult than those of their predecessors. Most were poor and uneducated, little housing was available, and the dingy rooms that were all that they could afford were often sweltering in summer, barely heated in winter. Sometimes a single room was shared by more than one family. Often all members of a family had to work twelve or fourteen hours a day merely to exist. Edwin Markham, a poet who earlier had aroused compassion for "the man with the hoe," wrote for *Cosmopolitan Magazine* (January 1907) an article that said, "In New York City alone, 60,000 children are shut up in the home sweatshops," because "a child may add to the family purse from 50 cents to $1.50 a week." When not sewing garments in a half-lighted room, the child might be responsible for deliveries: "Nearly any hour on the East Side of New York City you can see them—pallid boy or splindling girl—their faces dulled, their backs bent under a heavy load of garments piled on head and shoulder, the muscles of the whole frame in a long strain."

A high proportion of the new immigrants were Roman Catholics, and that fact posed added problems in a mainly Protestant country. True, most Irish were Catholics, too, but even they did not always equate the newcomers' religion with their own. Some of the new priests wanted to hold their flocks together as well as they could, so they encouraged enclaves of the same nationality or even from the same old-country region. They often preached against the ungodly ways of those not of their own kind and discouraged social mixing, let alone intermarriage.

About a third of each year's immigrants settled, at least for a while, in New York City, which thus gained much of its still-large Jewish population—many of them voluntary exiles from Russia—its hundreds of thousands of Italians, and its reputation as being the most variegated of the world's cities.

Others in the flow went to Massachusetts or Rhode Island, where they often joined Quebec French in the textile mills. Railroads were still to be built, and Italians and Poles and Lithuanians and others began to replacc the Irish and the Chinese who had done so much of the earlier building. The Scandinavians and the reduced numbers of Germans continued especially to the upper Midwest, although some lingered in eastern cities or intermediate places or pushed farther toward the West Coast.

Most Jews preferred cities, and many filtered from New York to Cleveland, Chicago, and other large places. Cities grew rapidly, for some Irish and Germans were still coming to them and many of the central and eastern Europeans had too little money to go to the farmlands some would have preferred. Six cities exceeded a half million people by 1900, and thirty-two others had passed a hundred thousand. Large populations required more shops, more transportation, more newspapers, more doctors and lawyers and teachers. Streets needed to be built or improved, electrical and telephone wires provided, sewer pipes buried and then dug up periodically. Fingerlike streetcar tracks reached out toward Manhattan suburbs, toward Chicago's south and west sides. Men like Potter Palmer, whose surname means ‹pilgrim carrying palm branches›, grew from small-shop proprietors to millionaire entrepreneurs whose wives could rule the society of Chicago or Newport.

Across the country, railroads encouraged would-be farmers with a little money to travel west by offering to sell them at low prices portions of the land earlier granted the railroad companies by the government. Sometimes a small abandoned farm in nearby New Jersey or Connecticut or upstate New York could be had for almost nothing; some of today's prosperous truck farmers are the grandchildren of the Italians or Poles who bought it.

More and more mine shafts needed to be dug, more iron ore smelted, more trees cut down, more houses and factories built. Company-owned houses could often be rented, and company stores would give credit so that their high-priced food and clothing could be purchased on time and paid for with interest. Some immigrants went hungry, a few may even have starved to death, but most eventually found niches of some sort in the American economy. Business flourished as the population grew, at a time when there still seemed no limits to what could be taken from the fertile soil and the deep mines or open pits.

The wealthy men were still usually those with the established names: Palmer, Vanderbilt (Dutch ‹dweller near the mound›), Gould (English ‹gold›), Drew (English, short for ‹Andrew›). Some Irish and Germans were coming up fast, and early Jews made the going a bit easier for some of the late arrivals. But the Di Vittorios (Italian ‹son of Vittorio, "victor"›) were not yet winners in the economic race; many of the Czechoslovakian Svecs still cobbled shoes or did equivalent work; some Polish Czapkas still made and sold caps; perhaps Italian Gaglione still raised chickens while Gagliardi danced. Their turns in the mansions—or rather their children's or grandchildren's turns—were still coming. As Voltaire said, the sounds of history are the sounds of wooden clogs going up the stairs and the sounds of silken slippers coming down.

Woodrow Wilson, who should have known better, had written of the "coarse crew" of people from Italy, Hungary, and Poland, who possessed "neither skill nor energy nor any initiative or quick intelligence," and who seemed to him less desirable than were the Chinese, who were excluded. In the campaign of 1912 these remarks were translated into most European languages and widely disseminated to newly enfranchised citizens in an effort to take their votes away from Wilson. He then told these ethnic groups how much he really loved and admired them.

The names of many of the immigrants retarded their acceptance. The Italian names were not so bad: it's not hard to pronounce Di Marco ‹son of Mark› or Rossi ‹ruddy, red haired›. Maybe it helped that macaroni, spaghetti, and later pizza were on their way to becoming popular American foods, and that the martini would be a favorite alcoholic beverage. But the names from farther north and east looked unpronounceable and sounded worse. How could anyone ever say a *c* and a *z* together, or an *s* and a *z*? Why, a few of these bohunks still wrote their names with a lot of added squiggles or dots over or under some of the letters: God's own alphabet wasn't enough for them to spell their weird names. And why did so many of their names seem to end in *-vich* or *-ic* or *-czak* or *-wicz* or, especially, *-ski?* Kazmier ‹seller of cashmere› might not be too bad a name, but why did it have to be Kazmierski?

So the natives or those who had come over a few decades earlier coined their own names for the strangers. Anyone who differs much from us in language and customs is likely to be saddled with an opprobrious name. The Czech might be called a cheskey or a bohunk; the Hungarian a bohunk or a hunky; the Italian a dago, wop, or guinea; the Jew a kike, sheenie, or yid; the Pole a polack (often with *dumb* as a prefix); the Scandinavian a scandihoovian or a herring choker. Some of the Irish led the ridicule, perhaps recalling their own days as mick and harp; sometimes the Germans—formerly known as heinie and kraut—joined in. Occasionally there were playground fights over the nicknames, and sometimes barroom tangles.

Some of the old nicknames still exist, but more recent arrivals such as the gooks and the slant-eyes and the greasers now receive most of the onomastic taunts. Kazmierski may by this time have changed his name to Casper or Cash or something else, and he's paying off his mortgage and his car like everybody else. Maybe he still goes to the Annual Polish Festival, and maybe he tries to talk his Irish wife into naming their firstborn son Stanley instead of Kevin, but perhaps only a half dozen times a year does he think of himself as anything other than American.

Immigration laws passed between 1891 and 1907 excluded paupers, polygamists, prostitutes, imbeciles, anarchists and other political extremists, and persons suffering from specified diseases. By a "gentlemen's agreement" in 1907–8 the Japanese government stopped issuing passports to laborers emigrating directly to the United States, although some might go first to another country and from there to America; a California law in 1913 forbade Japanese to buy agricultural land. The Immigration Law of 1917 excluded still other Orientals, required a "head tax" of eight dollars per immigrant, added alcoholics and "persons of constitutional psychopathic inferiority" to the exclusions, and required the applicant but not his immediate family to demonstrate an ability to read a short passage in English or another language.

Obviously not everyone favored such restrictions. Leading the oppostion was the National Association of Manufacturers (NAM), which welcomed a steady supply of cheap foreign labor to its factories. In general the Republican party had been restrictionists, but the NAM position led them to shift their views somewhat, and this shift was abetted by the fact that the Republicans hoped to gain more of the votes of new citizens, who tended usually to vote a straight Democratic ticket.

Those favoring more stringent regulation, however, were aided by events. During the war years many persons violently distrusted anyone or anything with a German name: hamburgers and sauerkraut became Salisbury steak and liberty cabbage, and thousands of Schultzes and others hurried to change to English surnames. The distrust of the Germans, after the war ended, tended to move to other, newer immigrant groups. Strikes and bombings in 1919 and 1920 were blamed on "all them foreigners," and several thousand aliens considered radicals were deported. There was an economic depression in 1920 and 1921, which left jobs in short supply even for "Americans."

The war had ended in 1918. The next year brought only a slight increase in immigrants, but in 1920 the number tripled to 430,000, and in 1921 it jumped to 805,000—close to prewar levels. New alarms sounded against foreigners. There was a short-lived Red Scare, anti-Semitism increased, the anti-Catholic Ku Klux Klan reached 2.5 million members by

1923. An argument in favor of new restrictions was found in the fact that wartime test results, when released, showed that soldiers of southern and eastern European backgrounds had made lower scores, on the average, than had the northerners and the westerners. The concept of cultural bias in intelligence tests was not yet known, nor was the comparative recency of the southerners and easterners considered.

In 1921 Congress passed a law restricting annual immigration of each national group to 3 percent of the number of that nationality who had been residents in 1910. Then, in 1924, the Johnson-Reed Act limited the total number of immigrants to 150,000 each year and assigned national quotas based on the 1890 census, which had been taken before large numbers of southern and eastern Europeans had come here. Western hemisphere nations were not included in this quota system. Japanese immigration was completely forbidden.

The national quota system was finally abandoned in 1965. Other than that, from 1929, when the National Origins Act of 1924 became fully effective, until 1981, when President Reagan proposed far-reaching changes in policies toward people from Mexico and the Caribbean, only a number of minor or temporary adjustments have been made to admit certain refugees or other selected groups, such as war brides. For fifteen consecutive depression and war years, 1931 through 1945, total yearly number of immigrants ranged only between 23,000 and 97,000. Since about 1950, however, the annual average has been about 250,000.

Among the immigrants of the 1930s were thousands of people, Jews especially, fleeing from Hitler's Germany, many of them prosperous, many well educated. Writer Thomas Mann ‹servant, man›, scientist Albert Einstein ‹mason›, musician Bruno Walter ‹descendant of Walthair, "rule, people or army"›, and philosopher Paul Tillich (of uncertain derivation) were among them. After the war many British and German craftsmen and white-collar workers came over, and, from various parts of the world, about 150,000 women and a few hundred men who had married or become engaged to American military personnel; their 25,000 children accompanied them. From 1947 on, the restriction against Orientals was sufficiently relaxed that a few hundred or in some years a few thousand Japanese, Chinese, or other Orientals arrived. Filipinos became increasingly numerous at our gates. The number of Asians increased somewhat during the Korean War and increased much more substantially when the Vietnamese War finally ended in 1974. A few thousand Africans fled here from Idi Amin's Uganda in the late 1970s.

Other war refugees had established a pattern of sorts. A Displaced Persons Act in 1948 had provided that up to 400,000 such persons might be admitted over a four-year period. A Refugee Relief Act in 1953 authorized admission of another 214,000. When the Russians put down a Hungarian uprising in 1956, some 35,000 persons from Hungary were granted admission.

From 1951 through 1973, immigrants totaled about 7½ million. Of these, close to 3 million were from Europe, with Germany, the United Kingdom, Italy, and Poland, in that order, providing the greatest numbers. Asia sent close to a million in the twenty-three years, of whom the Filipinos were the most numerous—about 200,000 of them. South America sent more than 300,000 people, Africa about 75,000.

From North and Central America and the Caribbean, however, came a more substantial number, over 2½ million. About 600,000 of these were Canadians. Mexico's official contribution was close to a million, but perhaps two or three times that number (some say more than that) entered the country illegally. Puerto Ricans shuttled back and forth between their island home and the mainland but do not count as immigrants. Cubans, including a quarter million refugees, totaled some 400,000 during this period, and Fidel Castro in 1980 found economic advantage in letting another eighth of a million cross in small boats to Florida.

If we look at the statistics concerning the number of foreign-born residing in the United States in 1960 and 1970, we may note some interesting trends. In both those years the largest number of foreign-born were of Italian birth, followed by Germans, Canadians, Poles, and Russians (mainly Jewish). But in the ten-year period the number of our foreign-born from every major European country except Greece declined. In contrast, our Asiatic foreign-born increased by 53 percent, our officially recorded Mexican foreign-born by 29 percent, and our officially recorded Cuban-born by 284 percent.

In all, though, we lost about a half million foreign-born during the decade—many because of deaths among the elderly. Despite the drop in our Europeans, Europe still accounted for twenty-three million of our foreign-born in residence in 1970, the rest of the world for only ten million. The Changs and even the Rodriguezes, although gaining, still had a considerable way to go before they caught up with the Joneses.

In the Cabinet of John F. Kennedy there was a Jew from eastern Europe (Abraham Ribicoff), a man of Polish ancestry (John A. Gronouski, Jr.), and an Italian American (Anthony J. Celebrezze). Kennedy was the first Irishman and the first Roman Catholic elected president.

Somewhere someone named Sanchez or Tagawa or Chin must have looked at the names of Kennedy and his cabinet and said confidently, "Someday a Sanchez, someday a Tagawa, someday a Chin will be in that group. That's the way this country works."

Part II

THE BRITISH AND THE NORTHERN EUROPEANS

5

THE ENGLISH:

The Jamestown Colony

STEPHEN VINCENT BENÉT (a French name equivalent to English Bennett ‹descendant of Benedict "blessed one"›), looking back at the Jamestown of over three hundred years before, remembered some of the names in his last and unfinished epic poem, *Western Star:*

> There were a hundred and forty-four, all told,
> In the three small ships. You can read the names, if you like,
> In various spellings. They are English names,
> William Tankard, Jeremy Alicock,
> Jonas Profit, the sailor, James Read, the blacksmith,
> Love, the tailor, and Nicholas Scot, the drum.
> One laborer is put down with a mere "Ould Edward,"
> Although, no doubt, they knew his name at the time,
> But, looking back and remembering, it is hard
> To recollect every name. . . .
>
> —It is so they perish, the cast grains of corn,
> The blown, chance pollen, lost in the wilderness—
> And we have done well to remember so many names,
> Crofts and Tavin and Johnson, Clowell and Dixon,

And even the four boys, come with the gentlemen,
In a voyage somewhat topheavy with gentlemen,
As John Smith found.

A hundred and forty-four
Men, on a five months' voyage to settle Mars.
And a hundred and five landed on the strange shore.

The Jamestown colonists are the first whose names we know, and not even all of them. As Benét reminded us, there were 105 in the first contingent, of whom 67 are identifiable by name. The names of 73 of the next 120, who came a year later in 1608, are also known. Among the first 300-plus, "a disparate crew of adventurers and roughnecks" Sigmund Diamond calls them, there were over 60 "gentlemen," often impoverished younger sons. In the first 67 a disproportionately high 29 were gentlemen, and there were 12 laborers, 4 carpenters, 2 bricklayers, 1 each mason, blacksmith, sailor, barber, surgeon, tailor, drummer, and preacher, and 12 others, including 4 boys, of unspecified occupation. The second tide brought more tailors and blacksmiths, an apothecary, some jewelers and refiners and goldsmiths (since current beliefs held that the New World must abound in precious gems and metals), and, ironically when one remembers the harsh life of the colony, a perfumer. A lack of realism and realists. That's probably why the colony fared no better.

"The first Plantation in Virginia," an early account says, was

> so slenderly provided for that before they had remained halfe a yeare in this new Collony they fell into extreame want, not havinge anything left to sustein them save a little ill conditioned Barley, [of which] one smale ladle full was allowed each person for a meale, without bread or aught else whatsoever, so that had not God, by his great providence, moved the Indians, then our utter enemies, to bringe us reliefe, we had all utterlie by famine perished.

These impoverished people "lodged in cabbins & holes within the grounde." They cut down cedar and black walnut trees to send back to England for use in shipbuilding or other construction, and they dug "goulde oare (as some thought) which beinge sent for England proved dirt." Pyrite, chalcopyrite perhaps. The colony was badly managed, the natives were unfriendly as a rule, and the surroundings were so unhealthful that few colonists survived.

But others replaced them. Women as well as men. Whole families sometimes. "A List of the Livinge" was prepared in February 1623. It had about 1,225 names, plus mention of 22 Negroes for each of whom only one name or none at all was given, "two Frenchmen" and "a Frenchman et uxor" otherwise unidentified, and a few others with only partial identification. One of these is "Thomas, an Indian"; another is "a boy of Mr. Cans." Almost all the names are English, Welsh, or Scottish. Two persons named Lupo have an Italian name; Deverell may be French, as may Martine de Moone, three Pollentins, and three Arrundells; Anthony and James Bonall and ——— LeGeurd are identified as Frenchmen.

Some of the names are unusual, even given the uncertain spellings of the seventeenth century: Pharow Phlinton, Dictras Chrismus, Thomas Thornegood, Lawrance Smalpage, John Lightfoote, Thomas Oage, Ebedmeleck Gastrell, and a man named Snow with the unlikely notation (orig.) Swnow. Some of the spellings may represent merely the compiler's preferences: Huges is probably modern Hughes; Reinolds and Reignolds are no doubt today's Reynolds; Perce and Perse may be Pierce or a modern variant (although Peirce is still pronounced like "purse" in Boston); Gouldsmith would later usually be Goldsmith (*gold* used to be pronounced "goold" in London); and Griphin is today's Griffin; Maddeson, Madison; Linkon, Lincoln; Graye, Gray; Thorogood and Througood, Thoroughgood; Yeardley, Yardley (who supplies Her Majesty's soap).

The most common names of 1623 are almost all still to be found among today's popular American names. Those borne by five or more persons are these (with the historical meanings added):

Baldwin	(5)	‹bold friend›
Ba(y)ley, Baly	(5)	‹estate manager›
Bennett	(5)	‹blessed one›

Biggs	(5)	‹large or powerful person›
Booth	(5)	‹dweller in a hut›
Brown(e)	(7)	‹dark complexioned›
Clark(e)	(7)	‹clergyman or scribe›
Davies	(13)	‹descendant of David, "friend, commander"›
Evans	(9)	‹son of Evan› (a Welsh form of John)
Fisher	(6)	‹fish catcher or seller›
Greene	(8)	‹dweller at the village green›
Hall	(7)	‹servant or dweller in the manor›
Harris	(9)	‹son of Harry›
Helin (Hellene)	(6)	(possibly a variant of Helland, in Cornwall)
Hill(s)	(6)	‹dweller on a hill›
Jackson	(10)	‹son of Jack›
Johnson	(9)	‹son of John›
Jones	(9)	‹son of John› (usually Welsh)
Jordan	(5)	‹descendant of Jordan› (from the river)
Loyd	(5)	‹gray or brown› (variant of Lloyd)
More	(5)	‹dweller near the marsh›
Osbo(u)rn(e)	(6)	‹descendant of Osborn, "god, man"›
Perce (Perse)	(5)	‹descendant of Peter, "a rock"›
Phil(l)ips	(5)	‹son of Phillip, "lover of horses"›
Powell	(5)	‹son of Howell, "eminent"› (Welsh); ‹son of Paul, "small"›; ‹dweller near a pool›
Price	(7)	‹son of Rhys, "ardor, a rush"› (Welsh)
Smith	(20)	‹worker with metal›
Thompson	(6)	‹son of Thomas, "a twin"›
West	(5)	‹one from the west›
Williams	(10)	‹son of William, "resolution, helmet"›
Yeardley	(5)	‹one from Yardley, "place where ships' spars were made"›

Those thirty-one names account for between a fifth and a sixth of the total population of Jamestown in 1623. In all, about seven hundred different names were represented in the colony at the time of this report.

Appended to the list of the "Livinge" was "A List of the Names of the Dead in Virginia Since April Last," which dramatizes the unbelievable amount of hunger, illness, and Indian danger in the first English colony even sixteen years after its founding. According to the list, 371 persons died in the ten-month period; in addition, 347 had been killed in an Indian massacre on March 22, 1622. Altogether the deaths totaled over a third of the colony's population in less than a single year.

In the list of the ten-months' dead the names are similar to those in the list of the living, with the Smiths, Clarkes, Jacksons, and the rest sharing in the bereavements along with folk with less common names like Usher, Thimbleby, Lullett, and Burnhouse. Christo. Ash, *uxor* Ash, and infant Ash were wiped out together, probably by a fever that plagued the colony; so were the three Winslows, the three Gulftons, and the two Rowsleys and "a maid of theirs." We must not forget Remember Michel or the very Welsh Thomas ap-Richard or Goodwife Redhead.

Other dead included "2 children of the Frenchmen," "Symon, an Italien," "2 Indians," "One negar," and "James, John, Irishmen." It is noteworthy that the compiler of the list seldom gave more than one name, if that, to Indians, Negroes, and "foreigners."

Mr. and Mrs. William Spence are described laconically as "lost." Even when there was no massacre, a number were reported "killed": John Wood, William More, Thomas Naylor, John Pattison and his wife, Jane Fisher, and two men identified only as Gilbert ——— and Nicholas ———, as well as others.

Whole families were wiped out in the massacre, as witness these entries: "Master Tho: Boise and Mistris Boise, his wife & a sucking Childe, 4 of his men, A Maide, 2 children." "Foreigners" massacred included "Mathew, a Polander," "A French Boy," and "Henry, a Welchman." One victim is memorialized only in this way: "One old Maid called blinde Margaret."

6

THE ENGLISH:

The *Mayflower*

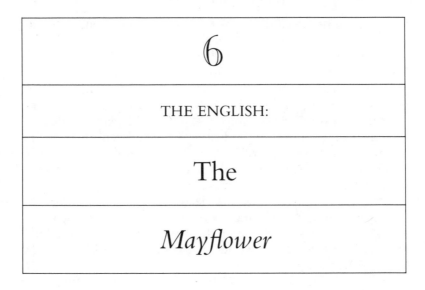

THE STORY of the *Mayflower* and the Pilgrims who arrived on it in late 1620 has often been told. Elementary school children learn the superficialities—that the Pilgrims wanted to worship God in their own way, that they landed at Plymouth Rock, and that friendly Indians taught them to grow maize and in return were invited to eat turkey at the first Thanksgiving.

Most of the children don't realize how small the ship was—only about ninety feet long. Nor are they likely to be taught that one group of the immigrants, separatists from the Church of England, had earlier established a church in Nottinghamshire and then moved to Amsterdam and Leyden, but left Holland in fear that the notorious Spanish Inquisition would harm them. And the children don't learn such commercial details as the fact that the *Mayflower* was chartered by a group of merchants called the London Adventurers, who thought of a colony as potentially profitable for them, at the risk of only ten pounds or so apiece.

Teachers usually soft-pedal the quarrelsomeness of some

of the 101 passengers, most of whom, including Captain Miles Standish, were not Pilgrims and had little or no religious motivation. Generally no mention is made of the unwisdom of their starting a voyage at a time when landfall was bound to occur in winter, or of the fact that the ship aimed at Virginia but missed because of stormy weather. Had the weather been different, the Pilgrim fathers and mothers would have been Virginians. Not until 1920, by the way, did the British see fit to erect a commemorative marker in the harbor in Plymouth from which the *Mayflower* sailed.

Of the passengers, thirty-five were from the group that had settled in Holland, and the other sixty-six were from Southampton and London. It is noteworthy that most early English settlers in America were from the south of England. Their dialects and some of their beliefs and customs differed from those of the north, which did not send many immigrants for a number of years.

We know the names of all the *Mayflower* voyagers, and all those names still survive in the United States. Twenty-eight of them, in fact, starred in the following list, are each held by ten thousand or more modern Americans, although obviously only a relatively small number of them can legitimately claim membership in the Society of Mayflower Descendants, founded in 1894. Here is the roll call of the surnames of the men on the ship:

Alden	Crackston	Langemore	Story★
Allerton (2)	Dotey	Leister	Thompson★
Billington	Eaton★	Margeson	Tilley★
Bradford★	Ellis★	Martin★	Tinker
Brewster★	English★	Moore★	Trevore
Britteridge	Fletcher★	Mullins★	Turner★
Browne★	Fuller★ (2)	Priest★	Warren★
Carter★	Gardiner★	Rigdale	White★
Carver★	Goodman★	Rogers★	Wilder★
Chilton	Holebeck	Samson	Winslow★
Clarke★	Hopkins★	Soule	
Cooke★	Howland	Standish	

★Held today by ten thousand or more Americans.

In all, the *Mayflower* names are still represented by about one-fortieth of present-day Americans, or one-thirtieth if more common spellings like Brown and Cook are counted as the same name.

The Pilgrims survived physically much better than their brethren in Jamestown. Governor Bradford ‹wide ford› wrote in 1621 that they caught "good store" of cod and bass and other fish.

All the summer there was no want, and now began to come in store of fowl, [including] wild turkeys, of which they took many, besides venison, etc. Besides they had about a peck of meal a week to a person, or now since harvest, Indian corn of that proportion.

Some settlers were "employed in affairs abroad," which usually meant trading with the Indians or opposing the uninhibited life-style of Thomas Morton ‹homestead by a marsh› and his fellows at nearby Merrymount.

Even in highly religious Plymouth, Bradford later complained, people were guilty of

. . . sundry notorious sins (as this year [1642], besides other, gives us too many sad precedents and instances), especially drunkenness and uncleanness. Not only incontinency between persons unmarried, for which many both men and women have been punished sharply enough, but some married persons also. But that which is even worse, even sodomy and buggery (things fearful to name) have broken forth in this land oftener than once.

In general, though, Plymouth Colony was highly respectable and well governed, and served as a model for many other English colonies.

7

THE ENGLISH:

Hingham and Some Other Colonies

THE STORY of Hingham, Massachusetts, near the highly irregular coast southeast of Boston, thirty miles from Plymouth, is much less known but no less informative. Its two waves of settlers illustrate the conflicts that often occurred among the English themselves—the conflicts and the eventual reconciliations once old disputes were forgotten.

The first wave, from 1631 to 1634, came from southwestern England, especially Devon, Dorset, and Somerset; the second was from southeastern England: Norfolk, Essex, Suffolk. Some eighteen families of the first group sailed from Bristol in successive voyages. They tended to be landholders, solid but not stodgy. "Probably the key element in their migration was a desire for greater estates and profits than England afforded them," according to John Jay Waters.

Among the names they brought with them was Thomas Andrews, then as now a frequent Scottish or English surname; it is a patronym that means ‹descendant of Andrew›. (A final *s* is often a short way to indicate ‹son of›.) The Otis family had a name going back to Old English Odo ‹rich, prosperous›. William Walton, a Cambridge graduate, bore the name of many small towns in England. Walton is an obvious combination of *wall* and *ton,* which can mean ‹town or homestead›; hence Walton is ‹a town or homestead with or near a wall›. Shipwright James Cade had a name that can mean either ‹big and clumsy› or ‹descendant of Cada, "the large, awkward man"›. Thomas Loring, who was Hingham's first seller of spirituous beverages and also the first deacon, had a name with various meanings: ‹descendant of Lawrence›, ‹one from the laurel tree›, or ‹a person from Lorraine (in France)›. Then there were the Strongs, with a self-evident name, the Phippenys, who probably owed their name to an ancestral Philip, and the Betscombs, from ‹Bette's valley›. And one of the leaders was Anthony Eames ‹the son of the uncle›.

These relatively wealthy pioneers were joined by craftsmen, especially weavers, from East Anglia, in the years after 1634. Some may have had Dutch blood, for immigrant Dutch families had mingled with them in England some years before. The East Anglians were unhappy with their wages in England, but they also considered themselves "members of the conscious community of God's people" who believed their freedom threatened by King and Church.

Among their leaders were the Peck brothers; although much of southeastern England is flat, Peck means ‹pointed hill› and is related to *peak.* Anthony Cooper's surname was that of an important occupation, making barrels or casks. An ancestor of Farrow had apparently lived near a medieval business sign showing a boar or pig, or may have raised pigs. The name-taking ancestor of Large was probably a big man, or perhaps generous. There was also the prosperous man named Henry Smiths ‹son of the smith› who brought with him a family of six and five servants. The Hobart family, a variant of Hubert ‹mind, bright›, was another influential one of the late-coming group.

Among the other East Anglians was one Samuel Lincoln, a weaver; his ancestors came from Lincolnshire. The name goes back to Welsh and Latin words for ‹lake colony›. Samuel Lincoln's great-great-grandson would become the sixteenth president of the United States. There was also Henry Chamberlain, a blacksmith whose nominal ancestor had been in charge of a royal or noble household. The name of Henry Rust, a glover, means ‹russet, redheaded›, and the name of the Jacob family honors the biblical Jacob.

Obviously these residents of Hingham represented the four chief ways in which almost all English and European surnames are derived: from ancestors or prominent persons (Otis, Andrews, Jacob), from places (Walton, Peck, Lincoln), from occupations (Cooper, Smiths, Chamberlain), and from appearance (Strong, Large, Rust). Some of their names, like many others, may have more than a single derivation (Loring), and some cannot be positively assigned to a source, so that only an informed guess is possible (Phippeny).

The two groups of English in Hingham did not get on well together. At first the West Countrymen were in control of public offices such as town clerk and constable, and could dispense whatever patronage such a small town had to offer. But the Easterners became more numerous, took over running the town, and almost completely shut out the Westerners. The Pecks, Allens, Jacobs, Beales, and the rest were dominant; even the pastor was a Hobart. Town squabbles mingled constantly with churchly squabbles, entering even into questions about which children should be baptized.

But just as in Shakespeare the Montague boy and the Capulet girl rejected the feud of their parents, so after a couple of decades did the children of Hingham's warring factions. Anthony Eames's daughter married John Jacob of the East. John Otis, Jr., of the West married Mary Jacob. The Jacobs must have been great mixers, for Hannah Jacob married Thomas Loring, Jr. There were other marriages in which East met West. "By 1660," says Waters, who has studied Hingham as a sociologist, "Hingham witnessed the disappearance of old-country differences as a major factor in its community life."

In various guises and in greater or lesser degree, the story of Hingham was to serve as a national prototype of bitter hostilities gradually being reduced and sometimes vanishing or at least being eventually ignored.

We tend to fear or dislike whoever is different from ourselves. At various times Americans who have themselves come from foreign lands have tried to keep out those who differed from them in race, national origin, moral standards, or religious beliefs. An early example was the citizenry of Massachusetts Bay Colony, founded in 1630 mainly by Puritans so narrow in their views that they sent back to England people who wanted to follow the Anglican ritual. Puritans, as well as the devil, it seems, could quote scripture for their purpose, as John Winthrop did in 1637:

7. A family is a little commonwealth, and a commonwealth is a great family. Now as a family is not bound to entertain all comers, . . . no more is a commonwealth. . . .
8. The rule of the apostle (II John: 10) is that such as come and bring not the true doctrine with them shall not be received to house, and by the same reason not into the commonwealth.

Winthrop ‹a person from Winthorpe, "Wina's dairy farm"› was the first governor of the colony, whose early settlers had been brought over by John Endecott ‹one who lives in the end cottage› in 1628. Eleven ships came across in 1630, their passengers settling north of Plymouth in Mishawum (later Charlestown), Shawmut (Boston—Shawmut is still the name of a large chain of banks there), Mystic (Medford), Watertown, Roxbury, and Dorchester. Somewhat later arrivals included clergymen John Cotton ‹person from Coton or Cotton, or one who lives in a group of cottages› and Thomas Hooker. Hooker would move to what is now Hartford, Connecticut, where he would espouse the novel view that governmental authority should rest upon the free consent of the governed, a view supported later by the Constitution, but in increasing danger in the twentieth century.

Roger Williams, bearer of what would become America's third most popular surname (in combination with the equivalent Williamson), quarreled with the religious bigotry of

Winthrop and other authorities, was banished, and became the founding father of tolerant Rhode Island. He fought a duel with John Cotton (using pamphlets instead of guns or swords), took into Rhode Island Jews and Quakers who were being persecuted by the Puritans, worked for peace with the Narragansett Indians, and so impressed Charles II that in 1663 Rhode Island was granted a charter explicitly providing for freedom in matters of religion.

Among other early Massachusetts Bay Colony names are those of Anne Hutchinson (literally ‹son of Hugh›, Hutch being a pet form of that name), who was excommunicated and, like Williams, banished from Massachusetts for unorthodox religious views, and killed by Indians in what some of her critics considered to be an act of divine judgment; the Reverend John Wheelwright ‹wheelmaker›, her brother-in-law; John Haynes ‹hedged enclosure›; the Reverend John Davenport ‹one from Davenport, "town beside the Dane river"›; and Theophilus ‹God loving› Eaton ‹home beside a river or an island›.

Most but not all the names are obviously English. One exception is that of Sir Ferdinando Gorges, who was really an English aristocrat despite his Frenchlike surname. Gorges never came to North America, but at one time he received a charter for all of the continent between the fortieth and the forty-eighth parallels—say from Philadelphia to the northern edge of Canada's New Brunswick. He planned to divide the land among his fellow gentry, bestowing generous grants in what could have amounted to a huge private kingdom. Massachusetts Bay and Plymouth prevented his doing so, but he tried again and received a much less generous charter for what is now Maine. But by that time—perhaps fortunately for democracy—Gorges was seventy-three years old and unable to carry through his dream.

The history of early American colonization is the story of one small group after another pecking away at the eastern edge of a continent whose magnitude and resources and variety they could not even dimly comprehend. Each of the colonies had its own characteristics and character; each had its own problems; each its own names. Here I can hardly do more than mention some of them.

Some two hundred colonists, many of them Catholics, sailed from Portsmouth, England, on November 22, 1633, and three months later completed the crossing and went up Chesapeake Bay to establish a settlement in what we call Maryland. The designated proprietor was Cecilius Calvert, 2nd Lord Baltimore (there's still a Lord Baltimore Hotel in the city of that name), but he did not visit the colony, entrusting the governorship to his brother, Leonard Calvert. Calvert originally meant ‹calfherd›; the name illustrates the possible social mobility of names, as does Marshall, who once took care of horses. Finding a Virginian, William Claiborne ‹one who lives near a stream with clay banks›, in their territory, Calvert and his men fought two sea battles with the Claiborne followers in 1635, and then drove them out by legal means only to have Claiborne later retake the island on which his trading post had stood.

More military and legal skirmishes followed, but in 1649, under the governorship of William Stone, a Protestant, Maryland passed its Toleration Act to grant religious freedom. It is significant that Stone designated a Roman Catholic, Thomas Greene, as his deputy. The Toleration Act did not bring peace to the troubled colony, which throughout the century fell into one internal or border dispute after another, but it did decrease the likelihood of serious religious conflicts.

In London in 1666 was published *A Brief Description of the Province of Carolina, on the Coasts of Florida,* intended to entice English persons, plagued that year by fire and pestilence, to come to a brave new world where "the woods are stored with deer and wild turkey, of a great magnitude," there were "two crops of Indian corn in one year, and great increase every crop," the meadows were large and the cattle in winter "keep their fat without fodder," the rivers had "great abundance of sturgeon, salmon, bass, plaice, trout, and Spanish mackerel," and the air was wholesome. And there were other inducements:

Third, every freeman and freewoman [note this early attempt at equal rights for women] that transport themselves and servants by the 25th of March next, being 1667, shall have for himself, wife, children, and manservants, for each 100 acres of land for him and his heirs forever, and for every womanservant and slave, 50 acres, paying at most ½ d per acre, per annum, in lieu of all demands, to the Lords Proprietors, provided always that every man be armed with a good musket full bore, 10 lb. powder, and 20 lb. of bullet, and six-months provision for all, to serve them while they raise provision in that country.

Fourth, every manservant, at the expiration of their time, is to have of the country 100 acres of land to him and his heirs forever, paying only ½ d per acre, per annum, and the women, 50 acres of land on the same conditions; their masters also are to allow them two suits of apparel and tools such as he is best able to work with, according to the custom of the country.

Queen Elizabeth I as early as the 1580s had granted a colonization right for Roanoke Island, in what is now North Carolina, to Sir Walter Raleigh ‹red meadow›, but a colony was not successfully developed. And King Charles I had granted Carolina land to some of his followers in 1629 (the name of Carolina is based on the Latin version of Charles's name), but again no permanent settlement resulted. In the 1660s and 1670s Charles II granted large chunks of land to already wealthy Englishmen, some of whom were the "Lords Proprietors" mentioned in the prospectus, and others of whom had such titles as landgrave, cacique, and lord of the manor, with holdings ranging from 3,000 to 48,000 acres each. Some of these large landholders remained in England as absentee landlords, but others or their successors and their families became the landed aristocracy of the area and some of the social and political aristocrats who flourished at least until the Civil War. Although small groups of Dutch, French, Scots, and Germans settled there from time to time, the Carolinas have always been predominately English. In 1970 South Carolina had proportionately fewer foreign-born residents (1 in 200) than any other state.

Early Carolinians who could afford to do so hired tutors or used private schools for the education of their children, and when possible rounded off the education with collegiate study in England or on the Continent. They stressed cultural activities (the seventeenth-century St. Cecilia musical society still flourishes) and developed elaborate social rituals such as debutante balls. Life in antebellum Charleston and other Carolina areas must have been ideal—for those fortunate enough to be born into the "right" class and color.

Among early governors in Carolina were Joseph Morton, James Colleton (equivalent to modern Colton, the name of several English towns), and Seth Southel, named for a town in Middlesex. One of the later governors was one of the Smiths (Thomas), who were so numerous in England and would become even more so here.

In 1732 James Edward Oglethorpe, whose name comes from that of a Yorkshire settlement, received a charter enabling him to settle the area between the Savannah and Altamaha rivers—now a substantial part of Georgia. Oglethorpe sympathized with the poor, especially with imprisoned debtors, and encouraged them to accept land grants in Georgia. A total of about four thousand English people —certainly not all poor—came in the next twenty years. They were joined by a thousand or so Ulster Scots and others, many of whom had earlier settled farther north. Among these thousand were Salzburgers from Austria who settled now at New Ebenezer and Savannah, Congregationalists from New England at Seabury and Midway, and Highlanders from Scotland at Darien. Nevertheless, like much of the South, Georgia has remained largely English in background, except for a black population that had reached 44 percent of the total by the Civil War. Most Georgian names thus were and are either conventionally English or those borne by the Ulster Scots.

In Georgia, as in the other colonies, the usual inducement to the new colonists was the promise of free land, usually fifty acres, sometimes more. A person who could not afford the fare for the long ocean voyage often could arrange to become someone's indentured servant, working for little or nothing for about seven years to pay the cost. According to

Oscar Handlin, in the colonies there were more immigrants of the servant class than any other.

Here is part of a typical eighteenth-century contract to which one William Mathews agreed. Although William would be an apprentice, rather than a mere servant, the terms of the agreement were similar. To learn the trade of a cordwainer (a shoemaker working with cordovan leather), William said that

> He will live and (after the manner of an apprentice) serve from August 15, 1718, until the full term of seven years has completed and ended. . . . He shall not waste his master's goods nor lend them unlawfully to any. He shall not commit fornication nor contract matrimony within the said term.
>
> At cards, dice, or any other unlawful game, he shall not play. . . . He shall not absent himself day or night from his master's service without his leave, nor haunt alehouses, but in all things he shall behave himself as a faithful apprentice toward his master. . . .
>
> The said master shall . . . teach or cause the said apprentice to be taught the art or mystery [craft] of a cordwainer. He shall find and provide unto the said apprentice sufficient meat, drink, apparel, lodging, and washing fit for an apprentice [a phrase that some masters found quite flexible]. During the said term, every night he shall give the apprentice one quarter of schooling. At the expiration of the said term he shall provide him with a sufficient new suit of apparel, four shirts, and two necklets.

Ship after ship brought more of the English to America. Most were poor. The rich tended to be held in England by their land and other possessions. Jean de Crèvecoeur emphasized the poverty of the immigrants from all countries, in his *Letters from an American Farmer* (1782):

> In this great American asylum, the poor of Europe have by some means met together, and in consequence of various causes to what purpose should they ask one another what countrymen they are? Alas, two-thirds of them had no country. Can a wretch who wanders about, who works and starves, whose life is a continual scene of sore affliction or pinching penury; can that man call England or any other kingdom his country? A country that had no bread for him, whose fields procured him no harvest, who met with nothing but the frowns of the rich, the severity of the laws, with trials and

punishments; who owned not a single foot of the extensive surface of this planet. No! Urged by a variety of motives, here they came. Everything has tended to regenerate them; new laws, a new mode of living, a new social system; here they are become men: In Europe they were so many useless plants, wanting vegetative mold, and refreshing showers; they whispered, and were mowed down by want, hunger, and war; but now, by the power of transplantation, like all other plants, they have taken root and flourished!

In 1630 the American colonies as a whole still had only about 5,700 white settlers, but the next decade saw a jump to 28,000, mainly in Massachusetts. After that the colonial population grew at a fairly steady rate of 30 to 40 percent per decade. Until the early 1700s the New England and southern colonies grew at the fastest pace, but later the middle colonies accelerated their growth to match that of New England, mainly because of heavy immigration to Pennsylvania. Even during the Revolutionary War decade the population grew by over a half million, and from 1780 to 1790, with the new nation being established, there was a leap from about 2.8 to 3.9 million. A comparable gain today would add about a hundred million in ten years.

Throughout most of colonial times Virginia was the most populous colony, with Massachusetts battling for the lead but falling behind after 1650. Connecticut and then Maryland held third place for a while, but Pennsylvania took over that spot in 1750 and in 1780 advanced to second. In 1790 the states (plus the not-yet states of Kentucky, Tennessee, Vermont, and Maine) ranked as follows in population:

1. Virginia	7. South Carolina	13. Georgia
2. Pennsylvania	8. Connecticut	14. Kentucky
3. North Carolina	9. New Jersey	15. Rhode Island
4. Massachusetts	10. New Hampshire	16. Delaware
5. New York	11. Maine	17. Tennessee
6. Maryland	12. Vermont	

The population of the colonies and then of the young states was predominantly rural. Boston was the largest American city until 1760, when Philadelphia moved into the lead with 18,756 persons, including its suburbs—a figure that today might classify it as only a large town, or in metropolitan minds as a small town.

New York became largest in 1810, although Philadelphia had continued to grow while Boston was just emerging from a slump that had lasted from 1740 to almost 1790. Charleston in 1790, with 16,359 inhabitants, was almost as populous as Boston, and Baltimore was fifth in size; no other cities had over 8,000 inhabitants. (Newport had reached 9,000 in 1774 but then had fallen off.) Virginia, although the most populous state, had no city larger than 4,000 in 1790, and North Carolina had none larger than 2,000.

One reason for the rurality of America was that the English who swelled the population during the eighteenth century tended to be rural folk, although a fair number had emigrated from London, Birmingham, and other cities. Many English farmers departed, especially in the second half of the century, because of the increase in enclosures in England. Earlier a farm worker would earn small wages but would also have for his use a strip of land in a plot owned in common by him and a number of others. On it he might keep a little livestock, grow some grain or other food, and maybe cut wood or peat for fuel. "I kept four cows before the parish was enclosed," one man said, "and now I don't keep so much as a goose."

Whenever an enclosure bill passed Parliament—there were 1,630 of them in the eighteenth century—the land was divided in such a way that a substantial landowner got most of it, and the small farmers were squeezed out. Rosamond Bayne-Powell describes the procedure:

> An enclosure bill began by a petition to Parliament from some local person, generally a big landowner who was lord of the manor. His signature alone was sufficient to set a bill in motion, and before the year 1774 he was not even obliged to acquaint his neighbours that he proposed to divide up their property afresh. After this date a copy of the petition was affixed to the church door, so that such as could read might be apprised of their fate. Parliament, having heard the petition, granted leave for a bill to be introduced, which was twice read and then referred to a committee. In the eighteenth century, the member in charge of a private

bill presided and packed the committee with his friends and supporters.

The announced motive of the large landholders was more efficient farming practices—the same motive declared by the twentieth-century American (and foreign) corporate giants that are gradually eliminating small farmers in this country. The practice obviously parallels that of big industry in general, which persists in buying out small bakeries, grocery stores, newspapers, and other privately owned enterprises. Oliver Goldsmith, in "The Deserted Village," which was second only to Gray's "Elegy" in eighteenth-century popularity, lamented the rural takeover in his day:

> Ill fares the land, to hast'ning ills a prey,
> Where wealth accumulates, and men decay:
> Princes and lords may flourish, or may fade;
> A breath can make them, as a breath has made;
> But a bold peasantry, their country's pride,
> When once destroy'd, can never be supplied.

What happened to the bold peasants, of course, was that some of them died, some moved to a city, and others set sail for a new world. Thousands of them emigrated to America, where the majority sought farms that they thought could never be taken away from them or their descendants. A few of them and many of their heirs eventually became big landowners themselves, holding maybe even more acres than the lord of the English manor would have dreamed of. Others, especially those who settled in the Appalachians, were hard put to scratch a living from the rocky soil; many of those moved to the cities or joined a westward caravan. Those who remained in the most secluded areas sometimes kept alive for centuries, and still keep alive, vestiges of Elizabethan, Jacobean, or later English language and customs.

City dwellers who left England were also often forced to do so—except for those who left because of adventurous spirits—by the economy or other factors beyond their control, such as undesirable living conditions. London was an unhealthful place: during parts of the eighteenth century no more than 25 percent of the children there lived to age five. Drunkenness was rampant; even infants were encouraged to sip gin. Prostitutes staggered through the streets, trying to exchange use of their bodies for a few pence to buy more gin. Mobs were often violent and found no sight more enjoyable than a public hanging. Wages were low, and only a relatively few people lived in housing better than hovels.

Byron described the smoky city near the dockside as he saw it a little later, in 1822, and pointed the way out that was found by thousands who had not become sottish and sodden:

> A mighty mass of brick, and smoke, and shipping
> Dirty and dusky, but as wide as eye
> Could reach, with here and there a sail just skipping
> In sight, then lost amidst the forestry
> Of masts; a wilderness of steeples peeping
> On tiptoe through their sea-coal canopy;
> A huge, dun cupola, like a foolscap crown
> On a fool's head—and there is London Town!

The "forestry of masts" offered a salvation that many a Londoner accepted if he could scrape together the few pounds required for passage for himself and his family. Once in the colonies he might choose to live in a city again, but sometimes chose instead the elbowroom and the freshness of the country.

Most of the early settlers have been largely or completely forgotten now, their wooden or soft stone grave markers long moldered away. One of the famous names that have survived is that of Daniel Boone, which is English and sometimes Welsh and may go back either to a French place called Bohon or, when Welsh, means ‹son of Owen, "young warrior"›. Boone's "autobiography" was actually written by John Filson ‹son of Philip› in 1784. Boone came of a family of English Quakers and spent most of his life as a trapper, a wanderer, an explorer, and the opener of the Wilderness

Road from eastern Virginia through Kentucky, which became one of the major routes toward the West in Boone's day. In the following passage Boone remembered for history the names of his companions on his first expedition into the wilds of Kentucky:

> It was on the 1st of May, in the year 1769, that I resigned my domestic happiness for a time, and left my family and peaceable habitation on the Yadkin River in North Carolina, to wander through the wilderness of America in quest of the country of Kentucky, in company with John Finley [Scottish ‹descendant of Fionnla, "fair hero, or one from Findlay"›], John Stewart [English or Scottish ‹keeper of the sty; estate manager›], Joseph Holden [English ‹one from Holden, "deep valley"›], James Monay [anglicization of French Monet, "descendant of little Mon"], and William Cool [English ‹one from Coole, "cows' hill"›]. We proceeded successfully, and, after a long and fatiguing journey through a mountainous wilderness, in a westward direction, on the 7th day of June following, we found ourselves on Red River, where John Finley had formerly been trading with the Indians, and, from the top of an eminence, saw with pleasure the beautiful land of Kentucky.

Some highly individualistic women—sometimes no less impressive, in different ways, than Martha Washington or Abigail Adams—were among the early settlers, and a few of them are remembered in sentences or paragraphs here and there. For example, there was the one encountered by Moses Austin (whose name is an English derivative of Augustine), who late in 1796 left his Virginia home for a sightseeing trip to the Mississippi. One snowy night, as he wrote later,

> After passing [Cumberland] Mountain, which we did this night, we stopped at Mrs. Davis', who keeps the tavern [inn] down the mountain, and met with very good accommodations. . . . On the 16th, by daylight, our horses being ready, we took our leave of Mrs. Davis, who I must take the liberty to say may be justly called Captain Molly of Cumberland Mountain, for she fully commands passage to the New World. She soon took the freedom to tell me that she was a come-by-chance—her mother she knew little of and her father, less. As to herself, she said pleasure was the only thing

she had in view and that she had her ideas of life and its enjoyments, etc.

Austin's "etc." leaves room for interpretation. People like Captain Molly must have made life on the Wilderness Road much more bearable.

8

THE ENGLISH:

Common Names and Amusing Names in the Census of 1790

THE CENSUS OF 1790 was a new venture not only for America but for the world, although Great Britain would have its own census in 1801; no other country had ever tried to enumerate itself completely. This American census provided less information than did later versions, but it did list the names of heads of families, divided white males into two age groups, and divided the black population into free and slave. The enumeration covered the thirteen original states plus Vermont, Kentucky, Tennessee, and Maine, which were not yet officially states. (Maine at the time was a province of Massachusetts and was included in the census of that state, although extrapolations can be made.) Unfortunately the detailed records of New Jersey, Delaware, Virginia, Georgia, Kentucky, and Tennessee have been lost; however, some comparable data for Virginia are available from another source. In all, we know the names of some 81 percent of the male white population of 1790.

The Annual Report of the American Historical Association for 1931 is an analysis called *Surnames in the United States*

Census of 1790. In it Dr. Howard Barker pointed out that the descendants of the people listed in the 1790 census represented "over half of the present population of the United States." Today, in the 1980s, the proportion would be smaller, perhaps two-fifths. The names that follow, then, may have belonged to some of your ancestors, although, as I'll explain, many of the names judged undesirable were changed.

Barker used elaborate demographic formulas to determine the ancestry of the 1790 residents and to classify their names by nationality. The extent to which the United States was a nation of English descent in 1790 is shown most clearly by the following adaptation of a Barker table:

Percent of English Persons in the 1790 White Population of the United States, as Indicated by Family Name

Area	**Percent English**	**Rank in "Englishness"**
United States	60.9	—
Maine	60.0	10.5
New Hampshire	61.0	8
Vermont	76.0	2
Massachusetts	82.0	1
Rhode Island	71.0	3
Connecticut	67.0	5
New York	52.0	14
New Jersey	47.0	15
Pennsylvania	35.3	16
Delaware	60.0	10.5
Maryland	64.5	7
Kentucky and Tennessee	57.9	12
Virginia	68.5	4
North Carolina	66.0	6
South Carolina	60.2	9
Georgia	57.4	13

The "most English" state was Massachusetts, and in general the New England states ranked high in this category, since the flow of Irish, Italian, and other groups was yet to come. The southern states were next in Englishness, and in the middle states, which had already attracted fairly large numbers of German, Dutch, French, Swedish, and Ulster Scots, only about half of the residents were classified as English.

The list of most common names varied from state to state, as indeed it still does. The top fifteen from Massachusetts in 1790, with the comparative ranks for three other populous states and, for comparison, the national rank in the 1970s are in the table on page 67.

The table shows Smith, in 1790 as today, to be the most common American name. Brown, Davis, Jones, and Williams were well represented in all the states. Johnson, however, today the second in rank, was still fairly far down the list in 1790, partly because many Johnstons had not yet dropped the *t,* but mainly because many Scandinavian, German, Dutch, and other names would later be simplified, anglicized, or otherwise changed to Johnson. In Massachusetts, Clark, Foster, Adams, Parker, and Richardson were common names, but much less so in the other states; the explanation appears to be that New England, through the chances of immigration and the great Englishness of those states, happened to draw heavily from families with those names.

The table does not show that the Millers of Pennsylvania in 1790 were almost as numerous as the Smiths and nearly twice as numerous as the Browns, largely because so many German Müllers or Muellers were already becoming Millers. Miller was third in New York. Moore ranked sixth in Pennsylvania and North Carolina but not in the top fifteen in Massachusetts or New York.

All the leading names in the 1790 list are English, or at least British, since Jones, Davis, and Williams may better be classified as Welsh; some of the others can be Welsh, Scottish, or Irish.

In all, only 27,237 different surnames are listed in the

Most Common Names, in 1790, in Several States and Nationwide

Name	Rank in MA, 1790	Rank in NC, 1790	Rank in NY, 1790	Rank in PA, 1790	Rank in all of US, 1974
Smith	1	1	1	1	1†
Brown	2	5	2	3	4
Clark	3	25	16	20	18
White	4	9	11	14	15
Allen	5	19.5	9	*	25
Davis	6	4	7	4	7
Foster	7	*	*	*	83
Adams	8	*	*	*	38
Williams	9	3	6	8	3
Wood	10	40.5	4	*	62
Jones	11	2	5	5	5
Parker	12	12	*	*	49
Johnson	13	21	12.5	26.5	2
Baker	14	33.5	10	*	33
Richardson	15	*	*	*	34

* Rank not available, but lower than any given in this column.

† The Social Security Administration reports that for 1974, the latest year tabulated, the most common fifty names were the following: (The SSA computer based its count on only the first six letters of a name; hence, for example, Anders includes Andersen, Anderson, and other variants.) 1. Smith, 2. Johnso, 3. Willia, 4. Brown, 5. Jones, 6. Miller, 7. Davis, 8. Martin, 9. Anders, 10. Wilson, 11. Harris, 12. Taylor, 13. Moore, 14. Thomas, 15. White, 16. Thomps, 17. Jackso, 18. Clark, 19. Robert, 20. Lewis, 21. Walker, 22. Robins, 23. Peters, 24. Hall, 25. Allen, 26. Young, 27. Morris, 28. King, 29. Wright, 30. Nelson, 31. Rodrig, 32. Hill, 33. Baker, 34. Richar, 35. Lee, 36. Scott, 37. Green, 38. Adams, 39. Mitche, 40. Philli, 41. Campbe, 42. Gonzal, 43. Carter, 44. Garcia, 45. Evans, 46. Turner, 47. Stewar, 48. Collin, 49. Parker, 50. Edward

surviving records from the 1790 census, in contrast to the more than a million of today. The Census Bureau compilers who authored *A Century of Population Growth* (1909) took an affectionate look at some of the strange names they found in the 1790 census, while admitting that what they did was "not properly a part of a report of this character."

Here are some of the unusual or amusing English surnames from their much longer list:

Household and Domestic Affairs

FOOD AND EATING Soup, Oyster, Haddock, Pork, Savory, Stew, Duck, Quail, Goose, Gravy, Tripe, Kidney, Liver, Hash, Ham, Eggs, Goodbread, Butter, Radish, Vinegar, Carrott, Squash, Brownice, Waffle, Honey, Pancake, Jam, Fudge, Tea, Diet, Slice, Greens, Alspice.

DRINK Brandy, Goodrum, Grog, Grapewine, Cider, Freshwater, Booze.

CLOTHING Dress, Raiment, Gowns, Petticoat, Redsleeves, Feather, Spangle, Shoe, Highshoe, Stockins, Jumpers, Overall, Socks, Cap, Bloomer.

SEWING MATERIALS Linen, Silk, Poplin, Buttons, Needles, Pin, Pattern, Spool, Threadcraft, Patching, Whitecotton.

Human Characteristics

KINDS OF MEN Countryman, Iceman, Sickman, Shortman, Toughman, Tidyman, Weatherman, Houselighter, Woolweaver, Landmiser, Pioneer, Pagan, Pettyfool, Passenger, Biters, Fakes, Equals, Drinker, Dancer, Cusser, Spitter, Booby, Dunce, Boor, Crook, Rascal, Swindle, Madsavage, Hero.

CONDITION Hunger, Thirst, Smell, Taste, Laughter, Reason, Clemency, Care, Wit, Devotion, Goodcourage, Fuss, Flurry, Piety.

APPEARANCE OR STATE Plump, Comely, Sallow, Supple, Bony, Barefoot, Busy, Idle, Careless, Gushing, Dumb, Howling, Daft, Looney, Dowdy, Fickle, Gadding, Sober, Maudlin, Severe, Naughty, Toogood, Prudent, Hasty, Allright, Lazy, Upright, Underhand, Measley, Cacklin.

AILMENTS AND REMEDIES Fatyouwant, Gout, Fever, Crampeasy, Measles, Swelling, Gripe, Ache, Blackhead, Fits, Quack, Physic, Pill.

PARTS AND ACTIONS OF THE BODY Brains, Forehead, Ears, Wrists, Hips, Gullets, Hearts, Bowels, Voices, Whisper, Murmurs, Grunts, Howls, Smack, Caress.

Religion, Music, and Literature

RELIGION Preacher, Chapel, Steeples, Spires, Organ, Pew, Sermon, Creed, Bible, Psalms, Psalter, Sinners, Miracle, Hell.

MUSIC AND LITERATURE Music, Harmony, Overture, Duett, Harp, Fiddle, Fife, Poet, Rymes, Jingles, Ballad, Parody.

Property

KIND OF HOUSE, BUILDING MATERIAL, AND BELONGINGS Lot, Brickhouse, Mahogany, Oldhouse, Halfacre, Laughinghouse, Brickroof, Gutters, Lumber, Scantling, Cranny, Lockkey, Buttery, Pump.

SURROUNDINGS Stable, Trough, Manger, Coolyard, Woodhouse, Milkhouse, Warehouse.

FURNITURE AND TABLEWARE Curtain, Vase, Clocks, Desk, Chairs, Bolster, Bucket, Snuffer, Platter, Newbowl, China, Knife, Forks, Saucer.

MERCHANDISE AND COMMODITIES Stove, Auction, Wondersale, Shovel, Poker, Hammock, Tubs, Ax, Nuthammer, Hatchet, Whetstone, Gouge, Oats, Husks, Barley, Bomb, Brass, Camphor, Cowhorn, Cutwork, Dipper, Ivory, Junk, Pencil, Sickle, Silkrags, Smallcorn, Stilts, Turnipseed, Whitehorn, Wigs, Hames, Surrey.

MONEY Money, Dollar, Milldollar, Thickpenny, Shilling, Nickles.

Nature

COLOR Colour, Ruby, Pink, Purple, Seagray, Orange, Lavender, Scarlet.

OBJECTS OF NATURE OR FEATURES OF A LANDSCAPE Tallhill, Widedale, Woodsides, Bogs, Chestnutwood, Hazelgrove, Woodyfield, Wilderness, Middlebrook, Gully, Taterfield,

Longwall, Maypole, Lowbridge, Drawbridge, Woodendyke, Saltmarsh, Oysterbanks, Sharpstone.

TREES Oaks, Greenoak, Chestnut, Willow, Tumbletree, Redwood, Sap, Acorn.

PLANTS AND FLOWERS Plants, Weeds, Shrub, Primrose, Ivy, Parsley, Marjoram, Wormwood, Fennel, Caraway, Bramble, Thistle, Barnthistle, Toadvine, Ragbush, Pollen.

WEATHER Weathers, Dry, Damp, Dismal, Sprinkle, Shower, Simoon, Slush, Blizzard, Coldair.

BEASTS Horse, Hoss, Hossies, Mules, Kicks, Ox, Bulls, Cows, Heifer, Redheifer, Cats, Leathercat, Mouser, Pup, Shoat, Sealion, Cub, Leopard, Tiger, Moose, Panther, Flippers, Canter.

BIRDS Eagle, Canary, Woodpecker, Peacock, Raven, Skyhawk, Buzzard, Snipes, Pheasants, Bantam, Gosling, Birdsong, Birdwhistle.

INSECTS AND CREEPING CREATURES Ant, Beetle, Fly, Hornet, Roach, Locust, Snails, Maggot, Worm, Snake, Turtle, Frog.

The Ocean and Maritime Subjects

Seas, Billows, Breeze, Ship, Sloop, Barge, Bigraft, Anchor, Commodore, Mariner, Shipsboy, Swab.

War

War, Campaign, Fight, Fightmaster, Boom, Guns, Trigger, Pistol, Bugler, Officer, Treason, Prison.

Death and Violence

Death, Deadman, Hearse, Vaults, Tombs, Moregraves, Murder, Demon, Ghost, Mummy.

Time

Months, Weeks, Shortday, Nights, Hour, Midwinter, August, Yesterday, Tuesday, Allday, Always, Friday, Sunday, Monday, Lunch, Supper, Christmas, Easter, Goodnight.

Unusual Combinations of Common Forms

Cathole, Clapsaddle, Clinkscales, Crackbone, Flybaker, Fryover, Goodbit, Goosehorn, Graytracks, Hogmire, Hungerpealer, Liptrot, Milksack, Moonshine, Spitsnoggle, Stophell, Sunlighter, Sydebottom, Threewits.

Striking or Ludicrous Combinations of Christian Names and Surnames

Joseph Came, Peter Wentup, John Sat, Sarah Simpers, Ruth Shaves, Barbary Staggers, Joseph Rodeback, Christy Forgot, Agreen Crabtree, Snow Frost, Wanton Bump, Adam Hatmaker, Darling Whiteman, Mourning Chestnut, River Jordan, Over Jordan, Boston Frog, Bachelor Chance, Anguish Lemmon, Unity Bachelor, Thomas Purify, Noble Gun, Hardy Baptist, Mercy Pepper.

It is difficult to imagine how some of these names came into being. Many of them, though, may be humorous descriptives. A catlike person, for instance, may have been called Mouser (German Mauser); an impoverished person who liked to dress up may have been named Silkrags; or Turnipseed may have been tiny. Tallhill, Saltmarsh, Brickhouse, and many more are clearly place names. Swab and Clocks, among others, may have had occupational names—sailor and clockmaker for these two. I must admit to having trouble in making reasonable guesses about Gravy, Kidney, Biters, Reason, Laughinghouse, Wondersale, Goosehorn, Hungerpealer, Threewits, and a few more.

It should be pointed out that a fair number of these names are still to be found in modern directories. In fact, I remember that once when I was to speak at Eastern Illinois University I spent some time in talking with President Buzzard while waiting for Professor Waffle. However, during the past two centuries there has been a tendency away from names that appear objectionable for any reason. So today we do not find many Deaths, Deadmans (although I've known a Dedman), or Murders, or many names of insects or snakes or names like Hogmire or Cathole, and although Hills and Valleys are not uncommon, Swamps and Bogs (with one *g*) are rare.

In all fairness, some of these names may not be what they seem. Bloomer, for instance, certainly in 1790 meant a flower rather than an article of clothing, since the garment called bloomers was named for a leader in the fight for women's rights, Amelia Jenks Bloomer, who was not born until 1818. Blackhead is probably not the name of a skin disorder but may be a direct translation of German Schwarzkopf, referring only to dark hair. Bomb may be a semiliterate spelling of German Baum ‹tree›. Toobald may be a variant of Theobald; Cacklin of Cochrane. A Crook need not be a criminal: etymology shows that he or she may have lived at a turn in a road or a stream, or may have carried a shepherd's crook, or may have come from Crook, the name of several places in England and Scotland. And, also according to etymology, Sydebottom or Sidebottom or Sidebotham was an Englishman who lived in a broad valley. Other names may likewise have been misdefined, perhaps willfully, by the Census Bureau personnel, but their list does offer moments of amusement.

Frederick Marryat ‹descendant of littly Mary› was in his day a popular English novelist. In his *A Diary in America,* published in London in 1839, he declared that "it is very remarkable how very debased the language has become in a short period in America." He went on,

> The names of persons are also very strange; and some of [them] are, at all events, obsolete in England, even if they ever existed there. Many of them are said to be French or Dutch names Americanized. But they appear still more odd to us from the high-sounding Christian names prefixed to them, as, for instance, Philo Doolittle, Populorum Hightower, Preserved Fish, Asa Peabody, Alonzo Wolf, etc. I was told by a gentleman that Doolittle was originally from the French De l'Hotel; Peabody from Pibaudiere;

Bunker from Bon Coeur; that the English Bumpus is a descendant of Mons. Bon Pas, etc., all [of] which is very possible.

Elsdon Smith's *New Dictionary of American Family Names* agrees in general with Marryat about these derivations, saying about Bumpus, for instance, "From Old French bon pas (good pace), probably a nickname for a messenger." Nevertheless Smith classifies it as an English name, perhaps assuming that it was one adopted by the Normans in England after their conquest.

9

THE ENGLISH:

Later Arrivals

THE FEDERAL GOVERNMENT did not begin keeping statistics on immigration until 1820, but the flow of immigrants, from England or elsewhere, was relatively slow until the mid-twenties, after which it increased rapidly.

The proportion of immigrants from England and Scotland and Wales was never again as great as it had been in colonial days. In general throughout much of the nineteenth century the number of immigrants from the British Isles, exclusive of Ireland, represented about a fifth or a sixth of the total each year, although there was considerable fluctuation. In the last years of the century the British share dwindled to a tenth or less. Figures for a few representative years are on page 75.

The total immigrants from England, Wales, and Scotland from 1820 through 1957 numbered only about 4.7 million individuals—well below the number of Germans or Italians, only equal to the number of Irish, and only about a third higher than the number from Russia. If the predominantly British pattern of surnames had not been established early,

Immigration Figures from the United Kingdom			
Year	**Total Immigrants**	**Number from England, Wales, Scotland**	**Percentage of Total**
1825	10,199	2,095	20.54
1845	114,871	19,210	16.80
1865	248,120	82,465	33.24
1885	395,346	57,713	14.60
1895	258,536	28,833	11.15
1900	448,572	12,509	2.79

we might today have a considerably higher proportion of names from non-English lands. Or, to look at it differently, if our nation had been settled first by Germans, Italians, French, Irish, or Russians, and 4.7 million British people had come in later, our surnames would much more heavily represent the Germans or others rather than the English.

The nearly 5 million Britishers who came here since 1820 were enough to reinforce an already established naming pattern, as did the millions of descendants of the Smiths, Browns, Johnsons, Williamses, and so on who were here earlier. In three nineteenth-century years (1870, 1882, and 1888) the number of British immigrants exceeded 100,000, and in fifty-one years (1846 through 1896) it only once fell below 20,000. So it was a fairly steady influx, a constant reinforcement, as contrasted with the periods of surge and decline represented by immigrants from Ireland, Germany, Scandinavia, Italy, Russia, and other countries.

What were the reasons for this rather steady English flow and for the occasional peaks? Each family had its own reasons for leaving and for choosing the United States rather than Australia, Canada, or some other place. (From 1830 to 1840, and in a number of other years, the British colonies did attract more English immigrants than did the United States.) One reason for moving to North America rather than to, say, Brazil, was simply the fact that the United States was an

English-speaking country and that many persons of English descent were already here—cousins, perhaps, or other relatives or acquaintances. Another was the glowing letters that some immigrants wrote home.

Also, during parts of the nineteenth century, food in England was in short supply and comparatively expensive. A flood of cheap American food later, after 1874, was deleterious to British agriculture and forced farmers to flee to the land where they could hope to be more prosperous. Life in the factory towns, which had sprung up as British industry developed outside the cottages, was often uncomfortable, sometimes sordid. Labor unions, if permitted at all, had little power to effect needed reforms.

The British spirit of adventure was not dead, and America was one of the places that promised adventure. Less adventurous people, though, also found America desirable. They no longer needed to dread an ocean crossing that might take two months or more: fast steamships had cut the time to days. Shipping companies and American railroads offered more and more special inducements, highlighted by low fares that often included the transportation of personal belongings. For all these reasons, and more, the British kept coming, and coming, and coming.

They still kept coming in the twentieth century: over a million of them in the first twenty-five years, few during the depression and World War II, but an average of some twenty thousand a year thereafter. They still come.

Of our 500 most common surnames, 345, or 69 percent, may be considered usually English in their derivation. This does not mean, of course, that every present holder of the name is entirely or even partly of English descent. Many immigrants changed their names to English ones after reaching this country, and many black people adopted common names, usually of English derivation. Conversely, some persons whose ancestry may be partly or mainly English may have "foreign-sounding" names because of marriage or change of name or for some other reason. I should mention also that there are some common names, like Jones or Williams, that may have started out as Welsh or something else but that have been adopted by so many persons in England or the United States that a present majority of the holders may be almost "pure" English.

Of the 3,169 most common names of Americans—names held by 10,000 or more persons listed on Social Security rolls —a count that I made shows 1,864, or about 59 percent, to be English or probably English. Of the over a million less common names, several thousand are or appear to be English, although the proportionate number decreases sharply because we now have names from all over the world to draw from.

An amusing game of solitaire may be played with uncommon English names in a city directory. In a few pages of a Manhattan phone book, for instance, I find that contrary to expectation only a few Manhattanites are Hasty. Apparently only one is Happy, although another, not English, is Happi. Unquestionably there are several Hazards in New York, and I surmise that the Hazard Powder Company makes gunpowder. Does Hasher run a restaurant? How did Halfhide get that namc? I know the source of Haycock—it's a little cone-shaped pile of British hay. I am glad that Robert Hascoat. I find several Haddock in Manhattan but no Halibut, and thoughts of fishing lead me (Hook) onward to discover in Manhattan Trout but no Tuna, lots of Salmon, Bass, and Pike, a solitary Perch, and a single Goldfish with a trio of Goldfishers ready to catch him.

The names of our presidents suggest the extent to which persons with Anglo-Saxon names have tended to dominate our history. All these are English, or sometimes Welsh or Scottish, names:

Washington	Harrison (2)	Buchanan	Arthur	Coolidge
Adams (2)	Tyler	Lincoln	Cleveland	Truman
Jefferson	Polk	Johnson (2)	McKinley	Nixon
Madison	Taylor	Grant	Taft	Ford
Monroe	Fillmore	Hayes	Wilson	Carter
Jackson	Pierce	Garfield	Harding	

The Dutch Van Buren was the only nineteenth-century "foreigner" to break the pattern. An assassin's bullet brought the Dutch Theodore Roosevelt to the White House in 1901, where he stayed until 1909, and a second Roosevelt was in office from 1931 to 1945. Hoover and Eisenhower, with a German-Swiss and a German heritage, and Kennedy and Reagan, Irishmen, were the only others to break the English hold. But it is no doubt indicative of the growing power of the non-English in American society that so far in just about half of the years of this century someone not of English descent or name has occupied the presidential office. The days of Presidents Serritella, Kaminski, and Gomez may not be far away.

10

THE WELSH:

How Green Is the Other Valley?

SLIGHTLY LARGER than Massachusetts, Wales is an irregular bump attached to England's west coast and looking across the Irish Sea at southern Ireland. Green much of the year because of its abundant rain, it is also a land of grays in many places: gray beneath an often overcast sky, gray with lines of bleak houses terraced on the hills of its two coal regions.

The people share in the grays and in the brightness. Many are rather dark complexioned, rather short, usually unsmiling, remnants of a Bronze Age heritage. Others—larger, some would say handsomer—may mingle with that a Teutonic element and God knows what more, for Roman legions and Norsemen and other trespassers have now and again moved in by land or entered on the long and rocky coast.

As in all people, but especially it seems in the men and women of Wales, the gray and the brightness contrast, clash, alternate. Actor Richard Burton ‹one from a fortified manor›, Welsh despite his English name, with his magnificently flexible voice ("He can make the rocks cry," someone has said), loves to recall bright days from his youth but remembers almost with affection grimy toil in the Welsh mines where his father and other relations risked their lives, and gray moods have sometimes driven him to long Lethean sessions with the bottle.

Poet Dylan Thomas ‹descendant of Thomas, "a twin"›—a hearty but moody man who could so tenderly describe a child's Christmas in Wales—could also improvise ribald, insulting verses and shout and sing them during evenings in Welsh pubs or even at American hotel bars. Preoccupied by death, he nevertheless told newspapermen that he had come to America to seek "naked women in wet mackintoshes." I once heard him tell an audience consisting mainly of collegiennes, "So much beauty, and none of it mine." His gray demon drove him to Welsh beer, American whiskey, and finally to his death at thirty-nine while he was on the way to California to write an opera with Igor Stravinsky.

The Eisteddfodau reveal the widespread Welsh love for music, poetry, drama, art. Local competitions climaxing in the National Eisteddfod that alternates between North and South Wales, they are attended by almost everyone in the country.

Over a century ago the Eisteddfodau were brought to America. At the first of them in California, July 4, 1860, two-thirds of the performers were named Jones ‹descendant of John, "gift of God"› and the others were all Evans ‹descendant of John› or Edwards ‹descendant of Edward, "rich, guardian"›. Two years later others got into the act: Owen ‹descendant of Owen, "well born"›, Ellis ‹descendant of Ellis, "God is salvation"›, Price ‹descendant of Rhys, "ardor, a rush"›, and Rowlands ‹descendant of Roland, "fame, land"›.

As this example suggests, the total number of Welsh surnames is not large. Sometimes only a half dozen names will be shared by twenty or thirty families in a Welsh village, and it has been estimated that about nine-tenths of the Welsh population answer to a total of a hundred names.

Among characteristically Welsh names, besides those just

listed, are Morgan, whose distant ancestor was so called because he was great and bright, Griffin or Griffith(s) ‹a lord of great fierceness›, Lloyd (from *llwyd* ‹brown or gray›), Llewellyn ‹descended from the lionlike›, which is often shortened to Lewis, and Meredith, whose name-taking progenitor was a sea lord.

Davies or Davis is Welsh for ‹son of David›, but Davis rather than Davidson has been taken over by so many English people that only a family historian can ascertain whether a given person called Davis is Welsh or English or a mixture. Since the boundary between England and Wales is essentially only a line of a map, the same comment applies to many other names. There are, for instance, thousands of Joneses and Evanses in England who have no Welsh blood in their veins, or if they do, are not aware of it.

A number of names starting with *P* are Welsh, and therein lies a little story. Sir Walter Scott's jester in *Ivanhoe* sang about a widow who had three suitors, one of whom was Welsh:

> Sir David ap Morgan ap Griffith ap Hugh
> Ap Tudor ap Rhice, quoth his roundelay.
> She said that one widow for so many was too few,
> And she bade the Welshman wend his way.

What the widow may not have known was that centuries ago a Welshman carried much of his pedigree with him. *Ap* is Welsh for ‹son of›. So Sir David was the son of Morgan who was the son of Griffith and so on.

Probably Sir David had only a little land, for in medieval Wales it was not infrequent that a father or a court would divide an estate among the sons, and thus plots became smaller and smaller. Sir David, though, could still point back with pride over a century and a half to his ancestor Rhice (or Rhys or Rees(e) or Reece as it is more often spelled), who probably owned a much larger estate.

The *a* in *ap* was often dropped, and that fact accounts for the frequency of initial *P*. Thus ap Hugh often became Pugh, which might also be spelled Pew or Pue. Powell is from ap Howell, Pri(t)chard from ap Richard, Pomfrey or Pumphrey from ap Humphrey, and Price (sometimes Brice or Bryce) from ap Rhys. Still other names in which *ap* survives as *P* are Parry or Perry ‹son of Harry›, Penry ‹son of Henry›, Plews ‹son of Lewis›, Ployd ‹son of Lloyd›, and Probert and Popkin, both of which mean ‹son of Robert›. Ap Evan, however, was condensed to Bevan and ap Owen to Bowen. *Ap* occasionally survives intact, as in Apjohn or Apdavid, or it changes to *Up* as in Upjohn ‹son of John›, or Uprichard ‹son of Richard›.

An *-s* rather than *-son* at the end of an English-sounding name often indicates Welsh ancestry, although the exceptions are many. Thus Williams and Roberts are more likely than Williamson and Robertson to be Welsh. I've already noted Jones, Evans, and Davis. Other examples are Owens, Rogers ‹descendant of Roger, "fame, spear"›, Edwards, Phillips ‹descendant of Phillip, "lover of horses"›, and Maddocks or Maddox ‹descendant of Madoc or Madog, "fortunate"›.

Maddocks has an interesting link with American history. Madoc ap Owain Gwynedd was a real or imaginary Welsh prince and sailor reputed to have landed in what is now Florida over three centuries before Columbus voyaged to the west. Richard Hakluyt told of Madoc's journey in his *Voyages* (1582),and David Powel reinforced the story in his *Historie of Cambria* (an old name for Wales), published two years later. English poet Robert Southey wrote *Madoc,* an almost forgotten epic, in 1805.

George Catlin, an American student of Indian life, in 1841 concluded that Madoc and his men had gone as far as the upper Missouri and were among the ancestors of the Mandan Indians. Unconfirmed stories exist of "white Indians" in the Louisville, Kentucky, area, and between 1650 and 1750 frontiersmen sometimes reported finding Indians who spoke Welsh. In 1953 the Virginia Cavalier Chapter of the Daughters of the American Revolution placed a marker outside Mobile, Alabama, that reads, "In memory of Prince Madoc, Welsh explorer who landed on the shores of Mobile Bay in 1170 and left behind, with the Indians, the Welsh language."

Whether or not a Prince Madoc and followers ever found America and left Indian-Welsh sons and daughters, it is certain that many thousands of Welsh came later. How many thousands we cannot say because since 1536 Wales has been unified with England and seldom separated statistically from it. English rather than Welsh is its predominant language, especially near the border; only about a quarter of its people speak or understand an appreciable amount of Welsh, which is a Celtic tongue using some sounds almost unattainable by English people's vocal apparatus.

No, we cannot say how many thousands, but perhaps an eighth of all those who came here from Great Britain were Welsh. We find in the Jamestown Colony names like Jones, Euans (Evans), and Davies, a Thomas ap-Richard, "Henry a Welchman," and others probably or clearly Welsh. We find more such names in other, later rosters that survive from other colonies.

In general the Welsh went where the English went, scattering across the continent with them, but sometimes they established their own little enclaves, especially in mining areas such those of western Pennsylvania or others not unlike the places where they grew up, or in steel towns or factory towns. In Wisconsin they were among the early settlers in Columbia and Waukesha counties and others; in Iowa, Louisa and Howard and Iowa counties; in Minnesota, Blue Earth County, where I once taught Lloyds and Powells and Llewellyns along with the more numerous Scandinavians and Germans. In the 1840s and 1850s a number of Welsh converts to Mormonism settled in Nauvoo, Illinois, where Dan Jones operated a Mississippi River schooner used especially in transporting Mormons across the river on their way west. Still later many other Welsh moved to the various western states.

Why did so many Welsh come to America? The usual reasons: occasional shortages of food, lack of land, a love of adventure, the call of the unknown, urging letters from those who had gone before, a dislike of their sometimes supercilious or imperious English neighbors.

How did they live? Variously. Some became rich, some

famous. Welsh or Welsh-descended signers of the Declaration of Independence were named Lewis, Jefferson, Williams, Floyd, and Lewis Morris. Daniel Boone's mother was a Welsh Quaker. Others of Welsh stock include such apparent opposites as John L. Lewis, once the president of the powerful United Mine Workers, and Benjamin Fairless, chairman of the board of U.S. Steel. Another labor leader was William Green, AFL president. The Cadwalladers became rich Philadelphia merchants, Frank Lloyd Wright one of the world's leading architects, the Duke family tobacconists and founders of a great university. The mothers of Daniel Webster and Calvin Coolidge were of Welsh stock. The names of Welsh-descended William Dean Howells and Jack London grace American literature. Many a Hughes, Evans, Jones, Howell, Powell, Walters, Perkins, Thomas, Morgan, Rice, Price, and other seeming Welsh have found entry to the pages of *Who's Who in America*.

But many more, especially in their first years here, lived like those depicted in 1861 in a short story in *Atlantic Monthly*. Its author was Rebecca Harding Davis, mother of novelists Richard Harding Davis and Charles Belmont Davis. This excerpt depicts the steel town where Hugh Wolfe (a not typical Welsh surname) worked. Frail of health, he dreamed of becoming a sculptor, even in this environment.

The idiosyncrasy of this town is smoke. It rolls sullenly in slow folds from the great chimneys of the iron-foundries, and settles down in black, slimy pools on the muddy streets. Smoke on the wharves, smoke on the dingy boats, on the yellow river—clinging in a coating of greasy soot to the house-front, the two faded poplars, the faces of the passers-by. The long train of mules, dragging masses of pig-iron through the narrow street, have a foul vapor hanging to their reeking sides. . . . Smoke everywhere! A dirty canary chirps desolately in a cage beside me.

. . . The Wolfes had two of the cellar-rooms. The old man, like many of the puddlers and feeders of the mills, was Welsh—had spent half of his life in the Cornish tin mines. You may pick out the Welsh immigrants . . . out of the throng passing the windows, any day. They are a trifle more filthy; their muscles are not so brawny; they stoop more. When they are drunk, they neither yell, nor shout, nor stagger, but skulk along like beaten hounds. A pure, unmixed breed, I fancy: shows itself in the slight angular bodies and sharply-cut facial lines. . . . Their lives are like those of their class: incessant labor, sleeping in kennel-like rooms, eating rank pork and molasses, drinking God and the distillers only knew what.

Despite all such difficulties, there can be a quiet determination among the Welsh. It is illustrated by a group of forty-seven of them who left Wales in 1795, determined to escape extreme poverty and what they regarded as the oppressiveness of the Pitt government. They went to Caermarthen to embark on the *Maria,* but the ship was too large to dock there. The men walked to Bristol (a week away) and boarded the *Maria* there; the women and children were to come to Bristol on a smaller vessel. But wind delayed that vessel's departure for three weeks, so the women and children decided to walk to Bristol, too. Before they arrived, the *Maria* had sailed. It met the smaller ship and the men found that their families were not aboard. They induced the *Maria*'s captain to return to Bristol, where all were finally reunited. Even then they had to endure an unusually stormy crossing, which took twelve weeks. At last they did arrive in Philadelphia and worked their way to Cambria County in western Pennsylvania. There they founded a place called Ebensburg. It now has a population of about 5,000, among whom one may still find the Joneses, the Evanses, and others with names like Lloyd and Bowen and Morgan.

11

ULSTER SCOTS AND OTHER SCOTS:

From the Lowlands and the Highlands

JOHN REID ‹red haired or ruddy› and Robert Lockhart ‹herdsman›, both born in Fifeshire, Scotland, founded in 1888 the St. Andrews Golf Course at Yonkers on the Hudson, the first organized golf club in the United States, although the game had been played here, with "the veritable Caledonian balls," before 1779. The game had been played in Scotland, though, as early as the fifteenth century: James II in 1457 decreed that "Fute-ball and Golfe [muste] be utterly cryed downe" since they reduced attention to archery, which was more valuable in warfare. However, others of the royal Stuarts ‹keeper of the sty; later a steward or manager› were enthusiastic about the game. For instance, Mary, Queen of Scots, is said to have been playing only a few days after her husband was murdered.

The United States is indebted to Scotland for much besides golf. For instance, Alexander Graham Bell, born in Edinburgh, invented not only the telephone but also a photophone, an audiometer, a device for detecting bullets or other metal objects in the body, and improvements on the phonograph. The less-remembered John McTammany, Glasgow, invented the player piano (1881) and a voting machine (1892). Allan Pinkerton, Glasgow, founded America's most famous detective agency and may have foiled a plot to assassinate Abraham Lincoln in 1861.

More instances: Andrew Carnegie, born in Dunfermline, made a fortune in steel, but he used large parts of it to provide funds for hundreds of American public libraries, endowed what is now the Carnegie-Mellon University, and built the Temple of Peace in The Hague. Mary Garden, Aberdeen, was one of our most famous operatic sopranos. Philip Murray, Lanarkshire, as a labor leader helped to win World War II by ensuring labor support for essential economic policies. Duncan Phyfe, born in Inverness to a family named Fife, has been called the greatest furniture designer of his day. John Muir, Dunbar, one of the early environmentalists, was the father of Yosemite and Sequoia national parks and the originator of forest preserves.

Most of our earliest Scottish settlers did not come here from Scotland. They came from Ulster.

In the northeast corner of Ireland, Ulster looks across the narrow North Channel at Scotland. Modern Ulster includes the counties Antrim, Down, Armagh, Fermanagh, Tyrone, and Londonderry in Northern Ireland, and just across a line to the south, Monaghan, Cavan, and Donegal in the Republic of Ireland. Its places have picturesque or evocative names like Coleraine, Dungannon, Ballymena, Carrickfergus, and of course Londonderry—city and county both. Belfast, often torn by civil war, is its chief city and port.

The proximity of Scotland is significant in Ulster's history and in that of America. In 1603 James VI of Scotland succeeded Queen Elizabeth, becoming King James I of England, Scotland, and Ireland. Mainly to demonstrate to his newly acquired English subjects how anti-Catholic he was, he confiscated much of Ulster from the Irish, resettling it with English and especially Lowland Scots, most of whom were Presbyterians. (This action by James I was in considerable part responsible for much of the bloodshed that still goes on in Belfast and other places in Northern Ireland.) In inviting the Scots, James said that he did so "out of his unspeakable love and tindir affectioun" for them.

The Scots who were brought in, and their descendants, are generally called Scotch-Irish, but obviously they were really Scots in Ireland—a quite different thing. For that reason some modern historians prefer to call them Ulster Scots. Most of them came to Ireland from southern Scotland, the Lowlands; some had lived almost within sight of Ulster.

A modern historian, James G. Leyburn, has said that in them were nine or ten blood strains: aborigines of the Stone Age, Gaels (ca. 500 B.C.), Britons (another Celtic folk), Romans (from the time when Rome invaded Britain), Scots (an early Celtic tribe that had invaded from Ireland), Norse (in the Middle Ages), Normans (after 1066), and (most recently) Flemish and English. In contrast, the Highland Scots, from farther north, were more Gaelic than anything else.

The Ulster Scots were a hardy breed—vigorous, bold, individualistic, some of them hard-drinking. Unlike the Highlanders, they seldom wore kilts, and they had no tartans, for they did not belong to clans, like those of Stuart or Douglas.

Life in seventeenth- and eighteenth-century Ulster was not smooth for the Scots. Even though they had been given the use of most of the choice land, they still had Irish neighbors who were understandably unhappy about the loss of that land. Scots on the southern edge of Ulster were on a frontier, with a couple of million angry Irishmen just across the boundary. English neighbors, also, were not easy to get along with, and British crown policies and tax rates often changed.

Besides, the Test Act of 1704 permitted only Anglicans, not other Protestants such as Presbyterians, to hold office. Rents took a large jump in 1717–18, when many original leases expired. A practice called rack-renting was especially pernicious: after a tenant spent much time and money on improving a farm, the landlord raised the rent because the farm was then worth more. A further problem arose as farms were divided and subdivided so much that some were too small to sustain a family.

Emigrants who went to America early in the 1700s wrote enthusiastic letters back, and ship captains, too, told of the wonders of America, thus drumming up business for themselves while they built up dreams in the Scots. Sometimes poor crops, as in the drought years of 1754 and 1755, convinced the hesitant that they should go to the land of plenty.

So they went, a few thousand each year. Sometimes a whole village would move together. In all, according to most estimates, there were about a quarter of a million Ulster Scots in the colonies before the Revolutionary War—perhaps twice as many as there were Irish. Some of the early ones went to New England, but many then proceeded elsewhere, because as William Douglass explained in 1755,

> being brought up to husbandry or raising of grain, called bread corn, New England did not answer as well as the colonies southward; therefore at present they generally resort to Pennsylvania, a good grain colony.

Some stayed, however, as one group did in Londonderry, New Hampshire, whose name they changed from Nutley. Some also went to New York, New Jersey, and Delaware. As early as 1682 a Scot colony was founded at Elizabeth, New Jersey, by James and John Drummond ‹one from a ridge›, Robert, David, and John Barclay ‹one from a birch wood (English)›, Robert Gordon ‹one from a large hill›, and Gawin Lawrie ‹descendant of Lawrence, "laurel"›.

In Pennsylvania they settled especially west of the Susquehanna, partly because the eastern part of the state was already pretty well filled by William Penn's Quakers, German immigrants, and others, and partly because those early settlers were happy to have the Scotch-Irish (as they generally called them) to serve as buffers against the Indians. This function was not new: New England's Cotton Mather in 1706 had wanted to put them on the frontiers of Maine and New Hampshire to protect his Puritans.

Much of western Pennsylvania, however, is too rugged

for good farming, and the choice parts were soon occupied. So later Ulsterites turned south and found their way down the Great Valley of Virginia—some stopping there and others, perhaps even more restless or adventurous, moving on into the Carolinas. There's a Scotland County in North Carolina, and others with such names as Graham ‹one from the gray homestead› and Forsyth ‹descendant of Fearsithe, "peaceful man"›.

In colonial days North Carolina had a Scottish governor, Gabriel Johnston, as early as 1734; an Ulsterman, Mathew Rowan ‹small and red haired›, was president of its council in 1753; another Ulsterman, Arthur Dobbs ‹son of Robert›, became governor in 1754. One "Scots agent," Henry McCulloh ‹son of Cullach, "the boar"›, was responsible for bringing three colonies of Ulstermen to the state, but no city or county bears his name.

In South Carolina most Ulsterites settled near the coast. Charleston, in fact, became a major point of entry for them. Its First Scotch Presbyterian Church dates from 1731. At Beaufort, another coastal settlement, a Scottish colony was wiped out in 1684 by Spaniards and Indians. Some inland cities had better luck, such as Laurens, in which a high proportion of the present-day inhabitants are interrelated because of their descent from founding Ulster families of the eighteenth century. Seventeenth-century settlers at Port Royal bore such Scottish names as McClintock, Buchanan, Inglis, Urie, and Cunningham.

In general non-Ulster Scots came later than those who had sojourned on Ulster soil. Some of them were criminals or supposed traitors whom the authorities sent into exile. Many were farmers hurt by the hard winter of 1771–72, by a cattle disease called murrain, or by rents that in the 1760s rose from 33 to 300 percent in the Highlands, 200 to 400 percent in the Lowlands.

In 1767 all of Prince Edward Island, Canada, had been granted to sixty-seven proprietors, mostly Scots, on condition that they would settle only Protestants there. They cheated a little by also bringing in some Highlanders who happened to be Catholic.

In his *Journal of a Tour to the Hebrides* James Boswell (the Scottish biographer of Dr. Samuel Johnson) reported on a party he attended in Skye in October 1773:

> We had again a good dinner, and in the evening a great dance. . . . And there we performed . . . a dance which I suppose the emigration from Skye has occasioned. They call it "America". . . . It goes on till all are set a-going, setting and wheeling round each other.

Some of the going and the wheeling round must have been performed by people like Lachlan Campbell ‹one with a crooked mouth›, who wore his Highland garb in the Saratoga, New York, area. Indians who saw him liked his colorful costume so much that they begged him and his friends to settle among them. But 350 Highlanders arriving in Wilmington, North Carolina, wheeled around a little too much. They frightened the officials so badly that they made the Scots take an oath to keep the peace. Many Carolinian Scots continued through the eighteenth century to wear their kilts, plaids, and sporrans (fur or leather pouches worn at the top of the kilt).

In 1769 some four thousand of the tenants of two major landholding families, the Macdonalds and the Macleods, left Scotland almost in a body, settling mainly in the Cape Fear valley of North Carolina, where some other Highlanders already were.

Most Highland immigrants spoke Gaelic rather than English, but the majority of their children quickly made the change. As late as 1805, however, Gaelic-speaking Highlanders moved from North Carolina to Jefferson County, Mississippi, baffling the good folk of Fayette and Church Hill with their incomprehensible tongue.

Many of the Ulster Scots successfully took up farming in America, often demonstrating a canny business sense. Some of them raised black cattle and sold the hides and sometimes the meat at considerable profit, in some places floating these products or grain and flour downstream on large rafts, disposing of them, and purchasing the smaller amounts of supplies they would themselves need for the more difficult upstream trip. Or they might find at the docks a British ship that was waiting for logs, dismantle their rafts, and sell the logs for shipment to the British Isles.

The Scots from Scotland were less likely to be farmers, more likely to be businessmen. Some opened shops in towns and cities. Others built up a profitable business with the fishing fleets putting out to sea. Some owned the fleets; others provided supplies. One group established a large transatlantic business with Glasgow merchants. In Virginia, Scots factors bought tobacco, sold it in Europe, bought manufactured goods there, and sold that to the Virginia planters who had grown the tobacco.

The Scots in general were fervent in their zeal to educate their children. As Louis B. Wright has said,

> If they did not literally believe that Latin and Greek would provide the passwords into heaven, Scotch schoolmasters and ministers managed to convey the suspicion that St. Peter would be more impressed by a learned man than a barbarian.

The Scots also gained a reputation for being conscientious workers. Harriet Martineau in the nineteenth century, for instance, described work in the textile mills of Massachusetts, much of it done by daughters of immigrants:

> I saw English, Irish, and Scotch operatives. I heard but a poor character of the English operatives; and the Scotch were pronounced "ten times better." The English are . . . on the watch that they should be asked to do more than they stipulated for. Their habits are not so sober as those of the Scotch, and they are incapable of going beyond the single operation they profess. Such is the testimony of their employers. . . .
>
> . . . at Waltham, . . . the girls earn $2, and some $3, a week. Most of the girls live in the houses provided by the corporation, which accommodate from six to eight each. When sisters come to the mill, it is a common practice for them to bring their mother to keep house for them and some of their companions, in a dwelling built out of their own earnings. . . . Some have cleared off the mortgages from their fathers' farms, others have educated the hope

of the family at college, and many are rapidly accumulating an independence.

During the Revolutionary War most Scots businessmen remained loyal to the British crown and were attacked sometimes viciously in the revolutionary press as money changers in the British temple. Unlike the Irish, almost all of whom sided with the colonials in the war, other Scots—both Ulstermen and the rest—were divided. Sometimes members of the same family could not agree on which side to support. Historian Maldwyn Jones tells, for instance, of two New Hampshire "Scotch-Irish" brothers named Stark, one of whom became a general in the Continental army, the other killed while a colonel in the king's forces. An Ulsterman named Alexander Chesney fought first for one side, then the other.

In general the Ulster Scots of Pennsylvania supported the revolutionary cause and provided most of the officers and men for a sturdy group called the Pennsylvania Line. Yet many others joined with the Volunteers of Ireland, a regiment formed in Philadelphia to fight for George III; many of these men had deserted the Continental army.

Jones describes the situation in the Carolinas like this:

> . . . it was in the back-country of the Carolinas that the Scotch-Irish were most sharply divided. Those in North Carolina, if not outright loyalists, were at least extremely hostile to the Revolutionary cause. In western South Carolina, too, there were many loyal Scotch-Irishmen, especially in the isolated frontier settlement known as Ninety-Six. . . . On the other hand, in the Waxhaws—the back country borderland between North and South Carolina—the British found that the population was "universally Irish and universally disaffected." When the Volunteers of Ireland were stationed there, their commander, Lord Rawdon, complained that the Waxhaw people used "every artifice to debauch the minds of my Soldiers," and persuaded many of them to desert.

Colonials who had signed the Declaration of Independence included Fifeshire-born James Wilson ‹son of William›, of Pennsylvania, who also contributed some of the most basic principles of the Constitution, and John Witherspoon, president of the College of New Jersey (now Princeton) and the only clergyman to sign the Declaration. William Hooper and Philip Livingston, both of Scottish descent, also signed. McKean and Rutledge, from Ulster, are claimed by both Irish and Scottish partisans.

John Paul Jones was a Scot from that wonderfully named place Kirkcudbrightshire. He added the Jones himself as an alias when he was in trouble with the law: he was born John Paul. A hot-tempered man who killed the leader of a mutiny and at another time flogged a sailor whose death may have resulted from the beating, he escaped punishment and became an officer in the Continental navy. His first ship there was the *Alfred,* and that vessel was the first on which the Grand Union flag was displayed. In another ship, in six weeks he captured eight enemy vessels, destroyed eight others. In the *Bonhomme Richard,* named for Ben Franklin's Poor Richard, he lashed his vessel to the much larger *Serapis* and after hours of hand-to-hand combat is alleged to have shouted, "I have not yet begun to fight."

Women of the revolutionary era often showed their courage, too. There was, for instance, Mary Murray, described by John H. Finley in *The Coming of the Scot* as "a charming rebel and a great beauty." Her husband was a Loyalist. When Washington's troops were retreating across Manhattan Island, "She detained by her hospitality on a warm September day General Howe and some of his officers (including Cornwallis) and troops, till the rear guard of Washington's little army could make their escape to the upper end of the island, where they on the next day fought the Battle of Harlem Heights, the only successful engagement won by the Americans in New York." Mary would be the mother of one of America's most famous early grammarians, Lindley Murray, and the Murray Hill district of New York is named for the house occupied by her and her Quaker husband.

Many of the names brought to America by Scots are identical with English names, or sometimes with Irish or Welsh. There are, for example, in Scotland as in England, more Smiths than anybody else (eighteen per thousand). But in

Scotland the MacDonalds are in second place—not Joneses as in England or Johnsons as in the United States—and there are three of these MacDonalds for every four Smiths. The Scottish Campbells, five-eighths as numerous as the Smiths, are in third place.

Of the names that are especially likely to be Scottish, Campbell ranks 41st in the United States, Ross is 77th, Graham 98th, Wallace 99th, Murray 106th, MacDonald or McDonald 128th, Gordon 131st, Shaw 136th, Johnston 150th, Ferguson 156th, Andrews 161st, Cunningham 172nd, and Duncan 183rd. Most Scottish names are patronyms or place names, not descriptive or occupational.

Because of people with such names, the Highlands and the Lowlands have greatly enriched the life of the United States. Ulster Scots and other Scots have given us presidents (or have at least contributed to their bloodstrains) Monroe, Jackson, Polk, Buchanan, Andrew Johnson, Grant, Hayes, Arthur, Cleveland, Benjamin Harrison, McKinley, Theodore Roosevelt, and Wilson.

King Robert the Bruce, a sentimental favorite of the Scots since the Middle Ages, is said to be an ancestor of four of those men: Monroe, Polk, Buchanan, and Roosevelt. Thomas Jefferson, though mainly Welsh, was partly Scottish and English, and his teachers were mainly Scots.

The Scots have given us Daniel Webster and Horace Greeley and Justice Oliver Wendell Holmes. Patrick Henry, who ranked liberty above life, was half Welsh, half Scottish. They have given us Stephen Collins Foster and Ethelbert Nevin; painters Gilbert Stuart and Thomas Eakins; Edwin Forrest, "the first great American actor"; and explorer George Rogers Clark. Davy Crockett is claimed by both the Irish and the Scots.

Inventors that proud Scots regard as theirs include Robert Fulton, of steamboat fame; Cyrus McCormick, who made grain harvesting less backbreaking; Robert Dalzell, who developed elevators for storing that grain; Duncan Campbell, who invented machines to help build shoes; William Malcolm, maker of telescopic gunsights; George Baird, who a hundred years ago could make fresh water from the sea; John

Barclay, who taught the telegraph to print its own messages. Oh, yes—and a man named Thomas Alva Edison, whose name means ‹the son of the rich protector›. The mother of Samuel Morse, inventor of the telegraph, was Scottish. Ironically, Morse wrote a book called *Imminent Dangers to the Free Institutions of the United States through Foreign Immigration.*

The Scots have given us, as I said, golf, and porridge, and haggis for the strong of stomach, and whisky without an *e,* and bagpipes, and the Loch Ness monster to talk about, and the eternal mystery of what if anything is worn under kilts, and Presbyterians, and have exported to us the poetry of Robert Burns and the novels of that man whose very tall monument you can see in a city park not far from the Edinburgh quarters where he did much of his writing, that most appropriately named man, Sir Walter Scott.

12

THE IRISH:

. . . Then Came the Careys and the Muldoons

ON MARCH 17, 1776, General George Washington ordered that the password for the night should be "St. Patrick."

The choice was appropriate, not only because of the date. In the Revolutionary War years Washington and other colonial leaders would find themselves increasingly dependent on the fighting abilities of the Irish, almost none of whom favored the Loyalist (English) cause. Some of them personally remembered years of English oppression on the Ould Sod, and others had heard their fathers and mothers and grandparents complaining of it.

Why, they had asked, should Ireland have had to pay a pension of £800 a year to the dowager queen of Prussia, the sister of George II? Why should three-fourths of Irish land belong to or be controlled by English landlords, many of whom were absentee? Why wasn't Ireland allowed to manufacture woolen goods or to sell wool to anyone who wasn't English? Why couldn't Irish ships trade with the colonies? Such economic restrictions had sent thousands of Irish into voluntary exile. Why did some Irish children have to go hungry? Jonathan Swift had proposed satirically that Irish babies be fattened so that wealthy English could buy and eat them.

So the Irish—then, earlier, and later—had no love for the English. The resentment went back a millennium, to the time when the Angles, Saxons, Jutes, and Frisians from the Continent had driven the Celts to the western and northern parts of the British Isles. It had been strengthened by the Normans and Norman-English blends in the Middle Ages, especially when they overthrew the Irish kings. Cromwell's cruelties had renewed and reinforced it in the mid-1600s. The intolerance of the English established church toward Irish Catholics was a constant irritant. So were economic and political restraints, including laws at least as harsh as those that the American colonies found intolerable. So, in a land west of the Atlantic, it was no wonder that the Irish were happy to fight against their oppressors as so often they had done in Ireland.

In May 1775, Maurice O'Brien, born in Cork, with his five stalwart sons and some of his neighbors in Machias Bay, Maine, took their fishing boats out to sea and captured the British warship *Margaretta.* The British sent two more ships, the *Diligence* and the *Tapnaquish,* to get it back. The O'Briens captured them, too. Maurice's son Jeremiah and others sailed the three ships to a provincial congress meeting in Watertown and turned them in to be part of the first American navy.

Several Irishmen signed the Declaration of Independence. One was a son of Fermanagh named Colonel James Smith, who also organized Pennsylvania's first company of volunteers. Dr. George Taylor and Dr. Matthew Thornton signed; they too were born in Ireland. Thomas McKean and George Read of Delaware and Edward Rutledge of South Carolina had Irish parents. Grandsons of Irishmen were Charles Carroll of Maryland and Thomas Lynch of South Carolina.

Where did the colonists who fought the British at Bunker Hill get their arms? Sure, it was from Major General John

Sullivan, who had stormed Fort William and Mary in New Hampshire and captured guns and powder which he gave them. The colonials at Bunker Hill and Breed's Hill used the captured arms well. They lost 367 dead and wounded, but the British lost 1,054.

Another Irish warrior, Richard Montgomery, after sixteen years in the British service, became a brigadier general in the Colonial forces but, still only thirty-seven, died while leading an assault on Quebec.

And there was John Barry ‹descendant of Barry, "spear"›, born in county Wexford. Some call him the father of the American navy. Made a captain in March 1776, he with his *Lexington* captured the English *Edward* in the first naval victory of the war. In other ships he won other battles and lost a few. It was he who triumphantly carried the great Marquis de Lafayette home to France in his *Alliance*. A little later the man who had started his share of the naval war with a victory ended it with another, capturing four British warships and some commercial vessels in the West Indies.

Not only in fighting did the Irish have a part. Charles Thomson, the secretary of the Continental Congress, was born in Derry. General John Sullivan's brother James was twice elected governor of Massachusetts—an early harbinger of widespread Irish political leadership. In fact, five of the first governors in the new nation had Irish blood: McKinley of Delaware, Rutledge of South Carolina, Clinton of New York, Bryan of Pennsylvania, and Sullivan. In 1780, when the revolutionary army was almost out of money, Philadelphia raised £300,000 to help. One-third of it came from an organization called the Friendly Sons of St. Patrick.

The Irish like to claim but cannot verify that the first white man to see America was St. Brendan in the sixth century. Known also as Brendan the Navigator, he assuredly sailed far into the Atlantic, and one tradition, repeated in 1931 by Edward Roberts, has it that "on the banks of the Ohio River he was halted by a stranger of unearthly majesty who directed him to return to Ireland, but assured him that others would follow in his steps."

Follow they did. Not many in Jamestown, although there were some with names like Farley and Higgins that can be either Irish or English. And among the 347 killed there in an Indian massacre on March 22, 1622, was one "Francis, an Irishman," who died "at Mr. Richard Owen's House—at Westouer, about a mile from Berkley-Hundred."

The early New England colonies were almost without Irish, but a few Irish were among the multinational "Dutch" of New Amsterdam. After 1650 other Irish trickled in, and the number increased slowly over the next century and a half, becoming largest when England's religious or political policies squeezed Ireland most tightly. During the numerous conflicts between English and Irish in the seventeenth century, the English seized many able-bodied men and women "not past breeding," and transported them as prisoners or virtual slaves to labor in the colonies. Other Irish, often at great risk and hardship, found their own, more satisfactory ways to cross the ocean.

Even so, at the time of the American Revolution only a fraction of 1 percent of our total population were Catholics, and some of those persons were of French or other backgrounds. (Today about a fourth of all Americans are members of the Roman Catholic church.) So the great contributions of the Irish Catholics to the Revolution were made by a relatively small number of persons.

Some of the early Irish were accused, rightly or wrongly, of extreme lawlessness, as by a South Carolinian who complained of "all our valuable horses . . . carried off," "families stripped and turned naked into the woods," "married women . . . ravished, virgins deflowered," "stores . . . broken into and rifled." A Reverend Charles Woodson asked the legislative body for help:

> As the back country is now daily increasing by imports from Ireland and elsewhere (most of whom are very poor), the number of idle and worthless must also increase if our settlements remain in their present neglected state. Many of these new settlers greatly repent their coming out here, to languish away life in a country that falls so very short of their expectations; and the sober part of them would more willingly return than remain here. . . . [If] a

spot of ground be planted (especially with fruit trees for cider, etc.), the proprietor cannot be certain of gathering the produce but may see it carried off before his face without control.

An English traveler, Charles Latrobe, expressed his mixed views of the Irish in 1832:

Here comes a ship load of Irish. They land upon the wharfs of New York in rags and open-knee'd breeches, with their raw looks and bare necks, they flourish their cudgels, throw up their torn hats and cry,—"Hurrah for Gineral Jackson!" They get drunk and kick up a row;—lend their forces to any passing disturbance, and make early acquaintance with the interior of the lock-ups. From New York they go in swarms to the canals, railroads, and public works, where they perform the labour which the Americans are not inclined to do; now and then they get up a fight among themselves in the style of old Ireland, and perhaps kill one another, expressing great indignation and surprise when they find that they must answer for it, though they are in a free country. By degrees, the more thrifty get and keep money, and diving deeper into the continent, purchase lands; while the intemperate and irreclaimable vanish from the surface. . . . Though the fathers may be irreclaimable, the children become good citizens,—and there is no finer race in the world both for powers of mind and body than the Irish, when favoured by education and under proper control.

In 1816 the Shamrock Friendly Association prepared a booklet for Irish immigrants. Much of it consisted of practical suggestions: come in the summer, when employment prospects are best, and leave the city soon, for work is more available in the country; eat lightly and avoid much strong drink; and especially, expect to work hard:

What is America? What sort of people may be expected to succeed in it? The immortal Franklin has answered these questions: "America is the land of labor." But it is, emphatically, the best country on earth for those that will labor. By industry they can earn more wages here than elsewhere in the world. Our governments are more frugal; they demand few taxes [today that statement would be followed by a derisive exclamation mark] so that the earnings of the poor man are left to enrich himself. . . .

Idlers are out of their element here, and the being who is technically called a man of rank in Europe is despicable in America.

> . . . Laborers, carpenters, masons, bricklayers, stonecutters, tailors, and shoemakers, and the useful mechanics generally, are always sure of work and wages.

The early nineteenth century saw only a few thousand Irish immigrants each year. There was a spurt to 20,000 or more a year starting in 1833 and then a huge jump to 105,536 in 1847 and a peak of 221,253 in 1851. In the decade 1847 through 1856 over a million and a quarter Irish checked in with American immigration authorities. In all of our history only Italian and eastern European immigrants at the beginning of the twentieth century outnumbered this flood of Irish.

A fungus that caused potatoes to rot was the chief reason why so many persons left Ireland during that decade. In the nineteenth century Ireland was mainly a nation of small farmers—very small farmers, partly because the land in 1840 had to support four times as many people as it had in the 1740s. Rural folk subsisted in part on the few pence that, when times were good, they could earn by doing work for an absentee English landlord or his representative. But chiefly they lived on what they could grow on the two or three acres of land that they rented, often at exorbitant rates. The luckiest had a couple of pigs and even a cow, but most depended for sustenance on kale, cabbage, beans, and especially potatoes, often a full acre or more of potatoes. Cabbage could not be kept much beyond the growing season, kale somewhat into the winter; beans would keep well but were not productive enough to provide bean soup for a large family over a long period. But potatoes grew well in the black soil, they required relatively little work, and they could be kept from the end of one growing season well into the next. Potatoes were the Irish bread and often the Irish meat as well, since the cost of a small piece of hog jowl might be a day's wages.

But in 1845 half the potato crop rotted, and in the following spring there was widespread illness caused by attempting to eat the spoiled food. The British government brought in some American maize to prevent starvation, but many persons could not afford the twopence a pound that was charged. Some farmers who had a little money or much resourcefulness decided to leave the hungry land and sail for Canada or the United States. A little later the government paid the transportation costs for many, justifying the expenditure on the ground that it was lower than if they had provided food or burial expenses for many thousands.

In 1846 the potato crop was an almost complete failure, and as a result twice as many Irish found their way to the United States in the following year, while many thousands more died of hunger or of "famine fever." Not all the emigrants were farmers. Many were shopkeepers, bakers, tailors, blacksmiths, and the like whose customers had been removed by the potato shortage. A winter that was much colder than is normal for Ireland accelerated the flight.

Sometimes the emigrants left from Liverpool, but more often from Dublin, Cork, Limerick, Sligo, or various harbors on the Shannon. Many did not want to depart from their lovely land, despite its troubles. A person left behind in Kerry wrote of a leave-taking:

> . . . the bright May morning with the summer sun shining in the heavens: the birds singing in the hedges, and the cuckoo's call echoing in their ears, as the sad procession wended their way down to the emigrant ship—men, women, and children—the very old and the very young—filling the clear summer air with their wails and lamentations.

The transatlantic voyages were not easy, especially in overcrowded sailing ships. Accommodations varied from ship to ship, but picture as one example a below-decks corridor perhaps a hundred feet long. On each side of a narrow aisle little compartments about six feet each way. Four persons—sometimes from one family, sometimes not—sharing each of these boxes. "Not much more room than in their coffin," says one account.

Single women sometimes next to strange men: modern Irish writers claim the men protected them from rough crew members and lascivious ship's officers. Twenty-one quarts of water a week per passenger, for all purposes, but less when the voyage proved exceptionally long. A pound of bread or potatoes a day, plus whatever food the passenger could afford to bring aboard, plus some that could be bought at outrageous prices from the captain if one had money. A restroom for women at each end of the corridor; men went to the upper deck. On that deck, too, grates called "cabooses" where the potatoes could be cooked.

There was little or no medical attention except possibly from a medically half-trained ship's officer. The expectation was that 10 percent of the passengers would die en route; in 1847 it was more than 20 percent. Fevers, something vaguely called "the plague," dysentery—a host of illnesses severe or mild. In 1847, eighty-four disease-ridden ships had to be held for days or weeks in quarantine below Quebec, and ten thousand Irish people died on those ships. Of these, says Oscar Handlin, "three thousand [were] so alone that their names were never known."

If we did know their names, they would probably be like the names of those other Irish who survived such journeys and landed in Boston, New York, Philadelphia, or other ports. Most Irish names are patronyms, and unlike Welsh names they are very numerous. No one of them, for that reason, has ever become so common as Welsh names like Jones or Evans. The most common distinctively Irish name in modern America is Murphy, and it ranks only fifty-first; Kelly is sixty-first.

Many of the patronyms are derived from names of Celtic princes or other leaders dating as far back as the eighth century. "The story of Irish surnames," says L. G. Pine, "is that of a people of great antiquity who began to use surnames earlier than most races in western Europe."

One of those leaders was Brian Boru, who was a king of Ireland from 1002 to 1014, having earlier been king of two smaller Irish areas. Brian means ‹hill›. He was a warrior and a diplomat, and countless O'Briens, O'Bryans, O'Brions, O'Bryants, and Bryans and Bryants still commemorate him.

The Irish *O'* means ‹grandson of› but is often translated loosely as ‹descendant of›. The apostrophe is only a scribal convention. Ordinarily *O'* shows that a name is definitely Irish, although I once taught a Slavic student who wrote his name O'Russa. When I questioned him, he explained that inserting the apostrophe and the capital letter had been his own idea "because I like the way it looks in O'Shea."

A prefix that the Irish share with the English is *Fitz-* ‹son of›. It can be traced back to Latin *filius* ‹son›, which in French is *fils*. The Normans brought it to England in 1066 as *fiz* or *fitz*, so that Fitzroy, for instance, meant ‹son of the king›. Later the prefix crossed into Ireland. The names Fitzgerald, Fitzgibbons, Fitzhenry, Fitzhugh, Fitzmaurice, Fitzpatrick, and Fitzsimmons for many years have been found among both English and Irish.

Amateur genealogists sometimes say with assurance that *Mc* is used by Irish, *Mac* by Scots. Actually many names of Scottish families are spelled with *Mc*, many Irish names with *Mac*. Elsdon Smith, in his authoritative *New Dictionary of American Family Names*, lumps all such names together under the spelling *Mc* but alphabetizes them as if the spelling were *Mac*. He says,

> Mc is just a shortened form of Mac. Both Irish and Scotch purists claim that the contraction to Mc is "wrong." In America, however, most people contract the prefix to Mc, the tendency being slightly stronger among the Irish.

A few people further contract *Mac* or *Mc* to *M'*, as in M'Neely ‹son of Conghal, "great courage"›, which in turn may come to be spelled Meneely. Especially among the Ulster Scots, *Mac* followed by *G* sometimes becomes *Ma;* this accounts for such spellings as Maguire from MacGuire or McGuire ‹son of the pale man› and Magee from MacGee or McGee ‹son of Aodh, "fire"›.

Many Irish names, though, have no markers like these prefixes. Sullivan is ‹grandson of Suileabhan, "the black-eyed one"› and Murphy is ‹descendant of Murchadh, "the sea fighter"›. Perhaps so many Kellys and Kelleys have been renowned battlers because their name means ‹grandson of Ceallach, "the contentious one"›.

After Murphy and Kelly, the most common American names likely to be Irish are Sullivan (79th), Bryant (116th), Ryan ‹grandson of Rian, "little king"› (152nd), Dunn ‹the brown man› (160th), Burke ‹dweller at the fort› (189th), Riley ‹grandson of Raghallach, "playful"› (193rd), and O'Brien (195th). Some other names might be on the list but are very often English or Scottish rather than Irish: Coleman, McDonald and its variants, Kennedy ‹he with a misshapen head!›, McCarthy and its variants, Boyd, Carroll, and Duncan.

How extensive were the departures from Ireland? Oscar Handlin gives us a hint. "Ireland in 1841 had held almost a half-million one-room cottages. In 1861 there were only eighty-nine thousand. The cottiers [impoverished renters] had not improved their housing; they had either died or emigrated." After the famine ended, as Marjorie Fallows says, "the journey to America had become institutionalized as a way of life." Between 1845 and 1881 Ireland's population shrank from nine million to five million. Even the wealthy joined in fleeing from a land that seemed cursed to a land they believed was blest.

But mid-nineteenth-century life for the Irish in America, especially the poor among them, was hardly blest at all. Many cottiers found that they had merely exchanged their little huts of mud and straw for even more cramped quarters in filthy tenements. Country men, women, and children, many of whom had hardly been out of sight of their birthplace before, did not know how to live in a city like Boston but also did not know how to get away from it to a rural area where they might again grow potatoes, cabbage, and the Indian corn that had been introduced to them in the old country.

Work was hard to find, especially for persons as unskilled and often illiterate as the majority of the Irish were. When work was advertised, often there was an accompanying notice, "No Irish Need Apply," as a song composed in 1848 or 1849 lamented:

I'm a decent boy just landed from the town of Ballyfad;
  I want a situation and I want it very bad.
I've seen employment advertised, "It's just the thing," says I,
  But the dirty spalpeen ended with "No Irish Need Apply."
"Whoo," says I, "that's an insult, but to get the place I'll
  try."
So I went to see the blackguard with his "No Irish Need
  Apply."

Chorus:
  Some do think it's a misfortune to be christened Pat or Dan,
  But to me it is an honor to be born an Irishman.

Honor or not, it was hard to be an Irishman in America in the 1840s and 1850s. "Americans" didn't like "foreigners," who were often willing to work for less money. Those of English descent had never cared much for the Irish anyway, what with their reputed dirt and their strange pronunciations and their stubborn refusal to behave as the English demanded and their kissing the Pope's feet and all. And now that they were coming to America in an unending stream, they might just take over the whole country if they were given some jobs. The South didn't want Irish at all: they already had their labor supply. The North did find menial jobs for many of the able-bodied, for there were floors to be scrubbed, canals to be dug, railroads to be built:

It's "Pat do this" and "Pat do that,"
  Without a stocking or cravat,
Nothing but an old straw hat
  While I work on the railway.

The concentration of many immigrants in the cities was to have a profound effect on industrial America. Oscar Handlin explains it this way:

Industry lost its rustic aspect after 1840. Immigration then piled up an abundant labor supply in the coastal cities. Thousands of penniless Irish and German peasants came ashore in Boston, Philadelphia, and New York with no resources and with a desperate eagerness to work at any wages. These people accepted what terms were offered; and if the labor of a man would not support his family, then the women and children could work, too. Their strangeness and the recollections of the hunger they had escaped kept these people from protesting. Some drifted off to the mill towns where they began to replace the girls and the casual farm hands. Others laid the streets and raised the buildings of the expanding towns; or they took to tailoring or similar tasks for contractors in the cities where they landed.

Within a decade the availability of cheap labor, unprecedented in America, sparked the appearance of many new industries and transformed those already in existence. . . . By 1860 manufacturing had become an urban pursuit.

Many of the boys who came over in the 1840s fought in the American Civil War of the 1860s, almost all of them for the North. They hated slavery, themselves having existed in Ireland in what many considered near slavelike conditions. Between 150,000 and 170,000 Irish-born fought to free the slaves and preserve the Union, according to some counts, and there were also many second and third-generation Irish. There were some large Hibernian units as well as many squads or companies.

Some of the Irish—long before the Kennedys—showed a genius for American politics. In 1817 in New York they protested Tammany's bigotry and forced their way into its membership, and by the 1840s they were in control of it. In the 1880s New York and Boston had Irish mayors. In 1894 a writer who was no friend of the Irish complained that over a dozen of America's cities, including St. Louis, Pittsburgh, New Orleans, Omaha, and San Francisco, were "led captive by Irishmen and their sons." The Irish potato famine of the 1840s had begun to have the unpredictable result of supplying America with many of its leaders. Even today, "National Opinion Research Center studies show that the Irish still have the highest political participation of any ethnic group in the country."

In only three years between 1844 and 1914 did Ireland send us fewer than twenty thousand persons. The total during those years was almost four million. Since 1914, however, two world wars, a long American depression, and restrictive immigration laws have kept the numbers much smaller.

The 1860 census showed that most of the 1,611,000 Irish-born who were then in the United States had stayed in New England, New Jersey, New York, and Pennsylvania, and that almost two-thirds of the men were classed as unskilled laborers. In 1855 Irish and Germans together had made up 44 percent of New York City's population. Boston had become the Irish center that it still is. In Philadelphia the Irish prospered more quickly than in most other places, largely because in the mid-century Philadelphia was undergoing a larger-than-most boom in industry and construction. A higher percentage of Irish there could already afford their own small homes.

But work on the railroads and in factories took other Irish across the country, as I have said. Of course they and others fought and drank and boasted in the saloons of gold-rush California. They worked, too, in the powder mills of Delaware, as this account from the diary of Father Patrick Kenny ‹grandson of Cionadh, "sprung from fire"› shows:

> Garesche's powder mill blew up. John Kelly, only 2 months from Ireland where he left his wife and 7 children, Dead. Also Wm Duffy [‹grandson of Dubhthach, "black"›] and Wm Delany [‹descendant of the challenger›]—all catholics. 4 Irish Cath wounded.

They worked, too, at Galena, Illinois, with its lead sulfate deposits. The first grand jury there, in 1827, had among its members Hogan ‹grandson of little Og, "young"›, Murphy, Riley, two Foleys ‹grandson of Foghlaidh, "plunderer"›, and a Scot named Finley and Englishmen named Coe and Lynch.

It was a cow belonging to Mrs. O'Leary ‹grandson of Leoghaire, which appropriately means "calf keeper"› that reportedly started the great Chicago fire of 1871. In later years much of the South Side became the Irish district described by James T. Farrell ‹son of Fearghal, "extremely brave"› in his novels such as the trilogy about Studs Lonigan ‹fierce little man› or Gas House McGinty ‹son of Fionnachta, "beautiful snow"› or Danny O'Neill ‹grandson of Niall, "champion"›. The Irish there lived in one of the ethnic islands so typical of our big cities. Writing of it in his book about Chicago's longest-serving mayor, Richard Daley ‹grandson of Dalach, "one who goes to meetings"›, Mike Royko says that the Irish island had Germany to the north, Poland to the northwest, Italy and Israel to the west, and Bohemia and Lithuania to the southwest. You could tell which "state" you were in, he says, "by the odors of the foodstores and the open kitchen windows, the sound of the foreign or function language, and by whether a stranger hit you in the head with a rock." Royko does not say which state had the most rock throwers.

With their love for fighting, many Irish became boxers, first in the bare-knuckle days when men fought virtually without regard for rules, fought until one of them could fight no more; later in the "civilized" fashion of today. The rolls of boxing champions before the 1930s consist largely of names like John L. Sullivan, John Morrissey ‹grandson of Muirgheas, "sea prophet"›, John Heenan ‹grandson of little Eidhean, "ivy"›, who trained by crushing rocks with a thirty-two-pound sledgehammer, and Jack Dempsey ‹grandson of Diomasach, "proud"›, who for years after his retirement welcomed customers to his restaurant on New York's Broadway, where I sometimes saw him seated near the door and looking out over the world that he had once in a sense ruled.

The descendants of other immigrating O'Briens, Murphys, Kellys, Sullivans, and others from the Emerald Isle have become teachers, lawyers, plumbers, heads of corporations, officers of labor unions, criminals, farmers—a cross-section of the American population.

- One named Croghan learned Indian languages, became a successful trader, and in 1765 negotiated with Indians in an attempt to end Pontiac's rebellion.
- One named Hoban, an architect from Dublin, rebuilt the White House after the British burned it in 1814.
- One named Grace, born in Queenstown, founded a major steamship line.

- One named Herbert, born in Dublin, wrote many operettas and in 1916 composed a score for *The Fall of a Nation,* probably the first musical score for a film.
- One named Holland, born in county Clare, built the *Fenian Ram,* a greatly improved submarine, in the years after 1877.
- One named McClure, born in county Antrim, founded the magazine that in the 1890s first published muckraking exposés of the Standard Oil Company and later of other companies and of crooked city and state politicos.
- One named O'Sullivan was one of the leading photographers of the Civil War and of the developing West.
- One named O'Reilly is memorialized in the Fenway in Boston; sentenced to be shot by the English but deported to Australia, he escaped from there to the United States and became a journalist and a hero to Irish on both sides of the water for his continuing leadership in Irish resistance.

Today almost no American reacts negatively to a name like O'Grady, Donnelly, O'Connor (once the name of a great Irish king), Carey ‹dark›, Muldoon ‹grandson of Maolduin, "commander to the garrison"›, or Cassidy. The O'Gradys and the others are no longer automatically classified as Irish; they are simply Americans whose names pass almost as unnoticed as if they were Johnson, Cooper, or Williams.

Marjorie Fallows opens her book *Irish Americans* by quoting a friend of hers:

> My name is Kelly, but beyond knowing the Irish songs that every American kid learns I hardly know what it means to be Irish. Here are the blacks with their history and their problems, and the Puerto Ricans with theirs, but what happened to mine?

13

THE GERMANS:

Germantowns, U.S.A.

A THOUSAND or more foreign-language newspapers and magazines were being published in the United States in 1920, and some still are today. There were a few as early as colonial times.

One of these, called *Philadelphische Staatsbote* ‹The Philadelphia Messenger of the State›, scored one of the major scoops of American journalism:

Philadelphia, den 5 July.

Gestern hat der achtbare Congress dieses vesten Landes die vereinigten Kolonien freye und unabhängige Staaten erkläret. Die Declaration in Englisch ist gesetzt in der Presse: sie ist datirt den 4ten July, 1776, und wirt heut oder morgen in Druck erscheinen.

Yesterday the respected Congress of this western land declared the united colonies free and independent. The text of the Declaration has been set in type in English: it is dated the fourth of July, 1776, and will appear in print today or tomorrow.

The Declaration of Independence was adopted on a Thursday, and the *Staatsbote* was the only Philadelphia paper to appear on Friday. Of course there were no telephones, telegraph, or radio to carry the news elsewhere. So the first public word of the Declaration was carried in a little German-language newspaper.

Until 1871 there was no united Germany. There was only a group of thirty or more separately governed and rather fluid states, duchies, principalities, and independent cities. Conflicts among these were frequent. Religious persecution was by no means rare, and a sect accepted in one place might be jailed a few miles away.

Some Germans were among the Dutch and Swedish settlers in the middle of the seventeenth century. In fact, the German Peter Minuit was the first director general of New Netherland and a leader in the founding of New Sweden a few years later.

Quaker William Penn of England as early as 1671 traveled in Holland and Germany preaching about the "inner light." Among those who heard him were some of the Mennonites, a soft-spoken religious group who believed almost literally in beating swords into plowshares and who tried to reduce or eradicate all temptations of the flesh. For a century and a half they had been forced to flee up and down the Rhine, and the peace-loving Penn, in 1671 but especially later, gave them hope of asylum in America.

One group of German Mennonites, led by Jacob Telner of Crefeld, on the Rhine, made a preliminary visit to Pennsylvania between 1678 and 1681, and in 1682 Telner and other Mennonites bought a sizable plot of land near Philadelphia.

Followers of Telner joined the next year with Francis Daniel Pastorius ‹shepherd, pastor›, a scholar who knew several languages but was not too proud to live in a cave until houses could be built. The small contingent of Crefelders arrived on October 6, 1683, on the *Concord,* subsequently nicknamed the German *Mayflower.*

Pastorius wrote that he and the others

> laid out and planned a new town which we called Germantown, or Germanopolis, in a very fine and fertile district, with plenty of

springs of fresh water, being well supplied with oak, walnut, and chestnut trees, and having besides excellent and abundant pasturage for the cattle. At the commencement there were but twelve families of forty-one individuals, consisting mostly of German mechanics [laborers] and weavers. The principal street of this, our town, I made sixty feet in width, and the cross street, forty feet. The space or lot for each house and garden I made three acres in size; for my own dwelling, six acres. . . .

I have also obtained 15,000 acres of land for our company, in one tract, with this condition: that within one year at least thirty families should settle on it; and thus we may, by God's blessing, have a separate German province where we can all live together as one.

Soon Pastorius and his followers joined with the Pennsylvania Society of Friends and were responsible for attracting many Germans to the New World. This group was also instrumental in preparing the first known protest against Negro slavery, in 1688, thus anticipating Lincoln's Emancipation Proclamation by 174 years:

Is there any that would be done and handled in this manner? viz. to be sold or made a slave for all the time of his life? . . . Now tho' they be black, we cannot conceive there is more liberty to have them slaves as it is to have other white men. . . . To bring men hither or to robb or sell them against their will, we stand against. . . . Being now this is not done in the manner we would be done at; therefore, we contradict, and are against this traffic of men-body.

Germantown would later be the site of the first paper mill in the colonies, erected by William Rittenhouse ‹house near the reeds› in 1690, and would become also a center for weaving, tanning, wagon making, and then printing. It is now a primarily residential Philadelphia section of some 150,000 persons.

Fleeing persecution and hard times in the Rhine valley, other shiploads of people came later, with many of these Germans settling along the Mohawk River in New York, a long, narrow finger of settlement reaching almost to Lake Ontario, a peninsula nearly surrounded by Indian territory.

Others followed, settling especially in Pennsylvania but also in New York and New Jersey, and later overflowing from Pennsylvania into Maryland, Virginia, and the Carolinas. Austrians, many of them from Salzburg, settled in Georgia in 1734 and later. Some five thousand of the Hessian mercenaries employed by the British generals during the Revolutionary War decided to make their homes on this side of the Atlantic.

Penn had been responsible for much of the early German influx. In March 1681, King Charles II of England had granted a land charter to him, and he founded Pennsylvania ‹Penn's woods› as a haven of religious tolerance. He prepared and distributed enticing pamphlets in English, French, Dutch, and German, describing the beauty of the scenery and the fertility of the soil, and offering a maximum of personal and religious freedom. He promised to sell tracts of land at low prices, and even the penniless, after serving a few years as indentured servants, would be given fifty acres.

Among those who received the leaflets were many residents of the Rhenish Palatinate, an area between the Rhine River and France that had been ravaged in the Thirty Years' War (1618–48) and had barely recovered when new turmoil hit, capped by French devastation in the War of the Great Alliance (1688–89), a short time after Penn's glowing description had been circulated. Tired of war and oppression and religious discrimination, hundreds and later thousands of people from this area made their way to Hamburg or Bremen or along the river to Rotterdam and then across the Atlantic.

Settlers from other parts of Germany followed, principally Hesse, Württemberg, Baden, Hesse-Nassau, and Franconia; a substantial number were German-speaking Swiss. The towns of Mannheim, Darmstadt, and Durlach were well represented, as well as Worms and Kaiserslautern. Relatively few of these early settlers came from northern Germany, although later such immigrants were frequent also.

By 1790, according to a study by the American Historical Association, the United States had a total of 276,960 Germans, or 8.7 percent of its total population. Almost exactly a third of the Pennsylvanians then living were German, 14 percent of those in the frontier lands of Kentucky and Tennessee (soon to become states), almost 12 percent of the Marylanders, and somewhat below 10 percent of the New Yorkers and New Jerseyites. In the South about 1 person in 20 was German, but in New England only about 1 person in 250 had a recognizably German name. One-half of all the American Germans, 140,980 of them, lived in Pennsylvania.

The newcomers found the limestone soil of that state much like what they had left in Germany. Black walnut trees flourished—a good sign to them. The agricultural practices that they had formerly followed would be successful here. "Their farms," says Oscar Handlin,

> quickly took on a neat settled look, were carefully tilled, never were burdened with debt, and year after year yielded an abundance of diversified crops. That the soil was fertile and close to market contributed to their success but did not altogether explain it.

Not all the Germans had an easy time, though. One of them, Gottlieb Mittelberg ‹one from the middle hill› in 1756 wrote this account of poverty-stricken Germans arriving in Philadelphia. Many were "redemptioners," whose services for several years could be purchased by someone who would pay the cost of their passage.

> At length, when after a long and tedious voyage, the ships come in sight of land, so that the promontories can be seen, which the people were so eager and anxious to see, all creep from below on deck to see the land from afar, and they weep for joy, and pray and sing, thanking and praising God. The sight of the land makes the people on board the ship, especially the sick and the half-dead, alive again, so that their hearts leap within them; they shout and rejoice and are content to bear their misery in patience, in the hope that they may soon reach the land in safety. But alas!
>
> When the ships have landed at Philadelphia after their long voyage, no one is permitted to leave them except those who pay for their passage or can give good security; the others, who cannot pay, must remain on board the ships till they are purchased and are released from the ships by their purchasers. The sick always fare the worst, for the healthy are naturally preferred and purchased

first; and so the sick and wretched must often remain on board in front of the city for two or three weeks and frequently die. . . .

It often happens that whole families—husband, wife, and children—are separated by being sold to different purchasers. . . .

When a serf has an opportunity to marry in this country, he or she must pay for each year which he or she have yet to serve, £5 or £6. But many a one who has thus purchased and paid for his bride has subsequently repented his bargain, so that he would gladly have returned his exorbitantly dear ware and lost the money besides.

Newspapers sometimes carried plaintive ads like two quoted by Maxine Seller in *To Seek America:* "A German female servant is for sale. She has five years to serve." "Rosina Dorothy Kost, nee Kaufmann, born in Waldenberg . . . desires to let her brother-in-law, one Spohr of Conestoga know through the medium of this paper of her sale at public auction."

The Germans spoke a foreign language at a time when most other whites in the colonies spoke some form of English. That fact, plus their tendency to live almost solely with other Germans, made many regard them as inferiors. Young George Washington is reported to have said, "I really think they seem to be as ignorant a set of people as the Indians. They would never speak English, but when spoken to they speak all Dutch." Benjamin Franklin called them "Palatine boors" and feared that they would "Germanize us."

German settlers usually got along well with the Indians, and until they themselves were attacked they refused to fight in the French and Indian Wars. When they did finally get into battle, however, they were courageous, and even the peace-loving sects provided food, money, and nursing, though not soldiers.

Although in the Revolutionary War many German colonists were Loyalists, thousands of others fought willingly for the revolutionary forces, and many farmers who stayed home from the war hauled wagonloads of food to the colonial soldiers. Again the most peaceful people, such as the Mennonites, Moravians, Schwenkers, and Dunkers, supplied nonmilitary help. The Reverend Peter Muhlenberg (a person from the mountain stream›, on completing a sermon in January 1776 removed his robe and showed that he was wearing a uniform. Outside the church he enlisted three hundred other men to join him. He became a revolutionary general, but his father, also a minister, moved to the country and tried to avoid the war entirely. In that way he was like many other Germans who were attracted to or repelled by both sides, or were indifferent to both.

A German-American woman became a legendary heroine of the war. Born Maria Ludwig, she married a man whose name is reported as either Hays or Heis. After he went to fight, she learned that he had become ill. She followed to nurse him, and on June 28, 1778 she found herself near Monmouth, New Jersey, Court House in the middle of a battle. Seeing wounded colonial soldiers lying in the hot sun and crying for water, she carried pitcher after pitcher to them, endangering her own life. No one knew then who she was, but someone began calling her "Moll." "Here comes Moll with her pitcher," they would say. So for that one day Maria Ludwig Hays or Heis was Molly Pitcher, and the history books still remember her.

Most Germans adhered rigidly to a work ethic unsurpassed by any other group in America. They labored long hours uncomplainingly. They were extremely well disciplined, often with iron-willed family heads who were strongly supported—physically and morally—by their *fraus*. Some of them, such as the Mennonites and the Amish, belonged to religious sects that reinforced the discipline of the home by strict codes of dress, speech, and unfrivolous behavior. Unlike some other settlers, most Germans took good care of their land, working to prevent erosion, manuring their fields, and even rotating their crops before that became a widespread practice. They protected their land, as Handlin says, "because they expected to stay where they were forever."

Some of their descendants are indeed still there, fields still neat, fat Holstein cattle grazing on the still-rich pastures or clustering outside bank barns that may have stood for a century or much more. But other descendants pushed on, of course, partly because they were adventurous, partly because the lessons of Europe had taught them what happens to farms too often divided and subdivided among heirs. So they moved south, and as the prairies and the Farther West became open, they moved there, sometimes living in Dakota or Kansas sod shanties until there was time to construct more substantially.

Religious disagreements certainly did not end when Germans reached America, and sometimes they became violent. Even different sects from the same denomination sometimes fought. In Pennsylvania, for instance, Count Zinzendorf ‹village tenant farmer› led a Pietistic Lutheran faction, and pastor Heinrich Melchior Muhlenberg led those he believed true Lutherans. (Muhlenberg College in Allentown was later named for this pastor and his numerous prominent descendants, one of whom was its first president.) Here is part of the pastor's narrative of one confrontation:

> On the Sunday reserved for the Lutherans, the Count sent to the church his adjunct, Mr. Pirlaeus, and the people he had enticed away from the Lutherans. When they found the lock there, they broke it off with a piece of iron, went in, began to sing, and Mr. Pirlaeus was about to preach. The Lutherans and the Reformed also gathered outside the door and saw that the lock had been broken off. A Lutheran elder thereupon went in and exhorted Mr. Pirlaeus to leave. When he repeatedly refused and accused the elder of not being a Lutheran and told him that he was going astray, the Reformed people rushed in and dragged the adjunct out. During all this rough work on a Sunday, they trampled, pushed, and knocked each other about, and the women began to scream; in short, there was a tumult. The Zinzendorfers brought suit in the affair, and the Reformed and Lutherans contested it; and the upshot is that it is in the hands of the court and has developed into a long, drawn-out lawsuit.

The Pennsylvania archives preserve a list of "foreigners"—people not of British origin—who took an oath of allegiance to the crown between 1727 and 1775, and others who came to Pennsylvania by ship from 1786 to 1808. There are 35,000 of these names in all, and most are German.

From them one may chose some that illustrate the various

types of German surnames. Occupational names among Germans rank higher than they do in England or most other countries, and are approximately tied with place names in total numbers. Patronymic and descriptive names are each less than two-thirds as numerous as the others.

Perhaps the German respect for work helps to account for the fact that in the name-giving period of seven or eight hundred years ago many persons were named for their occupations. These names represent occupations not only prominent in the Middle Ages but still vital at the time of German emigration, although it must be remembered that an eighteenth-century Schmidt was no longer necessarily employed as a smith, or a Seyler as a rope maker.

Among other occupational names of these early Pennsylvania Germans and their successors were the following:

Bauer	‹farmer›
Fischer	‹fisherman›
Gerber	‹worker with leather›
Jäger	‹hunter›
Kauffman	‹merchant, peddler, tradesman›
Kramer	‹shopkeeper›, or perhaps sometimes a peddler who purchased farm produce for resale in a town, hauling it in a *Kram,* a small cart that served as his shop
Metzger	‹butcher›
Müller	‹miller›
Schaffer	‹shepherd›
Schneider	‹tailor›
Schreiner	‹cabinetmaker›
Schultz	‹overseer› or ‹sheriff›
Schuman, Schumacher	‹shoemaker›
Schuster	‹shoe repairman›
Schütz	‹watchman›
Spengler	‹tinsmith, tinker›
Wagner	‹wagonmaker› or ‹carter›
Weber	‹weaver›

Ziegler	‹maker or user of brick and tile›
Zimmer-mann	‹carpenter›

Spellings for these and other German names might vary considerably, as these eighteenth-century variants of Schultz illustrate: Shilt, Shiltz, Sholes, Sholts, Sholtz, Shoults, Shoultz, Shults, and Shulz (as well as eleven others in the Pennsylvania records).

Surnames taken from places might refer to a landscape feature. For instance, Bachman lived close to a brook *(Bach)*, Wald in or near a forest, Brück close to a bridge. Hoff might come from a courtyard or from *Hof* ‹farm›, the name of many German villages. Baum ‹tree› may have lived near an especially conspicuous tree, or worked with trees, or resided at or near a shop or tavern that had a tree on the sign which welcomed possible customers. Schaub ‹sheaf› was also associated with a shop sign, or may have earned the nickname from work in a field of grain. Some surnames from places identified the city or other area from which a person had come. Thus Berlin or Berliner may have come from Berlin, Schwaab was from Swabia, a medieval duchy in southwestern Germany, Schlesinger was from Silesia, and Schweitzer had come to Germany from Switzerland or had some other association with the Swiss.

A few German patronyms, such as Johannes ‹John› and Karl ‹Charles›, indicate simply a descendant of someone named John or Karl or the like. Many more patronyms, however, are dithematic; that is, they are combinations of two themes, or words, usually with a militaristic suggestion. Thus Conrad combines the meanings of ‹bold› and ‹counsel›, and Reichmann is ‹powerful, man›. Such names should be interpreted in the way the comma suggests: as two separate meanings, not a unity like ‹bold counsel› or ‹powerful man›. Here are other examples:

Friedrich	‹peace, rule›
Gebhart	‹gift, brave›
Ludwig	‹fame, warrior›
Rudolph	‹fame, wolf›

Seiberth	‹victory, bright›
Ulrich	‹wolf, rule›

The smallest number of German surnames are those suggesting a physical or other description. Thus Lang was long (tall). Krafft was strong, Weiss had white hair or a pale complexion and Schwartz was dark and Roth was ruddy and Braun had brown hair, Gross was big and Klein was little. Funck or Funk was a lively person, and Vogel could either be birdlike or have lived at the sign of the bird.

As is often true of names from other countries, German surnames may have more than a single origin. Thus some Baumgartners worked at tree gardening (orchard growing) to earn a living, but others simply lived close to an orchard. The name has to be classified, then, as both an occupational and a place name. If your name is Baumgartner, you are unlikely ever to find out which it is, except in the improbable event that you have access to clear family records dating back to the name-giving period.

Some Mosers were vegetable sellers, but others lived near or in a swamp. Some Kuhns were sharp, keen people; others were descended from Kunrat = Conrad. Kesslers could come from Kessel ‹castle› or could have mended kettles. Rauchs may have smoked meat or may have been unusually hairy. Stumpfs perhaps lived near a stump or a large number of stumps, but other Stumpfs simply looked like stumps—short and broad. Brunner or Bruner, when his was an occupational name, dug wells, and when it was a patronym, he was descended from Brunheri ‹brown, army›. Hummel may have come from a town called Hummel ‹bumblebee›, or may have been a person as excitable as a bee, or may have been descended from Humboldt ‹bear cub, bold›.

Often it was a tearful experience for Germans, as well as many others, to leave their families and their homeland. The following account is by Carl Schurz ‹maker of aprons›, who came to America in 1852 at the age of twenty-three. He became a lawyer, a general, and a leader of the Republican party. In one of his many speeches he recalled the atmosphere of a German village when emigrants left.

> It is one of the earliest recollections of my boyhood that one summer night our whole village was stirred up by an uncommon occurrence. I say our village, for I was born not far from that beautiful spot where the Rhine rolls his green waters out of the wonderful gate of the Seven Mountains and then meanders with majestic tranquillity through one of the most glorious valleys of the world. That night our neighbors were pressing around a few wagons covered with linen sheets and loaded with household utensils and boxes and trunks to their utmost capacity. One of our neighboring families was moving far away across a great water, and it was said that they would never again return. And I saw silent tears trickling down weather-beaten cheeks, and the hands of rough peasants firmly pressing each other, and some of the men and women hardly able to speak when they nodded to one another a last farewell. At last the [wagon] train started into motion, they gave three cheers for America, and then in the first gray dawn of the morning I saw them wending their way over the hill until they disappeared in the shadow of the forest. And I heard many a man say how happy he would be if he could go with them to that great and free country where a man could be himself.

During the early part of the twentieth century both Irish and Germans were far outnumbered by the Italians, other southern and central Europeans, and immigrants from Russia and the Baltic states. Even so, more than 400,000 Germans settled here between the end of World War I and 1930, when our depression and strict laws cut all immigration to a trickle. In the 1930s many German Jews, including numerous scientists, doctors, artists, and other professionals, escaped here from the Nazis. After World War II we took in over 300,000 Germans in the single three-year span from 1950 through 1952—some of them refugees still seeking a permanent home, some of them new spouses of American military personnel.

Some of these relatively recent immigrants, like many before them, bore German names like Rosenblum or Goldstein that had been selected when Germany had permitted or required Jews to have surnames. But most of the twentieth-century names were essentially those revealed in the 1790 census: the Müllers or Muellers many of whom would make the easy translation to Miller, the Boettcher or Boettger whose eponymous ancestor had made barrels, the Weisbachs who had lived beside a stream whose water flowed white, the Wilhelms who were perhaps more peaceful than their ancestor whose name meant ‹resolution, helmet›, the big Grosses and the little Kleins and perhaps the supposedly fox-like Vosses, the quick Schnells, the handsome Schoens who would be likely to become Shanes or Shains.

Like the Irish, the Germans go by so many names that there cannot be huge numbers of them bearing a particular name. Also, as I have said, the same German name is often spelled in different ways. So the leader among probably German names in the United States is Myers ‹overseer, farmer›, which ranks only 78th, but if you added in all the Meyers, Meiers, and other variants the rank would be considerably higher. Schmidt is 117th. Snyder, basically a Dutch name for ‹tailor›, in America is often a simplified spelling of German Schneider; Snyder ranks 119th, Schneider 211th. But despite simplified spellings, Cincinnati, a city with a considerable German population, has more than twenty pages of *Sch* names in its telephone directory. And it has almost as many Fischers as Fishers, although nationally Fischer ranks only 337th, Fisher 87th.

Early Germans bearing such names were not only farmers, like those of the Pennsylvania Dutch countryside, or weavers, like those of Germantown. Their versatility extended to the building of the first organs in the colonies (and later to Steinway pianos; the original name was Steinweg ‹rocky road›). "Baron" Henry Stiegel ‹one from near the stile› blew glass that is now almost priceless. Others specialized in making pottery, stoves, furniture, farm implements, cutlery, barrels, and other items useful in a pioneer society.

Later German immigrants have variously changed and enriched Americans' lives. Conductor Leopold Damrosch, for instance, introduced to this country the music of Wagner, Liszt, Berlioz, and Brahms, and his son Walter introduced

Tchaikovsky, reorganized the New York Symphony, and in 1925 conducted the first symphony concert ever presented on radio. Adolphus Busch ‹one from the sign of the bush (generally a wine seller)› helped to establish the nation's largest brewery. Ottmar Mergenthaler ‹one from the muddy valley› invented the Linotype.

The list could go on and on. Anthropologist-linguist Edward Sapir. John Eberhard Faber, the first manufacturer of pencils in the United States and the first to attach erasers, which many of us now find indispensable. Architect Ludwig Mies, who added Van Der Rohe to his name, and who specialized in glass buildings and tubular steel chairs. John Augustus Roebling, who invented wire rope and used it in building the Brooklyn Bridge and other bridges. And Werner von Braun, who almost won a war for Hitler but later led the United States into the space age.

14

THE DUTCH AND THE BELGIANS:

We Could Have Used More of Their Ideals

IN the seventeenth century the Dutch illustrated some of the American ideals as fully, I believe, as anyone else who ever came here.

Consider, for instance, the treatment of females. At a time when few girls other than those in wealthy families got even a glimpse of a teacher, the Dutch in New Amsterdam, as in much of Holland, routinely sent their girls as well as their boys to school. In marriage, a man and a woman were often equal partners. Women, the Dutch knew, are as likely as men to have good business sense, so wives often managed the shop, the tavern, or other business while husbands worked beside them or somewhere else. The women generally worked conscientiously, hard. For instance, in New Amsterdam one Maria Provoost ‹manager› gave birth to a daughter one day and was back selling goods in her store the next. She did well financially, too. In all the colony, only the governor had a finer coach.

Or consider the Dutch treatment of people of other religions. When the New England Puritans were expelling people who differed from them even a smidgen in doctrine, Holland was accepting Huguenots, Calvinists, Roman Catholics, free thinkers—almost anyone (although sometimes they were reluctant to grant equal political and economic rights to Jews). A person who did not like the Dutch Reformed faith might in general follow whatever other faith he or she chose, or none at all. Desiring such freedom in 1639, entire little Massachusetts communities took refuge under the Dutch flag in New Amsterdam.

And as George R. Stewart has pointed out, the Dutch were not the "dull-witted and ox-like" folk that Washington Irving and others have led us to believe. None of them ever slept twenty years, certainly. Stewart says, ". . . those first Dutch settlers were as wild a crew as any that ever landed in Virginia, and they looked upon New Englanders as parson-ridden snivelers with no appreciation of rum or a bawdy song. . . ."

From the standpoint of building a lasting colony, however, the Dutch authorities did a very unwise thing. Instead of making land easily available to all, they granted it to only a few, in very large chunks. Thus there existed a system like that in much of modern South America, with a few rich landholders but a majority of people relatively impoverished.

Many of the settlers of New Netherland were not Dutch at all. Louis P. Wright explains:

> Almost symbolical of New York's later development as the greatest port of entry for foreigners was the make-up of the settlers whom the Dutch encouraged to come to New Netherland, for they were a mixed and polyglot people. Most of the families in the first contingent were French-speaking Walloons, refugee Protestants from the Spanish Netherlands. . . . One reason was the difficulty of finding emigrants in Holland, for the Dutch were happy at home and felt no compulsion to try their luck in the New World. . . . Among the diverse people who were counted in the early stages of development [of New Netherland] were Frenchmen, Germans, Danes, Norwegians, Swedes, Finns, Portuguese, Spaniards, Italians, Bohemians, Poles, and Jews. In addition, all

segments of the British Isles were represented. . . . A contemporary reported counting eighteen languages spoken in New Amsterdam.

Most of these colonists were religious, in their own ways, but they did not insist that every customary ecclesiastic form be followed to the letter. For example, in 1628, three years after the founding of New Amsterdam, pastor Jonas Michaëlius ‹descendant of Michael› arrived to establish America's first Dutch Reformed church. Previously the inhabitants had been served by a deacon and an elder, Bastian (= Sebastian) Krol ‹probably a variant of Carl or Charles› and Jan (= John) Huygens ‹descendant of Hugo›. Michaëlius wrote in a letter:

> At the first administration of the Lord's supper which was observed, not without great joy and comfort to many, we had fully fifty communicants, Walloon and Dutch, a number of whom made their first confession of faith before us, and others exhibited their church certificates. Others had forgotten to bring their certificates with them, not thinking that a church would be formed and established here; and some who had brought them had lost them, unfortunately, in a general conflagration, but they were admitted upon the satisfactory testimony of others to whom this was known and also upon their daily good deportment, since one cannot observe strictly all the usual formalities in making a beginning under such circumstances.

Washington Irving, with wit and more than an occasional touch of malice, described the fort that the Dutch built, and also the houses:

> Around this potent fortress was soon seen a numerous progeny of little Dutch houses, with tiled roofs, all which seemed most lovingly to nestle under its walls, like a brood of half-fledged chickens sheltered under the wings of the mother hen. The whole was surrounded by an inclosure of strong palisadoes, to guard against any sudden irruption of the savages, who wandered in hordes about the swamps and forests that extended over those tracts of country at present called Broadway, Wall Street, William Street, and Pearl Street.
>
> No sooner was the colony once planted than it took root and throve amazingly, for it would seem that this thrice-favored island

is like a munificent dunghill, where every foreign weed finds kindly nourishment, and soon shoots up and expands to greatness.

Irving wrote his pseudohistory under a pseudonym—Diedrich Knickerbocker. That surname did exist in Holland and still does (in small numbers) in the United States but now seems to have died out in the mother country. It referred to what sounds like a pretty specialized occupation ‹baker of clay marbles›. The current Manhattan phone book shows only one individual bearing the name, but a whole column of businesses and organizations such as Knickerbocker Synthetics Corp and the Knickerbocker Republican Club. There was once a New York Knickerbocker baseball team. Bloomerlike pants, formerly stylish wear for ballplayers and golfers, were called knickerbockers, since the early Dutch settlers wore baggy knee breeches or pantaloons. The New York Knicks professional basketball team has shortened both the name and the pants.

Those early settlers after thirty years lost their dominion to the English, but some hundreds of them remained, although scattered, and a few others joined them now and again. Albany at the time of the Revolutionary War was so Dutch that, as Maxine Seller has said, "it was difficult to assemble an English speaking jury."

The Dutch gave some of their own names, or the names of places back home, to places in New York. So skipper Adriaen Block is remembered today in Block Island, Amsterdam Avenue is still an important thoroughfare in Manhattan, Dutch Breukelyn and Haarlem are easily recognizable as parts of the metropolis, Hoboken was altered from an Indian Hopoaken to make it conform to the name of a village in Flanders, and the courtesy title "Jonkheer"—about like "squire"—applied to the rich Adriaen van der Donck and his domain a little north of New Amsterdam, is now recognizable as Yonkers. Dutch spellings of Indian names have given us Poughkeepsie and Hackensack, and a place spelled by the Dutch S-c-h-a-e-n-h-e-c-h-s-t-e-d-e eventually turned up not much better off as S-c-h-e-n-e-c-t-a-d-y.

Germantown, Pennsylvania, from its beginnings in 1683

had Dutch among its settlers, and some historians say that it was more Dutch than German until 1710. Its founder, Francis Pastorius, said, however, ". . . the Hollanders (as sad experience has taught me) are not so easily satisfied, which in this new land is a very necessary quality." Few, it seemed, were willing to trade their relatively tranquil lives in the Netherlands for the hardships, fighting, and dangers of the New World.

In the Revolutionary War most Dutch strongly favored independence. Far from separating church from state, many Dutch Reformed ministers preached in favor of revolution. In retaliation, the British sacked some of their churches. Among the active rebel families were the Schuylers ‹"schoolers," related obviously to *scholars*›, the Frelinghuysens, the Rutgers ‹descendants of Roger, "fame, spear"›, and the Cortlandts. Washington referred to the New Jersey–Hudson area as his "loyal Dutch belt." Dutch merchants supplied many war materials to the colonials.

In the 1790s a number of New Jersey and Pennsylvania Dutch families decided to go to what was then called Kaintuckee by many folk, a large proportion of them settling in what became Mercer County, southwest of Lexington. Meanwhile New York or "Mohawk" Dutch headed for Michigan.

An economic depression in the Netherlands in 1815 and especially the Dutch share of the potato famine of 1845–46 drove many more Hollanders than ever before to the New World. Large numbers of these newcomers joined their predecessors in Michigan. Followers of the Reverend A. C. van Raalte in 1847 founded Holland, Michigan, which today has a Netherlands museum, a Holland state park not far away, and an annual Tulip Time that attracts hundreds of thousands "to the Dutch hostelries to see wooden-shoe carvers, parades, & dancing in costume in scrubbed streets," as the *American Guide* says. Apparently nineteenth-century Dutch were less tolerant in religion than their forebears two centuries before. At any rate, van Raalte and his followers left the Netherlands mainly because they did not like what they called the "siren songs" in a newly adopted hymnal.

Dutch folk in 1847 also founded Zeeland, Drenthe, and Vriesland, all in Michigan, and Pella, Iowa, whose streets were given names like Liberty, Peace, Inquiry, Perseverance, Confidence, and Accomplishment. Residents of Pella, where their leader, Dominee Hendrik Peter Scholte, had managed to buy for them eighteen thousand acres of choice land at $1.25 an acre, easily recovered their investment two or three years later when they sold provisions to prospectors heading west for California gold. Still other newcomers later filtered into other midwestern states or into the Rocky Mountain area or other parts of the West Coast.

Three American presidents—Van Buren and the two Roosevelts—were mainly or entirely of Dutch descent. Dutch names are not held by large numbers of Americans, however. Only about 100,000 Hollanders lived here in 1900, and since then no more than a few thousand have entered during any single year. The grand total for 1820–1970 is only a third of a million Dutch immigrants. Lambert ‹land, bright›, which may also be English, ranks only 253rd among current American names, and if you put all the Van der Somethings and Vandersomethings together, they will rank only 277th. No other recognizably Dutch names rank among the four hundred most common American surnames.

The meanings of Dutch names may sometimes be figured out on the basis of their English or German cognates. Among those based on occupations, Smidt, Smit, or De Smet is pretty obviously a smith, Mulder a miller, Herder a herder (English Hurd). Snyder and Snider are Dutch spellings of Schneider ‹tailor›, although many Germans have taken over one or the other of the Dutch forms. Dutch Brower or Brouwer brewed beer or ale, and Tappan tapped the kegs and dispensed the contents. Bleecker bleached cloth.

Less obvious occupational names from Holland include Renner ‹runner, messenger›; Wynkoop ‹wine cup› and Schenk (one meaning of German *schenken* is ‹to sell wine›), both of whom were wine retailers; Boer or De Boer ‹farmer›, related to the English *boor;* Cuyler ‹crossbow archer›; Bogard ‹orchard worker›; Kloppman ‹cloth inspector›; and Wanamaker ‹maker and seller of baskets›.

Among Dutch descriptive surnames, Zwartz is obviously cognate to German Schwartz ‹black, dark haired or dark complexioned›, Licht or Lichter and Witt, Witte, or Witty are cognate to English Light and White and were used for the light-skinned or blond person. Groot or De Groot was large or tall, and Grootstadt ‹big city› may have come from a big city or may have been given the name to suggest that he tried to ape big city ways. Hartig, related to English *hearty,* was strong and virile. Buick, a less favorable name, was plump, fat, although perhaps just husky. Manke was lame, Groff gruff, and Conklin a person given to plotting or conspiracy. Link(e) was lefthanded. And De Jong, often spelled De Jonghe or anglicized to De Young, means ‹the younger person›. According to H. L. Mencken, in the Grand Rapids, Michigan, of the 1940s, a place with a large Dutch population, De Young was the ninth most common name. Sixth was the Dutch place name De Vries ‹a person from Frisia›, and eleventh was another place name, Van Dyke ‹one who lives near the dike›.

The prefixes *Van* ‹of› or ‹from› and *Vander* ‹from the› are the most frequent signals of surnames based on Dutch place names. Van Buren is from the neighborhood, Van Camp from the field, Vandenberg from the hill, Vandermeer from the lake, Van Devanter from a place called Devanter, Vanderbilt from near a conspicuous mound, Van Kirk from *Kerk* ‹church›, Van Ostrand from the east shore, and Van Winkle from a little town called Winkel or from a small shop. (The corresponding meaning of German Winkler is ‹shopkeeper›.)

Some place names have no *Van* or *Vander*. Haag came from a place with hedges, and Maas(e) lived by the river Meuse. Stuyvesant commemorates a place in Zeeland known for its quicksand. Voorhees was from ‹in front of Hess›, and Onderdon(c)k was ‹from the little town of Donk›. Rockefeller (earlier Roggenfelder) lived near a rye field, and Roosevelt near or in a field with many roses. Terwilliger had left Willige ‹Wille's town›. Olmste(a)d once lived in a place with many elms, and St(e)iger near a boat landing. The prefix *Ten* means ‹at the›, so Ten Eyck is ‹at the oak›. Ver Brugge or Van Brugge, like the German Bruggeman, lived close to a bridge or collected tolls from those crossing it. The ending *-stra* indicates ‹one from (a certain place)›. Hence Dykstra was from the vicinity of one of those dikes so vital to Holland, and Hoekstra, like Haack, van Hoek, or the English Hook(er), came from a hook or spur or odd-shaped piece of land or from a bend in the river.

Patronyms are rare among the Dutch and carry no consistent signals. ‹Son of› may be indicated by *-sen* as in Aarsen ‹son of Arthur›, by *-zen* as in Jan(t)zen ‹son of Jan or John›, or just by *-s* as in Roelandts ‹son of Roland› or in Pieters ‹son of Peter›. Occasionally a patronym is only a person's name, with no affix. Thus Joost may be the son of Joost ‹the just man›.

The number of Dutch Americans, as I have said, has never been very large. In 1790 they consisted of only some 57,000 persons, nine out of ten of whom lived in the state of New York. In all the years since then, that number increased only sixfold. One obvious reason for such low numbers is the small size of the Netherlands. If that country were spread over New Jersey and Connecticut it would cover those states with little to spare.

Those few square miles, though, have given us, as first-generation or later-generation Americans, the millionaire Vanderbilts and Rockefellers; Dr. Benjamin Spock, who perhaps has influenced the early care of more children than any other doctor in history; Lee de Forest, who earned more than three hundred patents for inventions relating to radio, movies, and television, and who in 1910 first broadcast live music —featuring Enrico Caruso; David Christian Henry, who built or was consulted about most large American dams constructed before World War II, including Grand Coulee and Boulder; Carl Norden, inventor of the bombsight that bears his name; Paul de Kruif, popularizer of medical science; Ralph Dykstra, who should be revered by pet lovers for his work in animal sanitation and disease control; writers Walt Whitman (part Dutch, part English), Carl and Mark Van Doren, Peter de Vries the modern humorist, John Updike the novelist; musicians Gladys Swarthout, who sang with the Met from 1929 to 1945, and Hans Kindler, who helped to found the National Symphony Orchestra in Washington, D.C., and conducted it from 1931 to 1949; artist Piet Mondrian, born Pieter Cornelis Mondriaan, leading practitioner of de Stijl, who was here only the last four years of his life but said, "I feel here is the place to live, and I am becoming an American citizen."

Belgium became an independent country only in 1831. Previously it had been successively a possession of Burgundy, the Hapsburgs, France, and the Netherlands. Some 5½ million Belgians today speak Flemish, 4½ million French, and about 150,000 German. The French-speaking Belgians, concentrated in the southern region and especially Liège, are called Walloons. In Brussels, in central Belgium, nineteen of the twenty-six cantons are bilingual, the others Flemish, which is hardly distinguishable from Dutch. Because there is no Belgian language, it is not often possible to say with semiassurance that a particular surname is Belgian. Elsdon Smith's *Dictionary,* however, does list fifteen or so names as Belgian.

Before 1831, obviously, there could be no immigration figures for Belgium, and later Belgian immigrants may sometimes have been counted as French or Dutch. I know of no distinctively Belgian areas of the United States, although a village in eastern Illinois is named Belgium.

The surnames that are least disputably Belgian are those referring to places in Belgium. Maeterlinck, for instance (Maurice Maeterlinck was the once well-known author of *The Blue Bird* and a few other delightful plays), is a Belgian town. Renault is from a largely French-speaking town, Renaix. Menin is from the town of that name. Waterloo, Belgium, the scene of Napoleon's final defeat, had its name taken over by Waterloo, in Iowa and several other states, as well as by Waterloo, Ontario, and by a few persons who found their way to America, where most probably they changed it to Waters.

Neef, clearly related to German Neffe ‹nephew›, may also be Belgian for the same relationship, and since some Belgian nephews seem to have had reputations as moochers, often means ‹parasite›. Nahon, according to Smith, may be either a French or a Belgian term for the ‹bird's nest hunter›. DeClerck, corresponding to English Clark, is sometimes used in Belgium for a ‹clerk or an administrator›; De Zutter is a ‹shoemaker›; De Caluwe has ‹rough skin›. Stephen Decatur, an American naval hero in the War of 1812 and the man who vowed to support "our country, right or wrong," apparently had a Belgian ancestor who lived near the sign of the cat; a city in Illinois owes its name to Decatur and hence to that cat. After Stephen Decatur died in 1820, President Monroe suggested that Alabama memorialize him, and in that way Decatur, Alabama, got its name.

Among others of Belgian birth immortalized in American history are missionary-explorers Pierre Jean De Smet and Louis Hennepin; Charles Van Depoele, inventor of electric trolley cars and a pioneer in color photography; Leo Hendrik Baekeland, inventor of photographic materials and of Bakelite; and George Sarton, a historian of science.

15

THE SWISS:

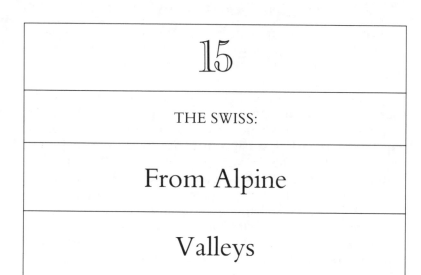

From Alpine Valleys

JOHN AUGUSTUS SUTTER was much more than the owner of a California sawmill near which gold was discovered. Born in Germany of Swiss parents, Johan August Suter ‹cobbler› or ‹one from the south› became an officer in the Swiss army but left Switzerland to avoid a bankruptcy suit. In the United States he lost more money in the Santa Fe overland trade, again fled his creditors, and after about eight or nine thousand miles of additional travel by land and sea got to California, which still was a Mexican province, on July 3, 1839.

A fast talker in Spanish as well as German, English, French, and Italian, he persuaded the Mexican governor, Juan Bautista Alvarado ‹John the Baptist from the white hill›, to grant him fifty thousand acres of land near the junction of the Sacramento and American rivers—the site of modern Sacramento. He named it New Helvetia (an old name for Switzerland) but quickly became a Mexican citizen. He erected a large house and a sturdy fort and in about five years built his ranch up to 2,000 horses, 2,000 sheep, and 4,200 cattle, and also engaged in a profitable fur trade.

So he was a wealthy man when one of his employees found gold on his property in January 1848. But the gold rush of 1849 ruined him. His workers stopped herding cattle and harvesting grain and started to seek gold; other prospectors killed his cattle or stole as many as $60,000 worth of them in one night. He was bankrupt in three years and this time could not escape. He had no legal redress. The government did give him a pension of $250 a month, which he spent in vain attempts to reclaim his fortune.

The Delmonicos ‹descendants of the monk› fared considerably better. Giovanni and Peter came to New York in the 1820s and started a pastry shop and a catering service. In a stroke of genius they brought in their nephew Lorenzo, as well as other family members who contributed to the growing business. It was Lorenzo who suggested opening a restaurant that, unlike others of the time, would be open all day and would serve quality food on a varied menu that would include many vegetables and salads and much fresh fruit as well as choice meat.

The Delmonicos moved several times to increasingly desirable locations, including a hotel at 25 Broadway and a midtown spot at Fifth Avenue and 44th Street, and a number of branch restaurants. They started a fashion of having dinner parties in a restaurant rather than at home. On a Brooklyn-area farm they grew much of the food they served, thus assuring its freshness. Among their early guests were Jenny Lind and Aaron Burr, and later came Emerson, Dickens, and several presidents, including Lincoln, Johnson, and Grant. Their restaurant finally closed in 1922.

Several decades before Sutter and the Delmonicos, another Swiss-born American had performed even more notable service for America. He was Albert Gallatin ‹the lively, joyful one›. After teaching French briefly at Harvard, he settled in western Pennsylvania, was elected to Congress, originated what has become the powerful Committee on Ways and Means, frequently opposed Treasury Secretary Alexander Hamilton, and then was himself secretary of the treasury for thirteen years. He was partly responsible for the Louisiana Purchase. Once he was a nominee for vice-president. In his private business as manufacturer and dealer in glass he developed in 1797 a profit-sharing plan that would also provide employees an opportunity to obtain stock in the business—an ingenious Swiss plan with which a number of modern businesses are again experimenting. He spent most of his last years as a foreign minister, the founder of a New York bank, and the author of a book on American Indian tribes.

I have chosen these three examples because they represent the three major national strains that have learned to live together in reasonable harmony in Switzerland. About two-thirds of Swiss people today speak German, as Sutter did; one-fifth French, like Gallatin; one-tenth Italian, like the Delmonicos; and about one one-hundredth Romansch, which appears to be a blend of ancient Celtic and Illyrian.

One estimate has it that there were only about thirteen thousand Swiss Americans in 1850. There couldn't have been many, for the total population of the homeland at that time was only about 2½ million. A few, of course, had come with the multinational "Dutch" to New Netherland, ten Swiss Mennonite families had come to Pennsylvania in 1710, and in that same year Christopher von Graffenried, of Berne, founded New Bern in North Carolina, where the state's first printing press and first tax-supported school would later be located.

After 1850 Switzerland's population began to increase. It doubled during the next century, and some people felt crowded enough to move. As a result, about ten to twenty thousand have come here each decade since that time. They are scattered widely. There is, of course, the Italian Swiss colony in California, and there is a Swiss belt across northern and central Ohio. But here and there a New Englander claims at least one Swiss forebear, and there are Swiss in the rural areas and the cities of New York, Pennsylvania, and the Midwest. Since 1930 a few have found their way to the Pacific Northwest.

Prominent Americans of Swiss Origin, by the Swiss-American Historical Society, includes biographies of about sixty persons. It reminds us that Herbert Hoover's ancestors were Swiss and that the name was then Huber, German for ‹tenant of a *Hube,* "farm" under feudal tenure›. About 1762 Huber was anglicized to Hoover.

Naturalist-geologist Louis Agassiz was Swiss-born, as was his son Alexander, a marine zoologist who as a sideline developed copper mines that made him rich. Other names in the Historical Society's book are undistinguishable from German, French, or Italian names, for as a mingle of other national strains Switzerland has few surnames of its own.

There are some, however, mostly based on names of Swiss places. Bern(e) is usually Swiss, although there is also a town called Berne in England. Basler and Bessler were both residents of Basel. Zu(e)rcher or Zurich of course came from Zurich. Schwitzer is a designation used by the Swiss for one from their country; Germans ordinarily use Schwei(t)zer for a person from Switzerland.

Other surnames likely derived from Swiss places include Ablanalp (one Ablanalp was widely publicized as a close friend of Richard Nixon), Effinger (from Effingen), Geis or a variant (from Geiss or Geis, or sometimes a patronym), Heidegger, a name made familiar by Nathaniel Hawthorne's story "Dr. Heidegger's Experiment" (from the fortress of Heidegg), Oberlander (from one of several places called Oberland ‹high land›), and Saxer (from Sax ‹crag›, or Saxon, a village in southern Switzerland).

Thies(e) is from a Swiss form of Matthew and therefore corresponds to English Mat(t)hews(on). Schnyder is a spelling often used in Switzerland for the German word for tailor. Klegerman is a Swiss public prosecutor.

Today, probably because of the fame or notoriety of secret Swiss bank accounts, we are likely to think of all Swiss as rich and to picture them as Scrooge-like "gnomes of Zurich." The stereotype is of course only fractionally true. In this country some have become wealthy, but others are no more prosperous than their neighbors. But something about their heritage or their upbringing has made them in general meticulous, craftsmanlike, careful, thoughtful.

16

THE SCANDINAVIANS:

Hans Olsa and Beret

MY MOTHER'S MOTHER died before I was born, but I think I understand this woman I never knew. She grew up in southern Denmark, just north of the then uncertain boundary with Germany. Somehow she met a young German man (though one of his grandmothers was Finnish), Chris Engel, and married him in 1860. He had been a sailor but settled down with her on a small farm in Denmark.

He was handsome, bluff, hearty, outgoing, an exuberant who in his boyhood had liked to stand on his head and play the harmonica (a recent German invention). As a grown man he laughed a great deal but spoke his opinion vigorously when he thought he should.

She was pretty, quiet, and thoughtful, and followed a not uncommon Scandinavian custom of subservience to one's husband. Whatever Chris did was right.

They had seven children in quick succession. In his dealings with his Danish neighbors, my grandfather's active tongue often caused trouble. He was a foreigner, a hated

German. The Danes resented the Prussians who in 1864 took Schleswig-Holstein from them. There was frequent bloodshed in the controversial border area. In conversation Chris sometimes defended the Germans, and the Danes called him names and threatened violence to him and even to his children. "We must go, Katrin," he finally told his wife in 1871. "To America. There we can live at peace."

"Yes, Chris," she said. But she did not really want to leave Denmark. She loved its quiet beauty, its unbelievably bright red and yellow flowers, her Lutheran church, the nearness of the sea which moderated the winter temperatures.

In Illinois they paused long enough for the birth of Rose, who would be my mother, then spent a few years in Iowa accumulating a little money through farm labor. Their last child was born there, and they finally settled on a farm near Creston, Nebraska.

My grandfather got along very well with Americans, whether Scandinavian or not. His physical strength and the high spirits that had returned after he left Denmark made him well-liked. His new friends and his ownership of enough land to support, even modestly, his large family gave him peace and contentment.

But my grandmother was much like Beret, the Norwegian wife in O. E. Rölvaag's *Giants in the Earth*. America had little for her. Like Beret she felt herself a stranger in a strange land. No close neighbors spoke a tongue that she could understand. The forms and rituals of the Nebraska church were wrong, and anyway Chris would rather put up hay than go there. Their house was much too small for a family of eleven, and a smelly livestock shelter was fastened European-fashion to its southeast side to protect the pigs, cattle, and horses against the north or northwest winds that pushed across the waves of prairie land in the winters. The winds howled unlike any Danish winds she had heard. They heaped snow higher than the fences. She and the smaller children hovered around an inadequately fueled stove, for wood was scarce and dried cow chips were not entirely satisfactory substitutes. Chris and the older boys would be outdoors except in the worst weather repairing fences, cutting wood, caring for the stock, occasionally going to the general store, but Katrin lived with quarreling children in an ugly little house buffeted by a wind that she felt would never stop.

As gradually became true of Beret, "Hidden forces were taking the children from her" once they were old enough to escape the house. The younger ones sometimes played with American children a mile or two away, and for two or three months a year they skipped gladly to the small school in Creston, and they returned with skills their mother did not have and information that she did not believe or want to possess. The older ones were soon working as hired men or hired girls and keeping company with other young men or young women whose ways were not Katrin's ways. As Rölvaag said of the Norwegian Beret,

> And never did she hear them so much as mention what pertained to them as Norwegians. . . . At times, as she listened to their talk, she would fall to wondering whether she actually was their mother —their language was not hers.

In earlier years, there were not many women among the Scandinavian settlers in America. The few Swedes, Norwegians, and Danes who were among the Dutch of New Netherland were mostly males. One of them, though, the Danish Jonas Bronck ‹brown›, did live with his family on a farm north of Manhattan Island. Says George R. Stewart: "People came to speak of 'going to the Broncks,' and in the English period, after the family was no longer remembered, the name worked into the present spelling." Thus the Bronx got its name and its article.

The first fairly large contingent of Scandinavians in the country consisted of Swedes, along with some Finns, who arrived at the Delaware River in 1638 to establish a trading company. Since their purpose was business rather than colonization, they brought few women. They built Fort Christina, the present Wilmington. Perhaps they built the first log cabins in America, although some Germans dispute the claim. At any rate the Swedes, Finns, and Germans, using notched logs and plaster, were responsible for cabins that were sturdier and warmer than the buildings of the English at Jamestown and Plymouth.

Some of the early Swedish leaders were Peter Ridder ‹knight›, the Reverend Reorus Torkillus ‹Thor's caldron›, Johan Björnsson Printz ‹prince›, and Johan Classon Rising ‹one from the lowlands(?)›. A Swedish clergyman named John Companius attempted to convert Indians to Christianity beginning in 1643. He even devised a system for a written translation of Luther's Shorter Catechism into the Lenape (Delaware) tongue. Since the Lenapes could not read, they must have been as much puzzled by the strange symbols as by the content of the catechismic questions and answers.

The Dutch drove out the Swedes in 1655, but some of those who survived continued to stay in Delaware, Maryland, and eastern Pennsylvania. They were joined in 1656 by a hundred or so others, who brazenly sailed past the Dutch forces up the Delaware to Fort Casimir, now New Castle.

Perhaps, over a century later, their descendants were among the farmers of the Delaware River area who rowed George Washington and his men across the stream for their surprise attack on the English and Hessians. Historians so surmise, but since those farmers are now nameless, one cannot be sure.

No large number of Scandinavians came to America before the middle of the nineteenth century, mainly because both state and church forbade or discouraged emigration. But there were a few notable early colonists.

In 1825 a sloop named *Restauration* arrived in New York with fifty-two Norwegian Quakers seeking religious freedom. They were met by Cleng Peerson ‹son of Peer or Peter›, who had come originally from near Stavanger and who served for a while as an unofficial American recruiting agent for Norwegians. In 1818 he had fallen out with the Norwegian state church and tried to discourage church attendance. At a time when the church tended to be domineering, one could not safely do that, so in 1821 he and Knud Olson Eide ‹descendant of Eden, "rich"› decided to leave for New York. There Peerson began seeking ways to attract Norwegians across the sea. He knew that most of them had little knowledge of seaports and sea journeys, so he sent many letters to spread information about the mechanics of leaving by way of Göteberg in Sweden, Le Havre in France, and any of several ports in England.

Theodore Blegen, a prominent historian of Norwegian Americans, says that the early immigrants

> particularly relished the tale of how, as the "Restauration" neared the harbor of Funchal [in the Madeira Islands], a floating cask of Madeira wine was hauled on board. . . . The contents of the cask were consumed by the crew, with the result that "the ship came drifting into the harbor like a plague ship, without command and without raising its flag." The immigrants narrowly escaped from being greeted by cannon.

Most of them settled near Kendall, New York, where Americans gave them supplies, but an unfortunate fire burned those, and much sickness also afflicted the new arrivals. The colony lasted only a few years.

Meanwhile, Peerson was scouting for other settlement sites much farther west. He walked along Lake Michigan to what is now Milwaukee, where he met the French-Canadian fur trader who a little later would be the founder of that town. Apparently Solomon Juneau did not want Scandinavians barging into his area, for he told Peerson that Wisconsin was heavily forested and unsuitable for settlement. It is ironic that today persons of German, Polish, and Scandinavian ancestry are the most numerous in the state, and that in Milwaukee itself are thousands of persons with names such as Peterson and Larsen but only sixteen Juneaus in the phone book.

Later, Peerson came to a hill overlooking the Fox River valley. Blegen says,

> Almost exhausted with hunger and fatigue, he threw himself on the grass and thanked God for having directed his steps to such an attractive land. In his enthusiasm he temporarily forgot his hunger and weariness, and his thoughts turned to Moses and the promised land.

Other Scandinavians also fancied themselves in the role of Moses. In the late 1830s and the early 1840s Gjert Hovland ‹in the land of the heathen temple› sent back to Norway rapturous letters about the New World. "This is a beautiful and fertile country," he said. "Prosperity and contentment are to be seen almost everywhere one goes." "The vote of the common man carries just as much authority and influence as does that of the rich and powerful man." But, he warned, "Everyone must work for his living here, and it makes no difference whether he is of low or high estate." Hundreds of Hovland's letters were circulated, and they were repeatedly published in newspapers.

Another Moses was Kund Anderson Slogvag. After five years in the United States he returned and, says Blegen, "From all parts of the diocese of Bergen and from Stavanger, people came to talk with him." He became in 1836 the leader of about two hundred new immigrants who crossed the sea on the *Norden* and *Den Norske Klippe*.

Ole Rynning used both the spoken and the written word to attract his Norwegian countrymen. In 1837 he led a group of eighty-four persons, some of them *bönder* ‹landholders› and others farm laborers, to New York, then to Albany by boat, to Buffalo by canal boat, to Detroit on Lake Erie, and then across Michigan to Chicago. The group settled on low-lying land in Iroquois County, Illinois, but were flooded out the following spring after losing many of their number to disease. "Nothing could shake [Rynning's] belief that America would become a place of refuge for the masses of people in Europe who toiled under the burdens of poverty," his friend Ansten Nattestad wrote. Gullich Gravdal added,

> Since many came long distances in order to talk with him, the reports of the far west were soon spread over a large part of the country. Ministers and bailiffs [in Norway] . . . tried to frighten us with terrible tales about the dreadful sea monsters, and about man-eating wild animals in the new world.

In a book published in 1838 Rynning tried to tell the simple facts. It was *True Account of America for the Information and Help of Peasant and Commoner*. Its thirteen short chapters (a fourteenth was deleted by prominent Norwegian clergy) were studied by thousands of Scandinavians. One passage contains a description and a condemnation of slavery and an early prediction of the American Civil War: ". . . there will in all likelihood come either a separation between the northern and southern states, or else bloody civil disputes."

Sometimes the advice givers found themselves imposed on. Lars Larsen, one of those who had come on the *Restauration* in 1825, settled in Rochester, New York. There many later immigrants came for counsel. Larsen reported in some despair in 1837 that about ninety persons from Stavanger had stayed with him for three days, but worse still, some were still there three weeks later, and although the Larsens wanted to be generous, they could not provide for so many.

Another generous soul was Even Heg ‹one from a hedged area›. In Wisconsin in 1843 he put up a large barn for the use of immigrants passing through and also for a social and religious center; during an epidemic it served as a hospital. Heg also established the first Norwegian-American newspaper, *Nordlyset,* which in its first issue prominently displayed a cut of the American flag and a translation of parts of the Declaration of Independence. *Nordlyset* later became the Norwegian organ of the Free-Soil political party.

Mormon missionaries from America converted large numbers of English and Scandinavians starting in the early 1840s. In the 1850s some 2,600 Danish Mormons found their way to the Deseret settlements in what is now the state of Utah. Later some 27,000 other Danes joined them, as well as numerous Norwegians and some Swedes, all of whom came, as some of them sang, "Homeward to Zion." In 1900 about 34 percent of the foreign-born in Utah were from Scandinavia.

Numerous utopian colonies were attempted in nineteenth-century America. One of the lesser known of these was Bishop Hill, in Illinois, founded by Eric Jansson, a Swedish Pietist. Some 1,500 Swedes joined him in a few years starting in 1847, moved by his hypnotic persuasiveness. Jansson's colony was more dictatorial than most, and his followers began complaining about his autocratic regulations, which reached even into family relationships. For one thing, he required complete celibacy—even between married couples

—during the first two years at Bishop Hill. Dissidents drifted away, and the colony was dissolved by 1870.

Fredrika Bremer, in her day Sweden's most popular novelist, an antislavery partisan and a thoughtful, thought-provoking advocate of women's rights, traveled in the United States in mid-century, met Emerson, Hawthorne, and Longfellow, and talked with Scandinavians in several parts of the United States. Her visit resulted in *The Homes of the New World* (1854). "In glowing terms," says Blegen,

> she spoke to her fellow Scandinavians of the upper midwest. Probably no other book, before or after, has had such an important influence on promoting emigration from all of the Scandinavian countries to the United States.

The extent to which rather recent arrivals influenced American elections was much debated in the nineteenth century. Daniel Webster and other Whigs in 1844 contended that immigrant votes in Pennsylvania and New York, many of them alleged to be fraudulent, had been responsible for James Polk's defeat of Whig Henry Clay in the presidential race. In 1847 Ole Raeder (which can mean ‹wheelwright›, ‹alderman›, or ‹thatcher›) expressed the belief that Norwegians were responsible for rejecting Wisconsin's first constitution and thereby delaying its statehood until 1848:

> . . . almost the only opportunity to vote that the great mass of the Norwegians have had was on the question of the proposed constitution, on which the legislature declared that every man over twenty-one years who had been six months in the territory and had declared his intention of becoming a citizen should be entitled to vote. . . .
>
> When the constitution was framed and came up for a referendum of all the voting citizens, most of the Norwegians at Rock Prairie and, as far as I have discovered, the great majority of Norwegians in the whole territory voted against it. Their votes were not without influence, because the Norwegian population, according to what I have heard from dependable men in the various settlements, must be at the very least 6,000 and, presumably, 7- or 8,000.
>
> The outcome of the whole affair was that the constitution was rejected and as a result Wisconsin must still be content to be classed as a territory without the privileges of a state.

In the New World immigrants found higher prices and different methods of doing business than those they knew at home, as an anonymous Norwegian merchant wrote from Minnesota in 1866:

> A barrel of salt costs about $5, coffee, 35 or 40 cents a pound, and nearly all other groceries are more expensive than in Norway. Almost all kinds of dry goods are twice as expensive as they are in Norway, but the Americans are not satisfied to make such a poor profit as people do in Norway. There seems almost to be a silent agreement among all kinds of businessmen here that everybody is to make a good profit on what he has to sell.
>
> It is also much more pleasant to wait on customers here than it is in Norway. All conversation and aggressive recommendation of merchandise, which was always so distasteful to me, is nonexistent here. We also have extensive barter with the farmers. They bring us wool, butter, and eggs and get in return the things they need. Butter and eggs sell to the people of the town at a profit of 33 per cent. In New York butter costs 60 cents a pound; in LaCrosse [Wisconsin], 15 cents, and here the price is 30 cents.

By 1850, according to census reports, there were only 18,075 persons of Scandinavian birth in the United States, two thirds of whom were Norwegians. The total quadrupled in the next decade, reached a half million in the 1880s, and had passed a million before 1900. Thus nine centuries after Norse Viking Leif Eriksson, whose father was Erik Thorvaldson, reportedly set foot on what he called Vinland (possibly Nova Scotia), many of those who were at least nominally his descendants followed him. Almost 100,000 Ericksons now live in the United States.

Some surprising statistics are those concerning Scandinavian sailors who jumped ship and stayed here. A Swedish-American consular report of 1846 stated that up to that time 502 Norwegian and 910 Swedish sailors had done so. Between 1856 and 1865, 11,000 more from the two nations decided not to go back, and an estimated total by 1890 was 34,000. Presumably most of these seamen were unmarried, and many of them may later have returned to Scandinavia.

The peak of the Scandinavian flow was from 1880 through 1893, a period when some 900,000 persons came to America. By 1900 the Swedes outnumbered the Norwegians by 573,000 to 337,000, and there were 154,000 Danes. There was a gradual subsidence until the predictably low World War I years. Since 1920 the average has been only about 5,000 Scandinavians a year, partly because the standard of living in the Scandinavian countries gradually became higher than that of the United States.

One reason for the influx during the latter part of the nineteenth century was that the Scandinavian countries removed their opposition to emigration. The state and church authorities had at that time seen poverty steadily increasing. Land customarily was bequeathed to the oldest son, but in large families that often left three or four other sons landless. (Daughters did not really seem to count because they would presumably marry someone, with or without land, and no longer be the family's concern.) Some of the landless might become tenant farmers—*torpare* as the Swedes called them —and some might become *statare*—farm laborers—and some might have to subsist on handouts or starve. The landless frequently resented the prosperity and snobbishness of the landholders, who might be their own older brothers.

To make matters worse, the price of grain dropped substantially, partly because world production had increased dramatically, especially in the United States, Canada, and Russia; partly because the recently invented harvester and binder were cutting labor costs; and partly because railroads and steamships—both nineteenth-century inventions—had reduced the time and expense and hazards of transportation. As a result of the low prices, Scandinavian landholders' pocketbooks were pinched and *torpare* and *statare* felt the results still more.

So in 1882 alone over 105,000 Scandinavians emigrated to the United States where in some places at that time the government would still give homesteaders 160 acres of land, a huge amount according to most European standards, and far beyond the dreams of most of the landless.

The majority of Scandinavians have always preferred to resettle in a climate and on land not very different from what they have known in Europe. And, as is true of most nationalities, they have tended to live not far from others from their homeland. So the Norwegians who went to Minnesota put down their new roots mainly in the central part of the state and in the Red River valley, the Swedes in the area north of the Twin Cities. The few Icelanders who came settled in frigid but lovely northwestern Minnesota, and small but scattered communities still mainly Danish or the non-Scandinavian Finnish may yet be found in the state.

Similarly in other parts of the Midwest, more or less extensive areas dominated by Scandinavian names appear on modern demographic charts. In Wisconsin, for instance, although Germans are by far the most numerous people in the east, Norwegians fill much of the west and south, Swedes the northwest and north. Western and central Iowa have many Scandinavians. And so on for Nebraska, the Dakotas, Illinois, and parts of Michigan, as well as pockets elsewhere. Swedes much more often than the others have settled in cities—up to 60 percent of them now living there. Chicago, for instance, had and perhaps still has more Swedes than any other city in the world except Stockholm. The Manhattan phone book has two and a half columns of Petersons, the Chicago phone book nine columns.

The Hansens and the Larsons and the Olsons and the Ekstroms and others have added their patronyms and place names to America's onomastic kettle. Many of these names obviously mean ‹son of› somebody, but deserve some special comment.

For one thing, although it must be emphasized that many exceptions exist, a Scandinavian name ending in *-son* is most likely to be Swedish but may be Norwegian, and one ending in *-sen* is probably Norwegian or Danish. If there are two *s*'s —Hanssen, for example—the name is more than likely Norwegian, although most from Norway, especially after they come here, do content themselves with a single *s*. Icelanders favor a double *s*, but not many from that small island ever reached our shores.

Even into the nineteenth century some Swedish and Norwegian families would change names from one generation to the next according to the first name of the father. Lars

Olson's son Hans would not be Hans Olson but Hans Larson ‹Hans the son of Lars›, and *his* son might be Nels Hanson ‹Nels the son of Hans›. The system provides a beautiful example of patronyms but gives headaches to genealogists and government officials such as tax collectors.

Another unusual feature is that many Norwegians had what are called "farm names," which usually end with *-by, -ga(a)rd, -heim, -land, -rud, -set, -stad,* or *-vin,* all of which refer to a large or a small farm, sometimes just a clearing of an acre or a few acres. All persons who lived on the farm would have the same surname regardless of whether or not they were related—Björnstad ‹Björn's farm› or Stensrud ‹stony clearing›, for example. If a Björnstad moved to Stensrud, he or she would change names accordingly.

The Swedish government has taken a special interest in surnames and supports a *Släktnamnskommitté* ‹family name committee›. During the past century Sweden has encouraged its residents to depart from the confusing repetitiousness of the patronymic system that could result in pages of Lars Olsons in Stockholm alone. It has recommended the use or combinations of various nature names that sound pleasant alone or together. Hence countless Swedes, both at home and in America, are named Dahl ‹valley›, Holm ‹island in the river›, Lind ‹linden›, Strand ‹shore›, Ström ‹stream›, and Wahl ‹well›, as well as any of some 56,000 recommended combinations such as Ekberg ‹oak hill›, Cederquist ‹cedar twig›, Asplund ‹aspen grove›, or Lundgren ‹grove branch›. As those examples show, combinations of a tree name with that of some other natural feature seem especially favored.

Some Swedes, upon entering the army, adopted or were required to take during military service a less common name than was their birthright. So Peterson, for instance, might become Sward ‹sword›, Tapper ‹brave›, Fisk ‹fisherman›, or something else. Often upon leaving the army, especially if the soldier liked his new name, he would keep it permanently.

Among America's most common names, there is considerable likelihood but not a certainty that an Anderson, the 9th most common name, will be Scandinavian. In Minneapolis there are more Andersons, Nelsons, Petersons, Olsons, Larsons, and Carlsons than there are Smiths. Across all of America, Peterson or a variant ranks 23rd, Nelson 30th, Olson 118th, Hansen 165th, Carlson 171st, Larson 197th, Hanson 218th.

The Petersons, the Olsens, the Hedstroms, and countless more with such names through ingenuity and persistence and intelligence and dedication and an eagerness to try something new have made the lives of the rest of us a little better.

You owe the zipper on your dress or your trousers to an American named Sundbäck, born in Sweden.

If you fish, it is Ole Evinrude, a Norwegian American, who is credited with inventing the outboard motor, in 1909.

If you drink, Max Henius, a Danish-American chemist, is said to have trained more brewmasters than anyone else. If you don't approve of drinking, you should know that the author of the Volstead Act, Andrew Volstead, was born in Norway. (American Danes, though, like many Norwegians, actively opposed prohibition.)

If you like classical music, you would have enjoyed hearing the first prima donna of the New York Metropolitan Opera, Swedish-American Christina Nilsson, who opened the original Met by singing Marguerite in *Faust*.

If football is your specialty, you know that Norwegian-born Knute Rockne coached the so-called Irish of Notre Dame to 105 wins, 12 losses, and 5 ties in thirteen years and that he was one of the greatest innovators the game has known.

If quick wealth appeals to you, you may admire Jafet Lindeberg, a Norwegian reindeer herder, who came to Alaska and in ninety days panned out $200,000 in gold (now worth perhaps six or eight million); he helped to found Nome, and in less than twenty years was the richest Norwegian in America. His American-born near-namesake (no relative), aviator Charles A. Lindbergh, has been called America's last authentic hero.

If you are a laborer, you may know of Andrew Foruseth, born Anders Andreassen in Norway, who became president of the International Seamen's Union but accepted as salary only what an ablebodied seaman would be paid.

If architecture interests you, you should know that another Norwegian American, Edwin Bergstrom, was the chief designer of the Pentagon complex.

If politics interests you, you probably know that the mother of Hubert H. Humphrey was born in Norway. You may not know that every Minnesota governor from 1925 to 1976 was Scandinavian.

If you scorn Alexander Pope's advice "Be not the first by whom the new is tried," it may interest you that Chicago's first electric lights were in the store of Norway-born Christian Jevne in 1880. Crowds assembled each night to see them. And Swedish Americans in 1888 were the first farmers to use electric lights in their houses and barns. Or so they say.

My grandmother, God rest her, had no electric lights, and probably would not have wanted them because there were none in Denmark in her girlhood. My grandfather would have welcomed electric lights, milking machines, the Metropolitan Opera, zippers, outboard motors, and Nebraska football teams like those that Knute Rockne coached in Indiana.

17

THE FINNS:

From Above the Sixtieth Parallel

MY GERMAN GRANDFATHER and *his* German grandfather both found their brides in foreign lands, so one of my grandmothers was Danish and one of my great-great-grandmothers Finnish. I don't know where she lived in Finland before she agreed to move to Germany with him—he was a sailor, so probably it was Helsinki or one of the many other towns on the Baltic Sea, the Gulf of Finland, or the Gulf of Bothnia, places with names like Turku, Kotka, or Rauma, or Hango on the southern tip from which many Finns emigrated, or Viipuri, now called Vyborg and in Russian territory, the locale of the *Kalevala*.

I don't know how they spoke their love, either, for her Finnish language is not at all like his German or like the Scandinavian languages. It is most like Estonian, spoken just across the Gulf of Finland (an Estonian and a Finn can converse) and is a little more distantly related to Hungarian.

Today's traveler, flying Finnair across interior Finland in summer, looks down on a patternless but never monotonous green and blue, with frequent tiny patches of a different green representing pasture land or fields of wheat, rye, potatoes, sugar beets, even turnips. Finland, or Suomi as the Finns call it, is still heavily forested, mainly with conifers. The areas of blue, small or large, may be some of Finland's estimated 55,000 lakes, or rivers with names like Kemijoki or Ähtävänjoki. Northwestern Finland, where a considerable proportion of the people are Lapps, has a few unambitious mountains.

I don't know my great-great-grandmother's maiden name. The odds are fairly good that it ended in *-nen,* which is attached to many patronyms but some other names as well. Hanninen is the Finnish equivalent of Johnson, Mattinen of Matthewson, Kallinen is the son of Charles, Mikkonen the son of Michael, Heikkinen the son of Henry, Penttinen the son of Benedict, and Waltonen or Waltari (Mika Waltari was a fine twentieth-century Finnish novelist) the son of Walter. Seppa or Seppanen is the Finnish smith, Kupiainen a supervisor of farm workers, and Kauppinen a shopkeeper.

Some names are descriptive. Thus Kettunen is descended from someone who resembled a fox, and Musta or Mustanen is dark complexioned or the son of the dark one; Valkoinen is the son of a light one; Peltonen's name-ancestor owned many fields; Partanen has a beard.

Or maybe my great-great-grandmother's name was one of those based on the physical features of the beautiful northern landscape. Järvi or Järvinen lives or lived beside a lake, Lahti beside a bay (or possibly in the town of that name). The original Kangas lived on a heath, Keto in a field, Hakala on pasture land, Neva in a marshy area, Niemi on a cape or headland, Saari on either an island or a ridge, Ranta on a shore, Laakso in a valley, Ojala near a ditch.

Compounding and prefixing are rather frequent in Finnish names. Put together Koski ‹one from a waterfall› and Maki ‹hill› and you have Koskimaki ‹one from a waterfall in hilly country›. Ruoko ‹grass› and Mäki give Ruokomäki ‹one from the grassy hill›. The prefix *ala* means ‹lower›, *yla* ‹upper›, and *keski* ‹middle›. Combined with Lahti as Alalahti, etc., these indicate which part of a bay the specific family came from.

There were a few Finns among the seventeenth-century Dutch of New Amsterdam. A much larger contingent, estimated at five hundred, came with the Swedes to New Sweden a few years later. (The Swedes and Finns at that time, unlike some other times in their history, were getting along rather well together.) These early Finns in America seem not to have left many traces, although Louis Wright says, "Some few bits of folklore may have their origins in the belief that the Finns were given to traffic with witches and devils." This odd belief was apparently widespread and persistent, for a nineteenth-century Michigan woman in a letter referred to old settlers' "fear of the Finnish sorcerers," and Richard Henry Dana, in *Two Years Before the Mast,* told of a Finnish sailor whose bottle was always half full, no matter how much he drank. (My own Finnish informant, Lillian Lahti, says, "The Finns probably did little to counter such accusations, either because of their somewhat perverse sense of humor or because they were thus left alone or because they may indeed have believed the stories themselves.")

A more respectful and tangible token of the seventeenth-century Finns is a monument erected in 1938, three hundred years after the coming of the first ship from Sweden. It was sculpted by a Finnish sculptor, Waino Aaltonen, and stands in Chester, Pennsylvania, an area once informally called Finland.

Alaska had some Finnish residents in the first half of the nineteenth century, and later two Finns served as its governors. Some Finns joined the Alaskan gold rushes of 1880 and 1896. For a while after 1900, Finns and Norwegians were the largest foreign-born group in the territory. Finnish settlements were especially prominent at Sitka, Juneau-Douglas, Fairbanks, and Anchorage. A Finnish church at Sitka, built in the 1840s, was the first Protestant church on the west coast of North America.

Finland's population zoomed from 900,000 in 1800 to

3,000,000 a century later, and there was too little work, too few resources for so many people. Finland had been a major producer of tar, but the bottom dropped out of the tar market. Demand for sailing ships decreased concurrently; again the Finns were hurt economically for they had been expert builders of sailing vessels but could not compete in construction of steam-driven ships of steel. In 1878 many young men became unhappy when military service became compulsory, and in the 1890s Russia, on Finland's eastern border, resumed recurrent threats.

Word of the possibility of a better life spread gradually from one *pitäjä* ‹parish› to another. Labor recruiters from America sometimes visited. They wanted both young men and young women. Servant girls in the United States were being paid four times as much as in Finland. In three years —1874, 1894, and 1897—more women than men immigrated. But there were especially good jobs, it seemed, for men who did not mind cold weather. It became a matter of pride in some families to say, "Our son (or daughter) is in America, you know."

Some of the recruiters were agents of the Quincy copper mine in Hancock, Michigan, in the Upper Peninsula, above the cold 47th parallel, farther north than any part of Wisconsin, farther north than Duluth. In 1865 they persuaded thirty-five Finnish miners to come to work, and in the next ten years a thousand more came. Others went to the iron mines of Negaunee and Ishpeming and Ironwood, the Iron Ranges of Gogebic, Iron, Marquette, and Menominee, or to the mines of Duluth and Virginia in Minnesota. A few Finns didn't get farther west than the New England states, where they got jobs in textile mills, cranberry bogs, or stone quarries. Others settled in Lake Erie cities, especially Conneaut, Ashtabula, and Cleveland, and others went on to Illinois. Farm families began to populate parts of Wisconsin, Minnesota, and the Dakotas.

In 1883–92, 36,000 Finns came to America, and from 1893–1900 there were over 47,000. The peak decade was 1901–10, when almost 159,000 came to these shores.

As a rule the Finns worked hard and played no less hard, and sometimes their play was so vigorous that others were afraid of them. An indignantly righteous Gloucester editor opinionated, "Finns are truly people, not beasts, though at the lowest stage of development." Another journalist wrote, "They carried on a raw life in the saloons where they caroused." And another told how they "danced bare-chested and bare-footed on the turf in New England towns, attracting groups of townsfolk who regarded them as bands of gypsies, but fled in fright when the drunken brawls began."

But the Finns, brawlers or not, opened their own college and theological seminary in Hancock in 1896 and fittingly called it Suomi Opisti ‹Finnish place of learning›, later just Suomi. Today the seminary is gone, and numerous black students mingle with the Finns and others. The Finnish national epic, the *Kalevala,* was taught in Suomi and eventually at some other colleges as well, and some American poets imitated its rhythms. The greatest Finnish composer, Sibelius, traveled in the United States, and American conductors Eugene Ormandy and Serge Koussevitzky introduced to American audiences some of the *Kalevala*-inspired music of his *Finlandia* and other works. Leopold Stokowski invited the son-in-law of Sibelius, Jussi Jalas, to celebrate Sibelius's centennial in 1965 by conducting in Carnegie Hall. Martti Nisonen, born in Finland in 1891, became an American citizen, taught at Suomi College from 1923 to 1946, and composed symphonies, cantatas, operas.

Finland gave us the architecture of Eliel Saarinen and his son Eero. In 1923 the two came here together, and later they jointly won awards from the American Institute of Architects for an annex to the Smithsonian, and the younger planned terminals at Kennedy International and Dallas International airports, designed the arch that towers beside St. Louis, and created architectural history with glass and stainless steel.

My Finnish-American informant tells me that five words can help the non-Finn to understand Finns: *Suomi* for patriotism and affection for one's native land, *Sibelius* for love of music and all the arts, *sauna, sana,* and *sisu.*

The sauna, pronounced "sow-na" by Finns, has become well known to many Americans, although the knowledgeable deplore the frequent bastardization of its form, equipment, procedures, and uses. To the Finn it was a versatile place, often built before the house itself, for it could serve as a shelter. Babies could be born in it, bodies be laid out for burial; drinkers sometimes used it to sleep off their indiscretions. In its major function, I am told, "It cleanses the soul as well as the body."

Sana means ‹word›, and symbolizes a love for reading and knowledge, a love shared by countless Finns. The Finnish language helps that cause along, for it may be the most sensibly spelled language in the world. Each grapheme (letter) has one phoneme (sound). As soon as a toddler can recognize and pronounce the printed symbols, he or she can read anything in Finnish that is within his or her intellectual grasp. The Finnish language is the strongest argument for thoroughgoing simplification of the horrendous English spelling system—or the lack of system, rather.

Sana covers too Finland's rich heritage of oral literature, of storytelling as an art, and of enthusiasm for good conversation. American Finns quickly formed Bible-study groups and book-discussion groups, even newspaper-discussion groups that would compare contents of various newspapers, both Finnish and English.

Sibelius defined *sisu* as "a metaphysical shot in the arm which makes men do the impossible." My own informant calls it "a combination of perseverance, bull-headedness, never-say-die, do it for the Gipper." *Sisu* is the quality of the long-distance runner who reaches deep for last ounces of energy. It helps to explain the challenge that Finns find in farming stony soil. It enables them to increase the heat in an already sweltering sauna. In 1939, Finns' *sisu* enabled them for weeks on end to hold off the might of the Russian army.

After World War I, most nations reneged on the debts they owed to the United States, but every year, on the appointed date, "Little Finland," as the newspapers used to headline, "Pays Again." Maybe *sisu* accounted for that, also.

I have no way of knowing how much *sisu* or *sana* my

great-great-grandmother had. If she had lived later, I don't know whether she would have preferred the complex resonance of Sibelius or the simple melodies of Oskar Merikanto. I don't even know whether her family had a sauna.

I wish that I knew. I wish that I knew at least her name.

Part III

SOUTHERN AND EASTERN EUROPEANS

18

SPEAKERS OF SPANISH:

Spaniards, Cubans, Mexicans, Puerto Ricans, and Filipinos

SPANIARDS who came earliest to the New World were interested in exploring and especially in finding riches for their Spanish rulers. A good example is Juan de Oñate, although his name is less well known than those of Balboa, Cortez, and Ponce de Leon. He held out great promises if the king's viceroy would give him enough backing:

With God's help I will . . . give new worlds—new, peaceful, and grand—to his Majesty, greater even than the good Marquis [Cortez] gave to him, although he did so much, if you, illustrious Sir, will give me the aid, the protection, and the help which I expect from such a hand. . . . I beg you to take note of the great increase which the royal crown . . . will have in this land. . . .

First, the great wealth which the mines have begun to reveal. . . . Second, the certainty of the proximity of the South Sea, whose trade with Pirú, New Spain, and China is not to be underestimated. . . .

Third, the increase of vassals and tribute. . . .

I will not mention the founding of so many republics, the many offices, their payments, the patronage, etc., the wealth of wool and hides of buffalo, and many other things. . . .

Unlike the English, who usually came to colonize, the early Spanish came mainly to conquer and to carry wealth back to Spain. Had their motives and strategy been different, North America might today be a Spanish-speaking land.

True, the Spaniards did convert a few Indians to Christianity, although their tactics were sometimes violent. As Father Francisco Palou wrote on one occasion, "[The Indians] retired after learning a good lesson when three or four of them were left dead with gun-shots and many more were wounded. . . . [For] a long time they would not approach the camp and the mission."

True, too, the Spanish founded St. Augustine, Florida, in 1565, forty-two years before the first English settlers reached Jamestown. It was to be Spain's most northern colonial outpost for over two centuries, and is now the oldest existing city in the United States.

North America, however, has never brought the Spanish people great wealth—not yet.

That may change. Today Spanish surnames in the United States are increasing at a faster rate than that of any other large group. Social Security lists for 1964 showed 292,600 persons named Rodriguez (possibly with a variant in the last letters). Rodriguez is the most common Spanish name in this country, now occupying twenty-one columns of fine print in the Los Angeles telephone directory. In 1964 the Rodriguezes were in forty-fourth place among all American surnames. Ten years later (there has been no more recent compilation) the list showed 416,178 with that name, which had advanced to thirty-first place. The table on page 165 shows similar gains for other Spanish names. (The 1964 figures are from Elsdon Smith's *American Surnames*.)

These nine names plus Rodriguez gained an average of forty places in Social Security rankings in only a decade. The percentage rate of growth for them averaged 47.9; that for the entire United States was about 13. So the Rodriguezes and others with these Spanish names were multiplying at a rate some three and a half times as fast as the whole population. With a great influx of Cubans, Mexicans, Puerto Ricans, and Filipinos since 1974, that proportion has probably

Increase in Spanish Surnames

Name	Number in 1964	Number in 1974	Rank in 1964	Rank in 1974
Gonzalez	189,600	360,994	85	42
Garcia	242,000	346,175	58	44
Lopez	178,000	254,535	93	65
Rivera	176,500	238,457	94	73
Hernandez	159,100	235,498	112	75
Perez	148,350	217,801	124	86
Sanchez	121,100	175,104	176	114
Torres	120,100	170,507	183	120
Ortiz	93,700	130,631	241	184

increased. If present growth rates continue, within a century there may be as many Spanish names as English in the United States, and de Oñate's sixteenth-century promises to Spanish people may, after a fashion, come true.

Most American speakers of Spanish, of course, have not come here directly from Spain. Rather, many of their ancestors went from Spain to Mexico, Puerto Rico, Cuba, Central or South America, or the Philippines, and often intermarried with the native populations. Then the descendants found and are finding their ways here.

Their receptions have often not been gracious. Back in the 1940s Helen Papashvily (of Scottish and Irish ancestry, but married to a Russian) wrote *Anything Can Happen,* an often-rollicking story of Mr. Papashvily's first years here. She also wrote, for the *English Journal,* an account of her own childhood and her meeting with Mexican children for the first time.

I told Aunt Maggie and Uncle Andrew about it that night.

"What do you think?" I dropped my bombshell. "There's Mexican kids right in our room at school. Dirty old Mexicans.

And you can't trust 'em around a corner. That's what Golden West M'Gilligan's father says."

"Don't brag, Lass," Uncle Andrew said, attending to his steak.

"Bragging?"

"Aye." He looked me over the top of his half-glasses. "For when you say somebody's dirty and not to be trusted what you have in your mind to let the world know is that they're dirtier and less trustworthy than you. 'Tis only a twisted way of givin' us to know that yer clean and yer honest. Such a remark, when it's true, comes with more grace from another. So let's have no more of it, but pass the potatoes."

Hernando Cortez arrived in Mexico from Spain in 1519 and, pretending to be a god, conquered the Aztecs in 1524. The conquistadors found diverse peoples speaking highly diverse tongues. Many of them represented old civilizations, in some respects more advanced than that of the Spanish themselves. Their agricultural production, sometimes aided by irrigation canals, was fairly sophisticated, they had an elaborately organized feudal-communal government, religious beliefs and ceremonies were complex, there was interregional commerce, sculpture and ceramics were esthetically pleasing, masses of stone weighing as much as forty-four tons were sometimes transported fifty miles to make monuments, there were huge and architecturally ingenious temples such as the two-hundred-foot-high Pyramid of the Sun in Teotihuacán, the Mayas had a calendar suitable for recording astronomical and historical information, and a writing system comparable in structure to the Japanese syllabary had been developed.

So the proud heritage of Spain mingled with the proud heritage of the natives throughout what we call Latin America. In today's Mexico, *mestizos* (people of mixed European and native ancestry) comprise some 55 percent of the population, natives ("Indians") about 29 percent, and Europeans 15 percent, of whom the majority were born in Mexico. Mexico's birth rate for many years has been among the highest in the world—45 per thousand or thereabouts. The death rate dropped by two-thirds from 1930 to 1970. In consequence, Mexico's population increased by close to 40 percent in one decade alone (from 1960 to 1970 it grew from 34.9 to 48.4 million); current projections forecast a Mexican population of well over 100 million to start the twenty-first century. Inevitably, large numbers of these people spill across the long border into the more prosperous United States. American immigration figures or other head counts are meaningless, because many of these immigrants are "wetbacks"—people who enter the country illegally and avoid calling themselves to the attention of the authorities. Uncountable numbers of these are not represented in the Social Security figures cited earlier.

The people of Cuba also represent a mixed heritage. The native stock, however, mainly Tainos from Haiti, was largely wiped out by sixteenth-century Spanish invaders. To make up for the lost native labor, the Spaniards over the years imported some 800,000 Africans. Centuries later, from 1919 to 1926, another quarter million blacks, chiefly from Jamaica and Haiti, came to the island as laborers and tended to stay there. Today, some 15 percent of the population is black and perhaps another 30 percent *mestizo*. The remainder are mostly Spanish, many of them the descendants of Spanish who immigrated in the first third of this century.

Like the Mexicans, the Cubans have a high birth rate, with over 27 percent of the population below ten years of age in 1970. Also like the Mexicans, they have come to the United States in large numbers. Especially during the regime of Fidel Castro, many thousands of Cubans have fled, mostly to nearby Florida. In 1980 alone, some 125,000 of them piled into small boats and came here, in general with Castro's blessing because of economic troubles in his country. Most were helped by family or friends to find housing and jobs, but others, including some mental patients and convicts, had to be retained in camps, hospitals, or prisons.

Puerto Rico has been another rich source of our Spanish names. Puerto Ricans are largely Spanish or African or a mixture of the two, although there are still traces of the native "Indian" physical features. Danes, French, Corsicans, and a few other Europeans have also contributed to the blend. The Puerto Rican birth rate has been lower than that of Cuba and Mexico, especially since the mid-sixties, but the fact that its citizens may enter the United States mainland without any formalities has led to a large inflow. New York City has been the major beneficiary, but Chicago also has a sizable Puerto Rican population, and fairly large enclaves exist also in other cities.

Since Puerto Ricans usually fly in, it has been said that they represent the first major air migration in history.

In 1930 only 53,000 Puerto Ricans lived here, and few came during the depression or World War II. But a combination of factors led to a gigantic influx after 1945: a low fifty-dollar air fare, a large population increase in Puerto Rico, labor shortages here and consequent recruiting by stateside employers, and urging by friends and relatives already here. Many settled in Harlem or the south Bronx or in the area of the Brooklyn Navy Yard. (*West Side Story,* popular as a stage musical and a movie in the 1950s and revived since, was set in east Harlem.) By 1950 there were 250,000 Puerto Ricans in New York City alone, and many also in the south end of Boston, the south and near north sides of Chicago, northwest Cleveland, and others in Newark, Camden, Bridgeport, Philadelphia, and other cities. By 1970 an estimated 1.5 million were living on the mainland, although many kept flying back and forth to their native island.

Their problems were probably as great as those of any other immigrant group. A Puerto Rican, Jack Agueros, in *The Immigrant Experience,* edited by Thomas Wheeler, has described some of the difficulties:

> The sudden surge in numbers caused new resentments, and prejudice was intensified. Some were forced to live in cellars, and were then characterized as cave dwellers. . . . In our confusion we were sometimes pathetically reaching out, sometimes pathologically striking out. Gangs. Drugs. Wine. Smoking. Girls. Dances and slow-drag music. Mambo. Spics, Spooks, and Wops. Territories, brother gangs, and war councils establishing right of way on blocks and avenues and for seating in the local theater. Pegged pants and zip guns. . . .
>
> Education collapsed. Every classroom had ten kids who spoke no English. Black, Italian, Puerto Rican relations in the classroom

were good, but we all knew we couldn't visit one another's neighborhoods. Sometimes we could not move freely within our own blocks.

Many Puerto Rican divorces came about because women often earned more than their husbands or had jobs when their husbands did not. Some men considered this situation disgraceful to them. Puerto Rican girls had a freer, chaperoneless social life on the mainland, but this too led to dissension, since many parents and grandparents believed that the girls were becoming immoral. Old and young alike tended to decrease their religious ties, going to church seldom or leaving the Roman Catholic faith and becoming, perhaps, Baptists or Pentecostals.

But slowly, as has happened with other ethnic groups, some of their names—as well as those of Florida's Cubans and the Mexican Americans of the Southwest—are gaining prominence. Herman Badillo ‹one from the small ford› of the Bronx was the first Puerto Rican to be elected to Congress. Jesus Maria Sanroma ‹holy one from Rome› became the pianist of the Boston Symphony. Playwrights include Florens Torres ‹one from the tower›, Rene Marques ‹descendant of Marcos›, Francisco Arrivi, and Emilio Belaval. The mother of poet William Carlos Williams was Puerto Rican. Blind guitarist-singer-composer Jose Feliciano ‹descendant of the fortunate man› taught himself, performed in Greenwich Village coffeehouses, eventually won two Grammies in one year.

Dolores Conchita del Rivero ‹one from near a brook› changed her name to Chita Rivera and starred in *Call Me Madam, Can-Can, Guys and Dolls*. Rita Moreno ‹dark› (nee Rosa Dolores Alverio) starred in *West Side Story*. Orlando Cepeda was a homerun hitter, and Roberto Clemente won four National League batting championships before dying in an airplane crash while taking off to carry help to earthquake victims in Nicaragua. Juan "Chi Chi" Rodriguez has won major golf championships. (Another golf champion is a Mexican, the irrepressibly comic Lee Trevino, called "Supermex.") Puerto Rican boxing champions include Sixto Escobar ‹one from where broom grows›, Jose Torres, Carlos Ortiz ‹son of Ordono the lucky›. A number of Cubans have become business leaders in the Miami area.

In 1981 his fellow Americans found out about the heroism of Jimmy Lopez, of Mexican ancestry. Jimmy was a Marine in Teheran when the Iranians took hostage the people in our embassy. Because of his quick thinking, six Americans were saved from imprisonment. He hurried them into a car of the Canadian embassy, and they were whisked away to be hidden there until the Canadians could smuggle them out of Iran. Jimmy himself, like fifty-one of the others who did not escape, had to spend 444 days in captivity.

The Philippines was ruled by Spain for 333 years. After 1898 it was controlled by the United States but was given its complete independence in 1946, following Japanese occupation in World War II. As a result of the long Spanish presence, Spanish is one of its three official languages, the others being English and Pilipino, which is the new name of Tagalog. Many Filipino names, as could be expected, are Spanish. Some of its leaders, for example, have been named Roxas ‹red haired›, Marcos, and Osmeña.

Before 1920 few Filipinos were in the United States, although a number had gone to Hawaii to work in the sugar and pineapple industries. By 1930 some 45,000 were on the mainland. Since then, somewhat larger numbers have immigrated, especially to the West Coast, where many do stoop labor; in Alaska they are frequently employed in fish canneries. Since relatively few Filipino women came with the early groups, the men often married Mexican girls. There are now, however, several thousand Filipino nurses in the United States, and in 1973 there were an estimated 6,000 Filipino doctors here, helping to alleviate the shortage of physicians that then existed.

In Spain or a Spanish-American country a complete name *(nombre completo)* has three parts, which have been most clearly explained and illustrated in a mimeographed booklet, *Spanish Personal Names,* by Raymond L. Gorden, to whom I am indebted. First comes a *nombre,* known in English as a given name or a Christian name. *Nombres* come from various sources. Thus Dolores and Felix are of Latin origin, Alberto and Armando were once Germanic, Abraham and Jesus obviously Hebrew, Alejandro and Delia Greek, Alfredo and Eduardo Anglo-Saxon, and Carlota and Raul French. Sometimes, but not usually, there is a *segundo nombre,* a second given name.

The middle name is the *primer apellido,* the father's name. The third name is the *segundo apellido,* the mother's name. So Esteban Garcia y Fernandez is the son of a father whose name is Garcia and a mother named Fernandez. Sometimes *y* ‹and› separates the names, but not always.

In some instances, especially in the past, an indication of the father's residence has been added at the end. Thus the father of Esteban Garcia Fernandez de Sevilla lived in Seville. On occasion these place indicators have become the person's legal name, with or without the prefix such as *de.*

Until about 150 years ago Spanish women did not take their husband's name after marriage. Today some of them retain both the mother's and the father's *apellidos.* So Sra. Leticia Maria Rios-Vega de Rodriguez has the *nombre* Leticia, her mother was Maria Vega, her father was Rios, and she is married to a man named Rodriguez.

Ordinarily, though, the wife retains only her *nombre* and her *primer apellido.* So if Ana Cabrera Leon marries Alejandro Otero Marquez, she becomes Sra. Ana Cabrera de Otero, their son would be Juanito Otero Cabrera, and their daughter Elvina Otero Cabrera.

When Spanish speakers alphabetize their names, the *primer apellido* comes first. So,

> Romiro Gomez Rueda is alphabetized Gomez Rueda, Romiro

A widow, however, would follow this pattern, using her late husband's *apellido:*

> Saturia Mogollon v. ‹widow› de Gomez is alphabetized Gomez, Saturia Mogollon v. de

The numerous Spanish names that one finds in American large-city directories, then, are usually arranged according to the *primer apellido,* not by the "last name" in the English sense. Some exceptions are created by persons who prefer to be known by the mother's maiden name. Second and especially third-generation Spanish speakers in this country are likely to follow the American custom of entirely ignoring the identity of the mother's family.

Patronyms outnumber other types of surnames, very decisively. In Mexico City and in a composite of South American Spanish-speaking capital cities, Gorden found the most common patronyms to be the following (in alphabetical order):

> Alvarez, Diaz, Fernandez, Garcia (which also may come from the name of a place), Gomez, Gonzalez, Lopez, Martinez, Perez, Rodriguez, Sanchez

These eleven names account for close to 25 percent of the population of those cities. Another fifty-four names account for the next quarter. So about half of Spanish-Americans in the capitals share only sixty-five names.

Considering Latin America as a whole, Rodriguez is the most-used patronym, followed in order by the other names in the list, which excludes Garcia because of its dual status:

2. Gonzalez	5. Lopez	8. Gomez
3. Fernandez	6. Perez	9. Diaz
4. Martinez	7. Sanchez	10. Alvarez

Others high on the list (not in order) are Benitez, Hernandez, Marquez, Ramirez, Enriquez, Vasquez, Velasquez, and Dominguez.

In Spain Garcia is the most popular of all names; it ranks third among all names in Latin America. Rodriguez, the Latin-American favorite and the leading Spanish name in the United States, is only seventh in Spain.

The characteristic ending for Spanish patronyms is *ez,* although the variants *-es, -az, -iz, -oz,* and *-uz* are not infrequent. Often it is easy for English speakers to translate these names. Thus Rodriguez is ‹son of Roderigo

(Roderick)›, Martinez ‹son of Martin›, and Enriquez ‹son of Henry›. Names like Sanchez ‹son of Sancho› derive from *nombres* not common among Anglos.

When Garcia is not a patronym ‹descendant of Gerald›, it is from the Spanish city Garcia. Other personal names from place names may use *de, de la, de los,* or *del,* or may have dropped these prefixes earlier. Examples include De la Fuente ‹from the fountain or spring›, De la Rosa ‹from the place of roses›, De los Puentes ‹from the bridges›, and de Mendoza ‹from Mendoza, Spain›.

Equivalents of English generalized place names like Hill, Rivers, Towers, or Meadows are fairly frequent. Acosta is ‹from the seacoast›, Aguilar comes from Aguilas ‹the place of eagles›, Cortez is ‹from a court or town›, Cardoza is named for Cardoso ‹where the thistles are›, and Figueroa is ‹where the fig trees are›. Navarro is ‹the plain between hills›, and Silva is from ‹a thicket or wood›. Medina ‹market› often refers to someone who has been on pilgrimage to Medina, Islam's most holy city after Mecca.

Spanish occupational names are rather rare. Two of the most common are Herrera and Ferrer, both meaning ‹smith›. Fairly unusual are Sastre ‹tailor›, Tejodor ‹weaver›, and Mayordomo ‹steward›. Arquilla operated a kiln, Vergara was a herdsman, Oliva raised or sold olives, Guerrero was a soldier, and Calderon dealt in kettles.

Among descriptive names from colors, only Blanco ‹white›, Castaño and Moreno, which mean ‹brown› or ‹dark›, and Pardo ‹gray› are found in the top one thousand Latin-American names. Plata ‹silver› occurs occasionally. A few dozen Negrons are in the Manhattan directory. Other descriptors, some of which were once probably nicknames, are Cuervo ‹hawk›, Calvo ‹bald›, Leon ‹lionlike›, Rico ‹rich›, Moralez ‹proper, right›, Alcalde ‹mayor›, Baquero ‹cowboy›, and Caballero ‹knight, gentleman›.

The most interesting and significant demographic development in the United States in the next fifty years is likely to be a continued rapid increase in the number of people with Spanish surnames. More and more Mexicans, in particular, are likely to arrive, legally or illegally. They will become an ever-stronger force—politically, economically, socially. They will certainly sometimes be destructive, sometimes constructive. They will profoundly influence American lifestyles, for instance in dress, food, and entertainment. If we are wise enough, we may be able to "Americanize" them as we have such other large groups as the Germans and the Italians, but since they may be much more numerous than any other group has been, they will probably go far in "Latinizing" the rest of us.

19

THE PORTUGUESE:

They Too Found Unknown Lands

SANDRA WOLFORTH, in *The Portuguese in America,* comments, "The Portuguese have quietly assimilated into the American mainstream, rarely if ever demonstrating or forcing themselves into conspicuous stances either as individuals or as a group." Usually they have been content to be manual laborers, but they have seldom been active in labor movements or reforms. They have not been active in politics, either. John Arruba, elected in Fall River, Massachusetts, in 1974, is said to have been the very first Portuguese-American city mayor.

Comparatively few of them have gone to college. They have a reputation for temperance, and their crime rate is very low. Until recently the women among them were regarded as distinctly inferior. In the words of a Portuguese folk song,

> Even the sea is married.
> Even the sea has a wife.
> He is married to the seashore;
> He beats her whenever he likes.

They have not been notably religious—though with many exceptions. Many Portuguese sailors thought that *priest* was an unlucky word and would not use it at sea. They said *fish buyer* instead. Superstition, including belief in witches, often supplemented or substituted for religion. They shared the widespread belief that a woman on board ship brought bad luck.

The ancestors of these quiet, solid, sometimes stolid folk were among the most important explorers of the New World. Historian Samuel Eliot Morison has called the years 1500–25 "an era of Portuguese supremacy in exploration of the north." Note some of their achievements:

- Gaspar Corte-Real ‹royal court› in 1500 and 1501 made two voyages to Greenland, on the second one heading south to Newfoundland and then vanishing.
- His brother Miguel, searching for him in 1502, also vanished, but there are legends about him—one that he became chief of an Indian tribe. Carving on a rock thirty miles from the mouth of Narragansett Bay says that he was there in 1511. The inscription is probably not authentic, but if it should be proved so, it would indicate that Portuguese, not English, were the first settlers in New England.

Other Portuguese expeditions reached down as far as South America.

- Italian Amerigo Vespucci sailed under a Portuguese flag.
- Fernando Magellan, leader of the first expedition to circumnavigate the globe, sailed under the Spanish flag but was himself Portuguese. His "real" name was Fernão de Magelhães.
- Five Portuguese horsemen took part in Coronado's search for the Seven Cities of Cibola in 1540: do Campo, Alvares, Martins, Pais, and Horta. Do Campo was captured and lived for many months as a slave of the Indians.
- Juan Cabrillo ‹goatherd›, believed to have been born in Portugal, in 1542 explored the California coastline and discovered the San Diego and Monterey bays.

- Luis de Gois was the first to take tobacco from America to Europe, in 1545. (Sir Walter Raleigh, sometimes given the credit, was not yet born.)
- Portuguese soldiers were the first garrison of the fortress of San Felipe del Morro in San Juan, Puerto Rico. Some of them, apparently not superstitious, brought their wives along on the ships; others married natives. "From these men descend the many Puerto Rican families with Portuguese patronymics."

More could be named. And the heroics did not end with the age of exploration. Twenty-eight of John Paul Jones's victorious crew in the battle against the *Serapis* were Portuguese. Others were in the crew of Jean Lafitte, the French pirate who helped the Americans in the Battle of New Orleans. A sailor known now only as "Portuguese Joe" was a hero of Great Lakes engagements in the War of 1812.

A final example. In 1866, according to Leo Pap,

> A fort built along the Bozeman trail, in the State of Wyoming, was suddenly threatened with extinction by a savage Indian attack. A volunteer was needed to break through the siege lines and call for help at the next fort. This meant riding some 240 miles through hostile territory, in freezing snow. John Philippe, a woodchopper employed at the embattled new fort and known there simply as "Portuguese John," undertook the almost impossible task—which has been called a much greater feat than the famous ride of Paul Revere. Born as João or Manuel Felipe in the western Azores, Philippe had settled in California after the Gold Rush, but later drifted into Wyoming, where he died in 1883.

A large proportion of Portuguese immigrants came from the Azores. The immigrants themselves generally differentiate carefully, indicating whether they are Continentals; or Eastern, Central, or Western Azoreans; or Madeirans; or Cape Verde Islanders (Portuguese and black mixed, called Bravas). Because of their frequent insistence on these distinctions, Portuguese Americans have less ethnic unity or solidarity than do some other national groups.

Portuguese settlers were few before 1850. Attracted by the

gold of California, several hundred in the early 1850s worked their way there on whaling ships. Today some of the largest Portuguese settlements in North America are in California, and some of the inhabitants trace their ancestry back to the early miners. Not finding much gold, some of the miners turned to dairying, in which they prospered. In 1939, Portuguese owned three-quarters of all the cows in California, and in 1974 the value of their cattle was estimated at $833,000,000. Other Portuguese, especially in San Leandro and San Diego, did well in fishing for tuna, albacore, and bonito. Still others became fruit or vegetable farmers. As early as 1828 Antonio Rocha ‹rock› owned the 4,600-acre La Brea ranch, and in 1883 John Avila ‹one from the city Avila›, who would become known as "the father of the sweet potato industry," reached California from the Azores.

On the East Coast, especially in Fall River, New Bedford, and Provincetown, fishing for cod or other species was for years a major source of Portuguese livelihood. Some men and women worked in the New England textile mills, or (especially the Bravas) did the hard manual jobs in the cranberry bogs.

Away from the coasts not nearly so many Portuguese settled. However, in 1849, Protestants in Madeira were driven out by Roman Catholics, and many of them settled near Springfield and Jacksonville, Illinois. "By 1855 there were 350 in Springfield," Paul Angle says in his history of the prairie town where Abraham Lincoln then lived. The people of both communities treated the new arrivals very well, assisting them with jobs and helping them to build houses. Angle says, "On the prairies of Illinois, three thousand miles from home, they had finally found contentment." They established two Portuguese Presbyterian churches in Springfield, three more in Jacksonville. One of their neighbors reported, "They were industrious and very honest. . . . Their word was as good as their note. . . . None of them ever saw a penitentiary."

Other pockets of Portuguese exist or existed in Biloxi, Mississippi; Fernandina Beach, Florida; and Brunswick,

Georgia. In 1930 about 7 percent of Hawaii's people were Portuguese. In all, 130,000 Portuguese came to the United States from 1820 to 1910. There was a great surge in 1965 to 1975, when about 30,000 came to Massachusetts alone. According to one estimate, which may be too high, about a million Americans have at least a little Portuguese blood.

Their names are similar to Spanish names, sometimes indistinguishable. The usual Portuguese patronym, however, ends in *-es* rather than the Spanish *-ez,* but since many Spanish also have names ending in *-es,* the distinction is not conclusive. Nor do first names provide adequate clues, since the Spanish and the Portuguese share many *nombres,* such as Carlos and Maria.

The most-used Portuguese names, by far, are patronyms. Place names are fairly common, often with the prefix *de, da, do, das,* or *dos.* The name of the American novelist John Dos Passos is said by some to mean ‹from the passes›, but according to Elsdon Smith is ‹a name adopted to express devotion to the passion of Christ›. To complicate matters further, the usual definition of *passo* is ‹step, pace›.

Less questionable is Davega ‹from the plain›. Costa means ‹coast›, Ponte means ‹bridge›, da Silva ‹from the forest›. Ferreira may have come from the town of that name or been a blacksmith or lived near a smithy. De Jesus is not a place name but expresses devotion to Jesus. Cruz (either Spanish or Portuguese) lived near a cross.

Descriptive and occupational names are infrequent. Cortes, which is perhaps more Portuguese than Spanish, is the name of some Spanish towns but also means ‹the courteous person›. Pacheco in both Spain and Portugal suggests ‹slow, lethargic, tranquil›. Santos may be ‹a holy man› or ‹a person from Dos Santos, "the saints"›. Favela grew beans and sold them, *fava* being a Portuguese word for ‹broad bean›. Furtado, a rare name, means ‹robber, thief›.

In America numerous Portuguese have changed their names. Thus Pereira ‹pear tree› frequently becomes Perry;

Ferreira, Ferry or Ferris; Rodrigues, Rogers; Fernandes, Ferdinand.

Unlike many immigrants, few Portuguese again became emigrants. Once they arrived in America, nearly all of them stayed here—"quietly assimilating."

20

THE FRENCH:

They Might Have Ruled America

STUDENTS in grades eight, nine, or ten used to be required to read Longfellow's *Evangeline,* a long poem that tells of French-speaking Acadians exiled from their Canadian homes during the French and Indian Wars of the eighteenth century. Evangeline Bellefontaine ‹beautiful fountain› is separated from her betrothed, Gabriel Lajeunesse ‹youth, young›, and spends her life searching for him in Louisiana, Missouri, Michigan, and other parts of North America.

Evangeline is largely fictitious, but the banishment of the Acadians from Nova Scotia and New Brunswick to what is now the United States was very real, very painful. Originally these French-Canadians had come mainly from Brittany and Normandy in France. In Canada they made their living from agriculture and fishing. The British, fearing that the Acadians would not remain neutral in the conflict with France, drove them forcefully and, according to Longfellow, cruelly to the lands toward the south. They were distributed among the colonies, but many came to rest in what is now Maine, because that was close to Canada, while others found their way to Louisiana, where the French, led by the LeMoyne ‹monk› brothers, had settled as early as 1699. The city of New Orleans had been settled by one of the LeMoynes, de Bienville ‹fine city›, in 1718.

In Maine the Acadians settled especially in the St. John valley, which is now the state's northern boundary. Later some French Huguenots along with some Germans settled along the coast, and after the American Civil War numerous French from Quebec also came to Maine to work in lumber and textiles.

Today more French speech than English is heard in the St. John valley, and French is the second language in Maine's industrial centers. And in the bayous of southern Louisiana live thousands of Acadians, now called Cajuns, who are descendants of the eighteenth-century exiles. Most of them speak the Cajun dialect, which is old-fashioned French blended with a smattering of English, German, and Spanish and with some expressions taken from Indians and blacks. They mingle little with speakers of English but live mainly in their own little communities or in isolated houses, some of them far back in the marshy lands. They are largely self-sufficient, catching fish, shrimp, turtles, and fur-bearing animals, growing their own yams, sugarcane, cotton, and livestock, and cutting logs and building boats.

Many of the names they bear in the heart of the Evangeline country, St. Martin's Parish, are the same as those of two centuries ago. Most common appear to be Broussard ‹shaggy haired› or ‹one from a brushy area› and Le Blanc ‹white›. Some of the other names are Bourgeois ‹townsman›, Thibodeaux ‹descendant of Thibaux, "people, bold"›, Benoi(s)t ‹blessed = Benedict›, Domont ‹from the mountain›, Boudreau ‹descendant of Botthar, "messenger, army"›, Mouton ‹sheep›, and Durand ‹lasting›. The name of Ron Guidry, a fine pitcher in the late 1970s and early 1980s for the New York Yankees, is no stranger to the area; the spelling Guidray is also found. A number of names, in fact, appear in variant spellings: for instance, Comeaux, Comau, Comaux ‹one from a dry valley›. More and more, too, one now encounters names that are not French at all—Alonzo, Johnson, Krewitz, Blaskowsky.

Germans who settled in the nearby "German coast" of the Mississippi were Catholics and, according to E. D. Johnson in *Names,* tried to adapt their ways, their speech, and even their names to those of their French neighbors. Weiss might translate his name to Le Blanc, Weber to a more French-looking Webre or Ouebre or Oubre, Bernhardt to Bernard, König to Roy. An Englishman named Littlejohn seemed to become half French after changing to Petitjohn, and a Johnson emerged rather oddly as Jeansonne. On the other hand, some French people have anglicized their names: Roy to King, De Clouet to Clewett, Geaux to Joe, Franques to Franks, and Arneau to Arno.

Scores or hundreds of French place names, especially in the middle third of the United States, are reminders of what might have been. Had a few battles turned out differently, much of what we call the United States might have become a French colony or a French satellite nation. For three-quarters of a century (1689 to 1763) in a series of struggles known collectively as the French and Indian Wars, France and Great Britain fought for control of the heart of the North American continent. Military fortunes varied, with now the French, now the British triumphant. In 1749 the governor general of New France attempted to limit British settlement to the area east of the Appalachians. From 1754 to 1757 it looked as though that attempt would succeed, for the British army and their colonial allies lost battle after battle to the stronger and better-equipped French troops.

But starting in 1758, approximately the time of *Evangeline,* the British began winning, partly because France was being bankrupted by military efforts here and elsewhere, partly because of a British naval blockade, and partly because the British and colonial fighters gained experience and increased in numbers and support. French forts at Ticonderoga, Duquesne, Niagara, and other places could not withstand the attacks, and a climactic battle on the Plains of Abraham outside Quebec in 1759 prepared the way for the

Treaty of Paris (1763) by which France gave up most of its claims to North America.

Hints of the French near-conquest remain up and down the center of the continent. Early French explorers have their names preserved in places like LaSalle, Joliet, Nicollet, and Père Marquette, and Louisiana (French Louisiane) was named for the Sun-King, "the most high, mighty, invincible, and victorious Prince, Louis the Great, by the Grace of God King of France and Navarre, Fourteenth of the Name."

Lake Superior was to the French only Lac Supérieur ‹Upper Lake›. Our custom of referring to most large lakes by saying *lake* first is a reflection of French word order: Lake Huron and Lake Michigan, for example, but not Lake Mud.

Sometimes the French adapted Indian place names, and we still keep some form of many of these hybrids. An Indian tribe named Aliniouek or Iliniouek (remember that the Indians could not write) was recorded by the French as Illinois; an Indian-garbed "Chief Illiniwek" still prances at University of Illinois football games. Ohio, Michigan, Kansas, Arkansas, Iowa (first shortened by the French from Ouaouiatonon to Ouaouia, which may hold a record for consecutive vowels), Wisconsin, Missouri, and Mississippi have Indian names that were adapted by the French and sometimes further modified by speakers of English. Some cities, too: Chicago, Milwaukee, Peoria, Des Moines, Omaha, and more. And the Osage River is named from an Indian word that the French recorded as Ouchage, the Wabash from what to the Indians was something like Ouaboukigou, to the French Oubache.

In Minnesota, according to some reports, a French explorer came upon a body of water that his Indian guide assured him was a lake. Impressed by its size, he exclaimed, "Un lac! Mille lacs!" ("A lake! A thousand lakes!") Thus the lake and its nearby town Milaca got their names, today anglicized in local pronunciation to "muh-lack" and "muh-lackuh." A hundred or so miles away is Lac Qui Parle ‹the lake that talks›. In neighboring Wisconsin at the foot of Lake Winnebago is Fond du Lac ‹foot of the lake›; Eau Claire celebrates ‹clear water› and Prairie du Chien is ‹the prairie of the dog› from a French translation of the name of an Indian chief. Illinois recalls the French royal family with Bourbonnais (but calls it "burr-BAHN-us"). Louisiana, of course, has its New Orleans, earlier Nouvelle Orleans, and Baton Rouge, a translation of Indian Istrouma ‹red post›, signifying a marker that separated the hunting grounds of two tribes.

Most interesting, perhaps, are the French place names no longer recognizable as such. George R. Stewart, in *Names on the Land,* mentions Terre Bleue ‹blue earth›, which became Tar Blue, Terre Noire ‹black earth›, now Turnwall, Mauvaise Terre ‹bad earth›, later Movestar "and doubtless children are already calling it Movie Star." In Minnesota, Frenchmen in talking of a small stream mentioned a place *aux embarras* ‹at the obstructions›; anglicized and clipped that became Zumbro, now the name of the stream, on whose banks the town Zumbrota stands. Strangers in Illinois, seeing signs denoting the Embarras River of course call it "embarrass," but natives still approximate the French pronunciation. Smackover, Arkansas, was originally French Chemin Couvert ‹covered road›, possibly referring to overhanging branches.

In the Jamestown Colony in 1619 were several Frenchmen who, the colonists hoped, could establish a wine-making industry, but the attempt failed and, as Louis Wright says, "The French workers disappeared from history." According to some accounts, about a quarter of the "Dutch" in New Amsterdam were actually French, and many of the others were French-speaking Walloons, Protestant refugees from the Spanish Netherlands. Dominee Jonas Michaëlius conducted some of his religious services in French. However, Wright reminds us, the French in the Hudson valley really thought of themselves as Dutch and

> served as a shield to protect the English to the north and south from the French, who otherwise might have come down from Canada and outflanked the English colonies before they were strong enough to protect themselves. A strong French segment in the Hudson valley might have changed the whole course of American history. This the Dutch forestalled.

It is possible that William Mullins of the *Mayflower* was really a Frenchman named Guillaume Molines ‹from the mill›. He and his wife and son died, but Priscilla survived and married John Alden after rejecting Miles Standish. Lucian Fosdick, in *The French Blood in America* (1906), romanticized this story:

How blind we were to the Gallic coquetry with which she held on to Miles Standish till she secured John! We must blot out, then, from the historic portrait the blue eyes and rosy cheeks of the English maiden . . . and we must paint in a slender, graceful, black-haired brunette with brown-black velvet eyes and long sweeping lashes, from under which shot such glances as melted the hearts of all the colony, and we must adorn the Puritan girl with some dainty ribbon. . . .

[She became] the ancestress of that celebrated New England family, the Aldens. From this descent, too, was John Adams.

Religious intolerance in France, late in the seventeenth century, led to the departure of many Huguenots—Protestants—who settled in groups in the Netherlands, England, and eventually the New World. One of them, Claude Requa, told this story of his family, as recorded by Fosdick:

They departed in the night, to save their lives, leaving the greater part of their property, which they could not convert into money. There were eleven other families. . . . The priests used to search every house where they imagined that Bibles might be concealed or meetings held. . . . The twelve families fled by night from Paris to La Rochelle, where they continued for some time. But intelligence from Paris to La Rochelle soon detected their several abodes. Their houses were to be broken into on a certain night. They would all have been cut off, had it not been for a good man, a Catholic, who had become acquainted with them. He gave them notice, so they fled the night before, at about one or two o'clock. The twelve families muffled the wheels of their wagons, so as not to make any noise, but they were discovered on the way and pursued to a river, before they were overtaken. Ten families got over the stream in safety, but two were taken. No others succeeded in getting aboard a ship which sailed to America.

Their troubles were not yet ended. On the ship a fever killed many of the passengers, including Requa's parents.

Numbers of Huguenots came to South Carolina, somewhat fewer to New York, Pennsylvania, and other colonies. They tended to be craftsmen, merchants, and professional men and to be better educated than most immigrants then or later. They contributed richly to colonial life. Henry Cabot Lodge, whose middle name and some ancestors were French, once said, "I believe that, in proportion to their numbers, the Huguenots produced and gave to the American Republic more men of ability than any other race." Apollos Rivoire ‹one from Rivière› was one of them, a silversmith and the father of America's best-known silversmith, Revolutionary War hero Paul Revere.

Later military figures included General Francis Marion, "the Swamp Fox"; Admiral Samuel Du Pont, for whom Du Pont Circle in Washington, D.C., is named; General John Fremont, western explorer and the Republican nominee for president in 1856; and Admiral George Dewey, who sank ten vessels of the Spanish fleet in Manila Bay in 1898.

The father of Peter Faneuil came to America as one of the Huguenot refugees. Peter built Faneuil Hall in Boston, a large market and hall. It became a favorite meeting place for revolutionaries. Faneuil gave it to the city of Boston, but the vote for acceptance was only 367 to 360. "Thus near did Boston come to losing Faneuil Hall and the 'cradle of liberty.' " Faneuil, by the way, would have married one Mary Jekyll, but she opted for the English Richard Saltonstall instead—another well-known New England name, it means ‹salt works›.

Stephen Girard ‹descendant of Girard, "spear, firm"›, once a penniless fourteen-year-old runaway from France, became the richest man in America through a variety of business ventures. He had the reputation of being a miser, but in 1814 he joined with John Jacob Astor (who was born in Germany) in bailing out the United States government financially. He left most of his estate to Philadelphia and to Pennsylvania, and six million dollars to found Girard College for orphan children.

Unlike Girard, Éleuthère Irénée Du Pont de Nemours came of a wealthy Huguenot family from Rouen and Paris.

His father, an economist, might have prevented the French Revolution if his proposed reforms had been accepted by the government. The son increased the family fortune by selling a high quality of gunpowder to the American government in the War of 1812, and later Du Ponts have made the chemical company into one of the largest in the world. The state of Delaware has sometimes been called the Duchy of Du Pont.

Among the people who reached Virginia was Valentine Sevier, from a Huguenot family whose name had been Xavier before they fled from France to London. Valentine's son John became an Indian fighter and while defending a fort in 1776 he saw, says the romanticizing Fosdick,

> a tall graceful girl running towards the fort pursued by a group of savages. Exposing himself above the walls, heedless of the peril, the gallant captain shot down more than one Indian who had raised his tomahawk to brain the girl, who succeeded in leaping the palisades and fell into his arms. [Quite a jump, if the palisades were the usual height.] It was in that exciting manner that the brave Frenchman first met the woman who was to be for forty years his companion in adventure, hardship, and success.

She was Catherine Sherrill, the daughter of a North Carolinian. Later, Sevier was a leader in the battle of King's Mountain (1780), in which the revolutionary troops captured about 1,100 Loyalists. Still later he became governor of the short-lived "Free and Independent State of Franklin," and then served six terms as Tennessee's first governor.

Presidents partly Huguenot in ancestry included Tyler, Garfield, and Theodore Roosevelt. Alexander Hamilton was Huguenot on his mother's side. Three of the first seven presidents of the Continental Congress were Huguenots: John Jay, Henry Laurens, and Elias Boudinot. Vassar and Bowdoin colleges were named for men with Huguenot blood, and writers Philip Freneau, Henry D. Thoreau, Henry W. Longfellow, Julia Ward Howe, and James G. Whittier were also in greater or lesser degree of Huguenot ancestry.

Life was obviously not easy for all Huguenots, especially because nearly all Frenchmen were distrusted by the English colonials who were fighting or had fought in wars against other French. Frenchtown, a Huguenot settlement in Rhode Island, was attacked by a mob in 1691, Pennsylvania imprisoned Huguenot "troublemakers," and New York refused to allow them close to the frontier for fear that they would assist the enemy. Despite such troubles, and because they scattered more widely than did other relatively small groups, Huguenots fairly rapidly became assimilated in the dominant culture, often joining the Church of England and frequently changing their names to something less obviously French. The changes from Rivoire to Revere and Xavier to Sevier are typical.

Some of the royalist sympathizers who fled France during the French Revolution came to the young United States. Shortly after came various Girondists and Jacobins whose lives were also in danger. After a Negro revolt in Santo Domingo in 1791 virtually the entire French population fled, with between ten and twenty thousand reaching the United States. Congress in 1794 furnished them with a small amount of financial help, perhaps recalling the aid given the Americans by Lafayette ‹one who lives near a little beech grove› and other French people during the Revolutionary War. Most of the French arrivals during the 1790s were genteel urbanites, described in one source as "dancing-masters, teachers of gentility and deportment, wig makers, entertainers and restaurateurs." The tradition of French chefs arose largely at that time. The Santo Domingan French settled in cities close to the East Coast, particularly New York, Philadelphia, Baltimore, and Charleston. Not all remained; when conditions in France permitted, many returned home.

An analysis of 1790 census figures shows an estimated total of 54,900 persons of French stock, or only about 1.4 percent of the whole population. New York had some 12,000 of them, Pennsylvania and Virginia had 6,000 to 8,000 each, and the others were scattered.

Since 1790 the number of French immigrants has seldom exceeded a few thousand a year and has never approached the great numbers of Irish, Germans, Italians, and certain groups from Slavic countries. In consequence, and also because the names were often anglicized, relatively few unquestionably French surnames are found in America today.

Of those that do remain, a number, usually prefixed by *De, Des,* or *Du,* are derived from place names. Du Pont has become the most famous of these in America; it means ‹from the bridge›. Others include Delacroix ‹from the place of the cross›, De Ville ‹from Ville, "town"›, Deveau(x) ‹from the valley›, Descartes ‹from the suburbs›, Desjardins ‹from the gardens›, Desmarais ‹from the marsh› (perhaps sometimes confused with Demaree ‹from the sea›), Duhamel ‹from the hamlet›, Dubois ‹from the wood›, Dupré ‹from the meadow›, and Dumas ‹from the farmstead›.

French patronyms are often derived from names of biblical figures or saints. Examples include Clements, Simon, and Paul, although some other nationalities use these same forms.

Descriptive names are represented by Le Grand ‹large, fat›, Le Blanc, Lenoir or Le Noir ‹dark, swarthy›, Lejeune ‹young›.

In the dreamland of Might-have-been, some French boys and girls today may read their history books and wonder what the world would be like now if the French rather than the British and British colonials had won that long eighteenth-century war, the war that caught the fictitious Evangeline and Gabriel in its netting. Would that land across the sea from them be even yet a French colony—all of it called, perhaps, Louisiane, for Louis XIV and XV both—and might it also include all of Canada? Or would it be an independent country, but called les États-Unis rather than the United States? Would there have been une Statue de la Liberté (a gift of France to the United States) standing in the harbor of what might have been called Nouvelle Paris?

21

THE ITALIANS:

Amerigo lo Bello

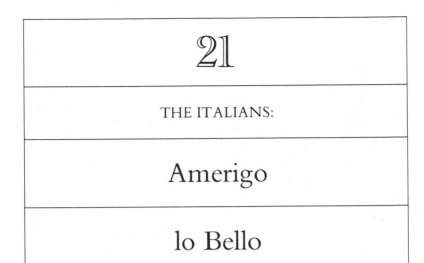

UNTIL 1507 world maps showed just three large land areas. In that year a German geographer and mapmaker, Martin Waldseemüller ‹miller at the wooded lakeside›, drew in not only the usual Europe, Asia, and Africa but also a fourth area which, he argued, should be named after the Italian Amerigo Vespucci ‹descendant of the wasp?›, in Latin Americus Vespucius, who had sailed on possibly four voyages of exploration along the coasts of what we call South and Central America and perhaps Florida.

Here is Waldseemüller's proposal:

> A fourth part [of the world] has been discovered by Americus Vespucius (as will appear in what follows). For that reason I think that nothing should prevent us from calling it Amerige or America, that is, the land of Americus, after its discoverer Americus, a man of brilliant mind, since both Europe and Asia are also named for women.

Other Italians contributed much to discovery and exploration in the New World: Columbus, of course, born in

Genoa, the son of Domenico Colombo ‹dove›, from whom the United States gets the alternative name Columbia as well as the names of a great river and a dozen cities. John Cabot, born Giovanni Caboto, who in 1497 planted English and Venetian flags in Maine or some place farther north, mistakenly considering it the mainland of China. The Florentine Giovanni da Verrazano, who in 1524 explored northward from the Carolina coast to Nova Scotia. Marcos de Niza, in the Southwest, whose imagination transformed Zuñi pueblos into the gold-inlaid Seven Cities of Cibola. Enrico di Tonti, claimed also by the French as Henri de Tonti, the "father of Illinois," builder of Fort St. Louis where Starved Rock Park now is, LaSalle's chief lieutenant in the Mississippi valley, Tonti with the iron hand. And others of smaller fame.

Before the nineteenth century, however, despite such an auspicious start, few Italians had come to the American colonies or to the United States. There were four Italian glassblowers in the Jamestown Colony in 1621, but they did not get along with the British. George Sandys, secretary of the colony, wrote unkindly on their departure, "A more damned crew hell never vomited." There were also a few Italians in New Amsterdam.

Later the Italian president of Georgetown College from 1812 to 1817, Giovanni Antonio Grassi ‹fat›, said that the Americans had their weaknesses, too. In his *Stati Uniti dell' America* (1819) he asserted that New Englanders were the "most knavish Americans," deplored fathers who "yield sadly and foolishly to their children . . . whose capricious wishes they do not restrain," and went on like this:

> The sight of gambling and drunkenness is more frequent here than in Italy, if that may be believed, and the consequences are fatal to individuals and to entire families. Behavior is generally civil, but one will find many deficiencies in the niceties. It is, for example, not regarded as uncivil to cut the fingernails and comb the hair in the presence of others, or to be seated, feet on the next chair or propped high against the wall. . . . Mothers have the praiseworthy custom of suckling their offspring themselves; they would be even more worthy of praise if they were to do it more modestly.

A few thousand Italians came across the Atlantic in small groups during the first six or seven decades of the 1800s. Some of them were prominent. Giuseppe Garibaldi ‹spear, bold› lived for a time on Staten Island. President Lincoln offered to make him a general, but Garibaldi was interested in uniting Italy, not in fighting for the American union. Lorenzo do Ponte ‹from the bridge›, the librettist for Mozart's *Figaro, Don Giovanni,* and *Così fan Tutte,* spent later years in New York. But the 1880 census reported a total of only forty thousand Italians in the United States—over a fourth of them in New York City.

That figure was destined to grow rapidly. Until Italy was unified in 1861, most emigration had been strictly forbidden, and for a couple of decades after that most emigrants were from northern Italy and left, often just for seasonal work, for France, Germany, Switzerland, or North Africa.

But after 1880 the south Italians began to depart in great numbers. With some exceptions they were poorer, less well educated, and much more provincial and unsophisticated than the northerners. Most were *contadini* ‹peasants›, including the *mezzadri,* or sharecroppers, who paid as rent to absentee landlords half *(mezzo)* of the wheat, grapes, and figs that they were able to coax from the rocky unfertilized soil. The *giornalieri* ‹day laborers› were even worse off, for they had no land to till and had to live mainly on the small amounts of money they could earn at harvest time.

As conditions steadily became worse, some of the illiterate *mezzadri* and especially the *giornalieri* ventured from their home areas, often for the first time, and sought work in places like Palermo, Taranto, Naples, or even Rome itself. There they heard—again perhaps for the first time—of a land called America, across a body of water much greater than the sea they knew or knew of. Many of them talked with their friends about going there, and some learned of a way to afford the thirty or forty dollars the voyage would cost—an amount that might equal what they could earn in south Italy in a whole year.

It was the *padroni* who, for a price, made many thousands of sea journeys possible. In 1901 the *Reports of the Industrial*

Commission on Immigration and Education in Washington carried a detailed and critical account of these entrepreneurs who brought other Italians here and found employment for them:

> The padrone provides transportation for the men [to work each day]. But in the rates, he overcharges the men, charging for first-class transportation or regular ticket rates, and receiving greatly reduced rates because of the large number. If the work is some distance from the city, the padrone often boards the men [and furnishes] lodging and wearing apparel, the cost of which is generally deducted from their wages. . . .
>
> If the men board themselves, their food must be bought at the shanty store, which is operated by the padrone. Notices are posted to this effect and fines are imposed for disobedience. Even dismissal is often the penalty. . . . For example, in 1894, Italian laborers were shipped from New York to Brunswick, Ga., for work on a sewage contract. Each man paid the padrone $1 for finding the employment. The passage money, $7 per head, was paid by the banker with the understanding that this was to be deducted from their wages. The agent of the banker paid $25 a month rent for ten huts, but charged each laborer $1 a month, which for 215 men was $215 a month. All supplies had to be bought at the shanty store, the penalty for disobedience being a fine of $5. . . .
>
> In New York there are large tenements owned by Italian bankers which serve as winter quarters for these laborers. Here the men are crowded together, a dozen or more in one room, under the worst sanitary conditions. It is frequently said that the padrone encourages the men in extravagance in order to have a firmer hold on their future earnings.

Earlier the *padroni* had induced children—abducted children, according to some accounts—to go to America as child musicians, street singers, and acrobats, and had kept most of their earnings, but Italian law had canceled that opportunity. So they now paid instead the fares of Italian men, and they did find them jobs and lodging, and they acted as interpreters and guides to the new life of America. Many of the jobs were in New York factories, or on the railroad tracks, or in construction, or in New England textile mills. Even though the lodgings were usually filthy, crowded rooms, perhaps they were not much worse than some of their hovels back in Italy.

The laborers did not even see most of what they earned. Each *padrone* had an arrangement with the employer. Part of each man's earnings should be paid to the worker himself, but the rest, often well over half, should be paid to the *padrone.* It was a profitable arrangement for a *padrone,* who might have a hundred, two hundred, or more men indebted to him and plenty more where they came from. In a short time the cost of the fare and other expenses would be paid, and after that, most of the *padrone*'s income was clear profit.

Even so, by scrimping constantly a good worker could save a little money, perhaps buy his first-ever suit of clothes and even a cheap watch and chain, and after a few years have enough money saved to return to Italy. There he could show off his wealth and perhaps settle down and tell his tales of America. Or instead he might stay in America, scrimp some more, and send tickets so that his family could join him.

In the 1880s, 268,000 Italians came to this country, although many of them went back home. In the 1890s, 604,000 came, and from 1900 to 1910 the all-time high of 2,104,000. The figures tapered off during the war decade to 1,110,000, and American restrictions held the number in the 1920s to 455,000. In the 1930s a sixth of New York's teeming millions were from southern Italy. Italians rank second in number only to Germans among America's ethnic groups.

Most ancestors of present-day American Italians continued to come from southern Italy. For example, in the period from 1899 through 1910, 1,900,000 south Italians came in and only 400,000 northern. Of the south Italians only 1 percent were classified as professionals, versus 3 percent from the north, and 77 percent of the southerners were officially called unskilled laborers.

To most Italians, family and community are important. Strangers are outsiders, not to be trusted until they have proved themselves. When the laborers finally were able to escape the *padroni* and leave their crowded rooms, they tried to settle with others of their kind, from their own Italian village, if possible, but at least from their own province. Nathan Glazer and Daniel P. Moynihan have written,

Among New York's Italians, for example, Neapolitans and Calabrians clustered together in the Mulberry Bend district; a colony of Genoese occupied Baxter Street and one of Sicilians a part of Elizabeth Street; west of Broadway in the Eighth and Fifteenth wards north Italians predominated, and a small group of Austrian and Tyrolese Italians was to be found on Sixty-ninth Street, near the Hudson.

The first Italian neighborhoods, they add, "proved remarkably stable. Areas that were Italian in 1920 remain so, somewhat attenuated, today [1970]." There are still heavily Italian areas in the North Bronx and in Queens "where Italians went to the end of the subway lines and beyond, seeking cheap land on which to build houses and raise vegetables and goats." Outside of New York, some of the mill towns remain predominantly Italian, some people still talk of "Little Italy" in Chicago, and most of the names in many a coal-mining town, like some I have known well in south central Illinois, still end in *o, i,* or *a.* Some Italian farmers or truck farmers live in every state, sometimes constituting whole communities as they once did in Tontitown, Arkansas, and Vineland, New Jersey.

As is true of other ethnic groups in America, Italian work patterns changed over the years. Once the Irish and some of the Germans did the "dirty work." Upward mobility was easier for them when the Jews and Italians and Slavs came in numbers, for by that time they had moved far toward acculturation. The Italians, once restricted to manual labor by their poverty, lack of education, and lack of knowledge of American ways, have now—many of them—become small or large business people, teachers, doctors, restaurant owners, secretaries, clerks, plumbers, carpenters, builders, politicians, and so on. New York, Toledo, Philadelphia, and some other large cities have had Italian mayors, and some Italians have been elected to Congress. Much of the unskilled work is now performed by Mexicans, Puerto Ricans, and blacks who have not yet found their way up the employment ladder. And although gangland news stories and novels like *The Godfather* have given much notoriety, in reality most Italians have no connections at all with the Mafia and lead lives no less or no more respectable than those of other Americans. Even Al Capone may have longed for a constructive life; at least he proclaimed, "Public service is my motto."

Italians have tended to keep the surnames they brought with them, save for the occasional dropping of a letter or two to simplify spelling. (Given names are another matter. The Giuseppes and Giovannis are decreasing in number, and Caterina is likely to be Catherine or Kathryn or Kitty.) The surnames they brought with them—these approximately six million Americans of Italian descent—are very numerous. None of the names are held by many people, however: in an American roll call there would be no Italian equivalent of Smith, Johnson, or even Rodriguez to which hundreds of thousands would respond. Italian names are more scattered, more evenly divided. No one of them ranks in the top five hundred American names.

Many of them have characteristics in common, however. Italians appear to love diminutives and pet names. In consequence many of their names end in *-ino, -ini, -etti, -etto, -ello,* and the Neapolitan *-illo,* all of which mean ‹little›. In contrast, *-one* means ‹big› and *-accio* may mean either ‹big› or ‹bad›. The suffix *-ucci* means ‹descendant of›. The endings *-dda* and *-ddo* are typically Sardinian. The prefixes *lo* and *la* ‹the› and *di* ‹from› are fairly common.

A considerable proportion of Italian names are descriptive. During the period when surnames were being adopted, Italians must have enjoyed identifying one another according to physical characteristics. As a result we find in Italy as elsewhere indications of complexion or hair color: Rossi, Rossa, Rosso, Rossetti, Rossetto, or Rossini for the ruddy or red-haired person; Bianco or Lo Bianco or Bianchi for one with light coloration; Moreno, Moretti, Moretta, and sometimes Morelli or Morello or Fosco for one who is dark. (*Mor-* stands for the dark-skinned Moors who for some centuries played a part in the history of Italy and a still larger role in Spain.) Longo was tall, and Basso, Curcio, and Piccolo were short.

Less universal descriptors abound in Italy. Pardo had gray hair, Riccio or Rizzo curly hair, Caruso close-cut hair, Cesario considerable body hair, and Luna no hair at all: his head looked like the moon. Mancini, Mancuso, or a variant was left-handed. Capone, Caputo, and Testa each had a big head, and Malatesta had a "bad," ugly, or malformed head, while Boccaccio (the name of a great medieval storyteller) had a large or ugly mouth. Bellagamba, however, had shapely legs, unless the name was applied ironically. (American slang *gams* for ‹feminine legs› may derive from Italian *gamba*.)

Allegretti, obviously related to some musical terms, was cheerful, Amato was a good friend or a beloved person, and various persons with *Bon* or *Buono* in their names (Bonelli, Bono, Buono, Bonomi, Buonomo) were recognized for their goodness; Buonoguidi was a good person named Guido, and perhaps Buongiorno was a good-natured person who cheerily said "Good day" to everyone. Gentile and Graziano were also courteous, and Fantasia, as the English *fantasy* suggests, was imaginative. Serio was an unusually serious person, and the dress and mannerisms of Zizzo showed that he was a dandy.

Gallo and Galliano made their contemporaries think of roosters, Izzo and Loizzo seemed snaillike, Marinello in somebody's opinion resembled a ladybug, and Mussolini and Muscarello were like gnats. Fasano suggested a pheasant, and Caliendo possibly sang like a lark.

Illegitimate children, often foundlings, tended to be given compassionate names in Italy. Damore is of course a child of love, and Innocenti ‹innocent, naive› is just a reminder that a baby is guiltless of the indiscretion of his or her parents. Trovato and Ritrovato are foundlings (remember our *trove;* a treasure trove is something worth finding). Names like De Benedictis, Dei Angelli, and De Santis suggest a blessed, angelic, or saintly origin of the illegitimate one.

Before literacy became widespread, in Italy and other countries, business signs were usually pictures and often portrayed animals. People might be named for the animal or other sign at or near which they lived. But the same name may also have been given to a person who resembled an animal in some way. We cannot be sure, then, whether Lupo and Lupino lived close to the sign of the wolf or resembled a wolf. The same kind of comment applies to Colombo and Palumbo ‹dove›, Gallina ‹hen›, Gatto ‹cat›, Capra ‹goat›, Chevallo or Cavallo ‹horse›, Volpe ‹fox›, Urso ‹bear›, and Rago ‹frog›.

Considerable numbers of Italians share various patronyms. These are seldom of the familiar Johnson ‹son of John› type (although Giannini, Di Giovanni, and a number of variants do mean ‹John› or ‹son of John›), but rather are likely to be names of less well known religious figures, especially saints, applied during the name-giving period and handed down. A few of the names are those of kings or other prominent figures. Here are some of the many patronyms with a few of the numerous variant forms:

Antonelli, Tonelli	‹Anthony›
Benedetto	‹Bennett or Benedict›
Bernardi	‹Bernard›
D'Allessandro, Alessi	‹Alexander›
D'Andrea	‹Andrew›
De Carlo, Carli, Carlo	‹Charles›
De Simone, Simonetti, Simonini	‹Simon›
De Stephano	‹Stephen›
Francisco, Cisco, Ciccolo, Ciccone	‹Francis›
Giacomo, Chiapetta, Como, Mazzucci	‹Jacob›
Henrici, Ricci	‹Henry›
Marzano, Marco, De Marco, Marchetti	‹Mark, Marcus›
Nicolo, Nicolosi, Nicolai, Nicoletti, Colonna	‹Nicholas›
Tomaselli, Tomasetti, Masi, Maso, Masello, Massi	‹Thomas›

As forms like Cisco and Massi suggest, often a name was shortened, and not necessarily to the beginning syllable. Occasionally a short form cannot be definitely traced to one name or another. Nardi, for instance, can be derived from both Bernardi and Leonardi.

Italian surnames from occupations are not numerous. Of course there is a smith—Ferraro *(-i, -io)* or Ferrero *(-i)*. Farina and Molinaro were millers, and Farinella was the carter who hauled the grist for their mills or was ‹the little miller›. Taglia or Tagliaferro (often anglicized to Tolliver) was an ironworker, roughly equivalent to the German Eisenhower. Pastore tended the sheep, Vaccaro the cows. Martello was a carpenter (the word means ‹hammer›) and Scarpello made shoes. Oliva, as in Spain, grew or sold olives. Pisciolo was a fisherman. Pusateri kept a tavern or an inn, and Calderone made, sold, or repaired kettles.

Among the more unusual occupations was that of hoe maker, Marrero; Marro could be the user of a hoe or a master in whatever his trade was. Fazio was a guard or watchman. A number of religious titles were also used, sometimes signifying that the person played the role in a medieval street drama or that he was a layman associated in some way with a clerical position—as an abbot's servant, for instance. Among these names are Prete and Quilici ‹priest›, Vicari ‹vicar›, Abbate ‹abbot›, and Papa ‹pope›. Rosario made and sold rosaries, and Santaro dealt in figures of saints.

Place names are moderately frequent, although one is not likely to find a large number of bearers of any single place name. Genova or Genovese came from Genoa, Messina and Serrano from the cities with those names, Napoli from Naples, and Siciliano from Sicily.

An example of a generic place name is Vinci ‹enclosed place›, but there is also a town called Vinci, from which Leonardo da Vinci's name was taken. Costa came from a seacoast, and Colletti and Zola are named for a lumpish little hill. Rocca is a cliff or a fortress. The first Fontana lived near a fountain or spring, Bosco in a wooded area, and Campo or Campagna in a field. Lo Verde was from a green place, but Arvia from plowed ground. Campanella or Campana may have lived near a bell tower or close to the sign of the bell. Serritella inhabited a valley, Padula a marsh. Dellacqua means ‹of the water›. Piazza lived close to the town square.

Fiore was from a place of flowers, and Fiorito perhaps grew flowers. Giglio was from the place of the lilies.

What would we lack if Italians had never come to America? A comprehensive list could fill a book. Here are a few excerpts from that book:

- The orphanages, hospitals, schools, and convents established by Frances Xavier, Mother Cabrini.
- Knowledge of the principles of "dynamic tension" that really did transform Charles Atlas (born Angelo Siciliano) from a "97-pound weakling" into the winner of the title "World's Most Perfectly Developed Man."
- The tender, sentimental movies directed by Frank Capra, such as *It Happened One Night, Mr. Deeds Goes to Town, Lost Horizon, You Can't Take It with You.*
- Light entertainment provided by Rudolph Valentino, Frank Sinatra, Dean Martin, Tony Bennett, Perry Como, and many more.
- Salvador Luria's genetic research and study of viruses.
- The serious music of Arturo Toscanini, Gian-Carlo Menotti, Renata Scotto, Luciano Pavarotti, and others.
- Enrico Fermi's and Emilio Segrè's work in atomic physics.
- The baseball feats of Joe DiMaggio.
- The Bank of America, founded by Amadeo Giannini as the Bank of Italy to aid immigrant farmers, fruit peddlers, and fishermen.
- The "mayor with a heart," Fiorello La Guardia.
- Thousands of examples of close-knit families; as Maxine Seller says, "Here, as in the old country, relatives were more reliable than outsiders, uncles hired young men when strangers would not, and aunts gave more reliable advice than social workers."
- The sort of humor displayed in this chapter title by Nicholas Pileggi: "How We Italians Discovered America and Kept It Clean and Pure While Giving It a Lot of Singers, Judges, and Other Swell People."

22

THE ROMANIANS:

Romanian Rhapsodies

AT the University of Pittsburgh is what is called the Romanian Classroom, moved there from the New York World's Fair of 1939. It has iron-grilled gates wrought in Romania. The room is finished in dark oak, with Romanian-made windows, and is decorated with Romanian-Byzantine floral arabesques like those in a seventeenth-century monastery built by Constantin Brancoveanu, Prince of Wallachia. Above the door are lines penned by a Romanian poet, Vasile Alecsandri ‹Alexander›: "The Romanian is like the mighty rock which amidst the waves of stormy and majestic sea remains unmoved."

Poetic exaggeration there, certainly, although the buffetings of this Balkan nation are as undeniable as those of its neighbors.

The tentacles of ancient Rome reached out in all directions. To the north and west they extended to the Danube in the first century A.D., and early in the second century the emperor Trajan crossed that river, in two difficult campaigns defeated the Dacians who had lived there for hundreds of years, and made Dacia a Roman province, speaking a Latin that was the ancestor of present-day Romanian.

In fact, the Romanian language retains more of the characteristics of Latin than do its sister languages Italian, Spanish, Portuguese, and French, despite the fact that in the intervening centuries the land that we call Romania (or Rumania or Roumania) has been repeatedly overrun by or in conflict with or strongly influenced by the Hungarians, the Turks, and the Russians. Moldavian, the only Romance language spoken in the Soviet Union, is the language of the Moldavian SSR and is actually a descendant or a variant form of Romanian. Moldavia was earlier known as Bessarabia and was a part of Romania until World War II. Some Romanian Americans came from there.

Few Romanians, though, came here before 1880. We do have records of a Transylvanian priest, Samuel Damian, who met with Benjamin Franklin in 1748, and a century later there were a few Romanians in the California gold rush.

Then there was George Pomutz, born of a Romanian family in a largely Romanian town inside Hungary. He fell in love with a girl of noble birth, whose parents opposed the marriage. They fled deeper into Hungary, and he joined Louis Kossuth's army, which was engaged in trying to free Hungary from Austria. But Kossuth was interested in liberty for Hungarians, not Romanians, so Pomutz and his lovely young wife fled again—first to Paris, then to New York, soon to Iowa. There Pomutz got rich in a few years, but a Hungarian stole his wife. To forget, he enlisted in the Union army, and in four years was a brigadier general. He took part in forty-one major engagements. Of thirty-seven officers in his regiment, only three survived. After the war he became consul general to Russia.

Most Romanian Americans, though, have had less distinguished or adventurous careers. Some 40,000 of them now live in New York, particularly the Bronx and Brooklyn, about 8,000 in Chicago, 5,000 each in Philadelphia and Detroit, somewhat fewer than a quarter of a million in the whole country. Many are waiters or bartenders; Petru Glafirescu in 1901 opened the first Romanian restaurant in New

York. Many others are in business or a profession. In 1945 a priest, Vasile Hatigan, gave the names and occupations of some Romanians that he knew—a cross-section of middle or upper middle class America:

> There are many prosperous small Romanian businessmen: Dumitru Balamoti owns a grocery store and Mihail Nibi a confectionary store; the Muha brothers are successful florists. . . . Emil Morarescu and Teddy Martin are barbers. Mr. John Buturuga has a successful auto repair business. . . . Constantin Gheorghiu owns and operates a tugboat. Emilian Ovesian is in the real estate business. . . . Christy Batsu is the owner of a fashionable beauty salon. . . . Stefan Serghiescu is a professor of mathematics at Columbia University. Radu Irimescu, former Romanian minister to America, is a member of the powerful holding company, the Atlas Corporation. . . . Among those qualified to teach [is] Mary Nedescu.

Often, too, Romanians are artistic or musical, as witness sculptors George Zolnay and Constantin Brancusi, movie director Jean Negulesco *(Three Coins in the Fountain),* composer I. V. Ivanovici ("Waves of the Danube," known also as "Anniversary Waltz"). Sometimes they become humorists: Mircea Vasiliu in 1963 published *Which Way to the Melting Pot?,* a spritely account of his attempts to learn English and to adjust himself to America.

These people or their parents or grandparents were driven here, like so many of their predecessors and contemporaries, by poverty and by yearning for freedom and peace. Most were rural folk or small-town folk, with little education. Although the majority spoke Romanian, the Balkan nations in general are so culturally mixed that there were among them many whose names would suggest that they might be Hungarians, Germans, Jews, Gypsies, Ukrainians, Turks, Serbs, Slovaks, Czechs, Bulgarians, or Armenians.

The ending *-escu* was most common in the names the "real" Romanians brought with them. It ordinarily indicates a patronym and is frequently based on the name of a saint or other religious figure. Thus Ion Antonescu, who was dictator of Romania during World War II, was ‹John the descendant of St. Anthony›. Constantinescu obviously honors

Constantine; Georgescu, George; Petrescu, Peter. Descendants of John may be Ionescu, Iovescu, or Jonescu, and in this country sometimes slip in quietly with the Jones or Johnson family. Dramatist Eugene Ionesco used a slight modification of the spelling. Georges Enesco, composer of "Romanian Rhapsodies," originally spelled his name in the traditional Romanian way but changed to an *o* when he went to Paris. Lupescu is the descendant of Lup ‹the wolf› (Latin *lupus*). Popescu ‹son of the priest› is the equivalent of Greek Pappadopoulos. The Teddy Martin named by Father Hategan may have started life as Teodor Martinescu.

A few of the patronyms are derived from descriptive words. Thus Murgulescu comes from *murg* ‹dark›, and Bucurescu, clearly related to Bucharest, which is spelled Bucureşţi in Romanian, goes back to a word for ‹happy›. The ending *-eanu* or *-anu* occurs in some surnames from places: Birladeanu ‹a person from Birlad›, Dobrogeanu ‹. . . Dobrogea, a province›, and Codreanu ‹. . . codru, "forest"›.

Some Romanian names are of Slavic origin. Bogdan ‹gift of God› or Bogdanovich is a frequent Russian, Polish, or Bulgarian patronym. Grigorovici and Popovici are other patronyms, this time from Serbian sources, in which *-ovici* often replaces or is equated to *-ovich* or *-ovic.*

Many Romanian given names reflect modern Romanians' interest in their Roman past. Although saints' names like Matei, Stefan, Petre, and Ion or Ioan are common, many others go straight back to Roman emperors and writers: Tiberiu, Virgil, Octavian, Liviu, Corneliu, Ovidiu, and Traian. An added reason for the popularity of these names is that at a time when Hungary controlled Transylvania (part of Romania) the government insisted that Romanian names be altered to Hungarian forms—Ion to János, for example. Transylvanian parents began naming their children after the ancient Romans because the Hungarians had no corresponding names.

The Irish Bram Stoker called more attention to Transylvania than did any other author to any part of Romania. Unfortunately, his book, *Dracula,* is about a vampire. Radu Florescu and a coauthor with the very un-Romanian name of

McNally wrote a book called *In Search of Dracula,* published in 1973. They dispelled any fantasies that anyone may have held that Romanians ever had such an unpleasant preoccupation as vampirism.

23

THE WESTERN SLAVS:

Poles, Czechs, and Slovaks

THE Poles, Czechs, and Slovaks, although their differences are many, are linked by being the westernmost of the Slavs and by speaking languages rather closely allied. Czechs and Slovaks can understand one another and read one another's books despite some differences in alphabets, and some words of the Poles are basically the same as those of their Czechoslovakian neighbors to the south. All three groups use the Roman alphabet but vary it in unlike ways.

Poland is among the countries that claim a pre-Columbus discoverer of the New World, although the claim is shaky. One Jan z Kolna (variously spelled) is said to have led in 1476 a Danish expedition that touched Labrador and a little later sailed into the Delaware River.

Much more definite is the early presence of Poles in the Jamestown colony. John Smith in wandering about Europe had been impressed by the quality of Polish soap, glass, and pitch and tar, and shortly after helping to found Jamestown he decided to bring over some Polish artisans. On the ship

Mary and Margaret, which arrived October 1, 1608, were Zbigniew Stefanski ‹son of Stefan›, a glassblower; Jan Mata ‹descendant of Mathias or Matthew›, a soapmaker; Jon Bogdan ‹gift of God›, a shipbuilder and maker of tar and pitch; and three other Poles with unspecified talents: a nobleman named Michael Lowicki, Karol Zrenica, and Stanislas Sadowski ‹one from the orchard›.

In the old country the Poles had become accustomed to fighting Germans, Russians, Austrians, Lithuanians, or others for what they considered their rights, so it is not surprising that over here they made what has been called "the first civil liberty protest in the English colonies of the New World." In Jamestown in 1619 they were denied the right to vote because they were not of British descent. They called a strike and as a result were enfranchised. (More than 350 years later, in Poland, they were still struggling for their civil rights with the Russians and the Russian-dominated puppet government.)

In the late eighteenth century Poland underwent a series of partitions that eventually divided the entire country among Prussia, Austria, and Russia. A number of Polish officers fled to America, and some of them made important contributions to the revolutionary cause. In all, about one thousand apparently Polish names are listed in the muster rolls of the American forces. Especially remembered are the names of Kazimierz Pulaski and Tadeusz Kosciuszko. Pulaski, the son of a count, was made a brigadier general by Congress and placed in charge of Washington's cavalry. A bold, dashing, but quarrelsome and not always successful man, he antagonized General Anthony Wayne, resigned from the army, and then organized his own corps of cavalry and infantry, which he used mainly to harass the British with hit-and-run tactics. He was killed leading a charge against British lines, ribbons flying gaily from his cap.

Kosciuszko became a colonel of engineers. Some military experts give him a sizable share of the credit for colonial victories at Ticonderoga and Saratoga, and he was responsible for building the fortifications at West Point. After the war he served as a Polish officer, but returning to America he switched his attention to slavery and the living conditions of black people, and in 1798 wrote about the matter to Thomas Jefferson, who called him "the greatest son of liberty . . . that I have ever known."

> I beg Mr. Jefferson that in case I should die without will or testament he should buy out of my money so many Negroes and free them, that the restant [remaining] sum should be sufficient to give them education and provide for their maintenance. That is to say, each should know before the duty of a citizen in the free government; that he must defend his country against foreign as well as internal enemies who would wish to change the Constitution for the worse to enslave them by degree afterward; to have good and human heart sensible to the sufferings of others.

Although Kosciuszko's wishes were not followed precisely, his estate was used for the founding in Newark, New Jersey, of one of the young nation's first schools for blacks.

In the following century the outstanding Pole in the Civil War was Vladimir Krzyzanowski, but his promotion to general was delayed for some time because no one in Congress —and presumably not President Lincoln either—could pronounce his name.

Before America's entry into World War I, President Wilson called for volunteer troops. Of the first 100,000 volunteers, 40,000 were of Polish descent.

In her book *The Polish Americans: Whence and Whither,* Theresita Polzin has divided Polish immigration into four periods:

Colonial	1608–1776
Political	1776–1854
Economic	1854–World War II
Exile	Post–World War II

During the political period a number of Polish groups were given American land. A polish National Committee reported in 1835, for instance, "After undergoing several months of Austrian captivity and more than a four-month journey, 235 of us laid foot on the free soil of Washington

[D.C.] on March 28, 1835." Congress granted this group 22,040 acres of land near the Rock River in Illinois.

Another settlement, in Panna Maria ‹Virgin Mary›, Texas, was begun in 1854 by one hundred families, about eight hundred persons, from Prussian-occupied Poland. Their leader was a Franciscan clergyman, Leopold Moczygemba, who had scouted the area earlier. This group came unusually well equipped with household goods, farm equipment, a large crucifix, and even church bells.

They arrived on Christmas Eve and almost immediately started to build houses and soon thereafter the first Polish Catholic church in America. They decided that the church should serve the Spanish speakers of the area as well as the Poles themselves. Symbolically, the first marriage performed in it was of Carmen Mauricio and Antonio Esparza, but the chief witnesses were Josepha Jarzombek and Joseph Krawietz.

The Poles who came to the United States mainly for economic reasons were much more numerous than their predecessors—so numerous that by 1930 there were 4¼ million Poles or people of Polish descent here. (In 1870 there had been only 50,000.) By 1970 Chicago alone had half a million Poles, the second largest Polish community in the world. Detroit, including the largely Polish Hamtramck—to which large numbers had been attracted by the opening of the Dodge Brothers automobile plant in 1914 (and to which other Detroiters drive when they want some of America's best *kielbasa,* an uncooked smoked sausage that the Slovenes and Czechs call *klobasa* and the Russians *kolbasa*)—had 300,000 in the entire city, Buffalo a quarter of a million, New York City 200,000, and Cleveland, Pittsburgh, and Philadelphia 100,000 each.

In all, about two-thirds of the "economic Poles" settled in urban areas. They were not always happy. As Polzin says,

> Ironically, the Polish peasant who had been lured away from his hut and plot of land which he loved, by the hope that in America he would be able to reconstruct his Old World life without its drawbacks, hardships, and sufferings, found himself thrust into the underground chambers of the mines, the reeking air of the slaugh-

terhouses, the heat of the steelmills, and the dust and smoke of the factory.

But there were compensations, as some of them wrote home: "We eat here every day what we get only for Easter in our country." "Schools here are free for everyone."

In World War II over six million residents of Poland lost their lives, more than half of them Jews in the Nazi gas chambers, and many of the rest killed as political criminals. The Russian takeover of Poland following the war drove large numbers of Poles into exile, many to the United States. These included numbers of professionals and artisans. Settling mainly in American cities, most found work easily and became naturalized quickly.

Poles in general have assimilated rapidly into American life, typically losing their Polish language in two generations and many of them simplifying their natal names. Mixed marriages increase with each generation. Polish-Irish marriages are especially common, with Polish-Italian second, Polish-German third, and—especially in California—Polish-Chinese, Polish-Filipino, and Polish-Korean not uncommon. Poles and American Indians sometimes marry in places like North Dakota, and Kowalski-Goldstein marriages are not infrequent in New York and some other cities.

Among especially prominent Polish Americans of the twentieth century have been biochemist Casimir Funk, the discoverer of vitamins and a specialist in deficiency diseases such as scurvy, pellagra, and rickets; semanticist Alfred Korzybski, who studied the ways that we use and misuse language; and concert pianist Artur Rubinstein, who could still play beautifully at age ninety.

Czechoslovakia. An elongated hilly or mountainous land in the center of Europe, bounded by topography slightly less rugged. East Germany and Poland to the north, West Germany to the west and southwest, Austria and Hungary to the south, a narrow strip of Russia to the east.

In the west of the little country (about the size of New York State) live the Czechs, Bohemians and Moravians mainly, who often look like Germans and Austrians. In the east the Slovaks, only half so numerous, could sometimes be confused with Russians or Yugoslavs.

A long tradition of painting, sculpture, decorative arts, and music. A saying, *Co Cech to muzikant* ‹Every Czech a musician.› (In Cleveland, one of the American centers for Czechoslovakian immigrants, the American Federation of Musicians in 1921 listed among its members 179 with Czechoslovakian names, 12 from the Hruby family alone, "and almost as many Zamecniks." In St. Louis in 1854 a Czech had offered to "trade 40 acres . . . for a good piano.") Five copies of books published per person per year in Czechoslovakia. More theaters, in proportion to population, than any other country in the world. The source of countless experimental plays and films.

Czechs started coming to the United States mainly after 1848, when an attempted revolution against Hapsburg (Austrian) rule failed. Jan Novak, an emigrant of 1852, described the departure of his family:

> So many neighbors gathered that the highway leading around our house was full of people, who came for the last time to shake my hand, and with tears in my eyes I said for ever good bye to them. I was accompanied three hours of the way to the river Kamejka by at least forty faithful neighbors, and from there I took off by ship to Prague with my wife Anna and our one year old daughter.

Says Vera Laska, in *The Czechs in America, 1633–1977:*

> The Czech immigrants came with their families: they came to stay. They were settlers, not seekers of dollars to be repatriated. They were mostly simple farmers, laborers, artisans, and tradesmen, hoping to own their own homes. They contributed to the mainstream of America not only as hewers of wood and drawers of water, but also their skill, music and humor. They brought as a dowry their traditional respect and love for learning and for freedom of conscience.

Over a century before 1848 they had founded Moravian College for Women, the first interdenominational college for women, in Bethlehem, Pennsylvania, a town started by Moravians. The college curriculum was based on statements by the most famous Czech educator, Comenius (Jan Amos Komensky, 1592–1670), who thought that education should be conducted in the vernacular rather than in Latin, that it should have some relevance to everyday life, and that girls and women have as much right as boys and men to gain knowledge—all earthshaking ideas in his day.

The 1900 census revealed 157,000 Czechs in the United States, with 10,000 or so per year still coming. A third of them were farmers, especially in the Midwest and Texas, but Chicago had the largest colony in the nation. A third of a century later the city's first Czech mayor, Anton Cermak, would be killed by a bullet intended for President Roosevelt. Anton Dvořák had come to New York and Iowa, had directed the National Conservatory of Music in New York, and had composed his *New World Symphony* before returning to Bohemia. His pupil Rudolf Friml would soon arrive here to accompany violinist Jan Kubelik, whose son would be Rafael Kubelik, a famous conductor. Friml would remain in the United States until his death at the age of ninety-four, in 1972, and would be known for such operettas as *Rose-Marie* and *The Vagabond King*.

One of the leading anthropologists, Dr. Ales Hrdlicka, had come here in 1882 and in 1909 would become director of the Smithsonian. In 1923 Karel Capek's *R.U.R.* (Rossum's Universal Robots) would be first performed in translation in New York and London. Capek had the distinction of coining a word that would become international—*robot*.

Many of the Czechs and Slovaks, like other immigrants, had no easy life in this country. Sometimes it was less difficult for the girls and women to get work than it was for the boys and men. In particular, because of their digital dexterity, they often got work in New York's cigar factories or made cigars in their homes. One result of this was a much earlier than usual reassessment of sex roles. One social worker wrote early in this century:

The most noticeable effect of having the mothers go to factory is that the ordinary masculine aversion to doing woman's work is greatly moderated. The boys run home from their play after school hours to start the kitchen fire, so that the water may be boiling when their mothers get home. They make beds and sweep and clean house. . . . Several times I have come into a home and found the strong young husband washing, and not at all embarrassed to be caught at the wash-tub.

Certainly back in the Middle Ages, when surnames were first adopted, few if any men were ever "caught at the wash-tub." One of the pleasures that I find as an onomatist is in recreating the ordinary lives of that era of six or eight hundred years ago. I find in people's names evidence of how they earned their bread, whom they respected, what they ate and wore, what the topography of the area was like, what animals, birds, fish, and trees they knew best, what physiognomies or other human physical features caught their attention, and much more. If the entire social history of a medieval region were covered over by time but we managed to uncover a list of the people's names, we could piece together a great deal of the lost heritage.

In the rest of this chapter I'll talk about what I have found concerning Slavic occupations in the name-giving period. I'll not confine myself to western Slavs, since many of their names are quite similar to those of the southern and eastern Slavs. There are, however, certain endings or other identifying marks that are fairly reliable, although seldom unquestionably so. For example, the ending *-ski* is likely to be Polish, and an American whose name ends in *-sky* is more likely to be Russian. (Russian-American names, being originally in the Cyrillic alphabet, have had to be transliterated in this country; Polish names, already in a modified Roman alphabet, have not often been.) The ending *-enko* is almost infallibly Ukrainian for ‹son of›. Among other patronymic indicators, *-vic* is likely to be out of Yugoslavia, although because of its pronunciation it has often been written *-vich* in this country, thus making it indistinguishable from Russian *vich; -vici* is almost always Serbian. The ending *-wicz* or any other *cz* combination is probably Polish, and *-ov, -off, -ev,* and *-eff* are most likely Russian.*

In looking at Slavic occupational names, one of the first things I noticed is that the Slavs during the naming period were not seafarers. They were almost a landlocked people. There is a *YS* name Mornar that means ‹sailor›, but not much else that is suggestive of the sea. In contrast, England and the Scandinavian countries have a fair number of names associated with the sea.

The Slavs were mainly agricultural people. *CS* Ovcik was a shepherd, as was *CS* or *Pol* Baca. *Bulg* Beranich raised lambs, as did *Pol* Beran. Goats must have been numerous: the Poles called the goatherd Koziarz or Kozierski or Kosinski or Koslowski, and sometimes used goats on their business signs, as Koziel and Kozielski attest. Goatherds in Bulgaria or Russia could be Kozin or Kozinski, with Kozlowsky sometimes showing up in Russia. The *Rus* Kozloff was the descendant of the goatherd. *Uk* and *CS* Kozel and Kozelka took care of goats or reminded someone of goats; so did *CS* Kozelak, although he sometimes tanned their hides.

Pol Krowa herded cows, and Bicek, Byczek, or Bykowski raised bull calves, probably for beef. *Pol* Gomolka made cheese from whey, and *Pol* or *Uk* Maslow or Maslowski churned butter. *Rus* Shifkin dealt in cream. *Uk* Maslanka sold buttermilk.

Pol Konicki drove horses, and Konikowski took care of "little horses," ponies. *YS* Koncevic and *Rus* Konen also were in charge of horses, and *Uk* or *Pol* Kolybecki tended the mares. *Pol* Gniadek had the specialty of bay horses. *Rus*

*To save space, the following abbreviations will be used in this chapter and the next: *Bulg,* Bulgarian; *CS,* Czechoslovakian; *Cz,* Czech; *Pol,* Polish; *Rus,* Russian; *Sl,* Slovakian; *Uk,* Ukrainian; and *YS,* Yugoslavian. These Slavic categories are those used by Elsdon C. Smith in his *New Dictionary of American Family Names,* upon which I have relied heavily for classification by nationalities and for translation. I have made no attempt to include *all* variations of any name, since sometimes there may be a dozen or even a score or more.

Droski and *Pol* Formanski drove coaches, and *Pol* Fornek was a carter. *Pol* Levandoski lived close to the meadow where livestock might graze. *Pol* Kosiba or *Cz* Kosiara cut the hay or the grain.

The existence of pigs is shown by *Pol* Swiniuch ‹piggish, like swine›. There were professional butchers, like *Rus, Uk,* or *Pol* Resnick, some of whom slaughtered and dressed carcasses in accordance with Jewish ritual; *Rus* Resnikoff was the butcher's son.

Many people kept chickens. *Pol* Kurczak made a living selling young hens, Kurinski sold hens and chicks, and Jajko was an egg dealer; *Pol* or *CS* Kokoszka dealt in both chickens and eggs. *Uk* Kurinsky raised chickens. *CS* or *Uk* Kohout or Kohut lived close to the sign of the rooster. *CS* or *Pol* Kurek and *Pol* Kogut apparently strutted about like cocks. *Pol* Gasior or Gasiorowski raised ganders—perhaps tender young ganders for the main course on feast days.

The farmer went by various names. The *Rus* Kulak was rich (later the Communists deemed him excessively rich), but Muschek or Muschick was only a peasant who owned at best a tiny plot of land. *Pol* Kmiec was a farmer, Kmiecik a little farmer. Klos(e) specialized in growing grain. *YS* or *Sl* Kmet(z) was a peasant, and *CS* Sedlac(e)k also earned his living by following the plow. Slavic plows of that time were made of wood, as *CS, Pol, Rus,* and *Uk* Socha tells us. *Sl* Gazda and *YS* Gazdziak signify the landlord or other superior being. One of the landlord's tenants might be *Pol* Dzierzowski ‹one who rents land›. Gardeners included *CS* Zahradnik and *Pol* Jarzyna and Sadowy. *CS* Teplitsky was a greenhouse worker.

What the farmers and gardeners grew was of course what the people ate. A staple crop was barley, as attested by *Uk* and *Pol* Krupa ‹dealer in groats and barley›. *CS* Zito means ‹rye field›. There were granaries, as *CS* and *Pol* Suski or Suskey bear witness. Some of the rye in granaries was used for vodka, already a favorite Slavic drink centuries ago; *Pol* Stopka ‹vodka drinker› perhaps overindulged. The keeper of a tavern in Yugoslavia was Krema, in Russia Kabac.

Pol Krupinski made and sold groats, consisting of coarsely cracked grain, and Krupnik made a soup from peeled barley. *Pol* Kapustka grew and sold cabbages, although the name may also have been contemptuous for someone thought to have no more sense than a cabbage head. *Pol* Rzepka specialized in turnips, Groch or Grochowiak (or some other variant) and *Uk* Groszek in peas, *Uk* and *Pol* Bura(c)k in beets (essential to borscht), *Uk* Bobich or *Pol* Bobin in beans, *YS* Kumar in cucumbers.

Rus Sadoff and *Pol* Sadowski and Sadecki had something to do with orchards. *Pol* Yablon(ski) or Jablonowski lived near apple trees and presumably raised apples; *CS* Hruska and *Pol* Dulski grew pears; Jagodzinski grew, picked, and sold berries. There must have been cranberry bogs in the Ukraine, for Kolinsky harvested the tart red fruit there, as did Kolinski in Poland. *Rus* Wishnov and *Uk* Wyszynski were growers of cherries; *Rus* Wenograd had a vineyard, and *CS* Winitz lived near one.

Some of those who supplied condiments were *Pol* Gorczyca, who grew mustard plants and made yellow paste from the seeds; Szafran, the grower of the saffron then widely used as dye as well as flavoring; Ziolko or Zuelke, who gathered herbs and acquired a reputation as a clever person, perhaps a sort of medicine man; and *Rus* Perchonock, who sold pepper and other condiments. *Pol* Kopera or Kopernik grew and sold dill and fennel. *Pol* Solarz or Solnick gathered and sold salt. For use in beer or ale, *CS* Chmelar picked pungent-smelling hops from their tall vines. *Pol* Grzyb or Rydzewski grew or harvested edible mushrooms.

Still other persons were involved in the preparation of foods. Important in every village was the miller who ground the grain. In Czechoslovakia he was Melnick, and Mlynak, perhaps a term of affection rather than description, was the ‹little miller›. *Uk* Melnyk(chuk) was the miller, and his son was Melnyczenko, who in Russia was called Melnikoff.

The households of the nobility and other wealthy folk employed cooks. Pisch was a cook in the Ukraine and Poland, and Kuchar or a variant cooked in several Slavic countries. *Pol* Kucia made porridge, Kwasiborski was named for his specialty, borscht, and Placek made pancakes. Kuchta was a kitchen boy. *Uk* Kulesa and Kulis and *Pol* Zacierka made gruel and porridge; *Rus* Zaluszka was known for dumplings, Kiseloff for puddings. *YS* or *Uk* Pekarek was a baker; so was *Pol* Piekarski as well as Pieczynski and Bochniak and Sucharski.

Fishermen provided some of what the cooks needed to prepare. In the streams and lakes *Pol* Karpinski found carp, *Rus* and *Pol* Okun caught perch, *Uk* and *Pol* Schupak hooked the long, slender pickerel, and *Pol, Uk,* and *CS* Rak or *Pol* Rakowski supplied crabs. General names for fishermen were *CS* and *Pol* Rybak, Ryba, or Rybar, *YS* Ribar.

Hunters like *CS* or *Pol* Jelinek provided venison; *Pol* Bibro or Bobrich trapped beavers, which were valuable for furs and parts of which were considered table delicacies; *Pol* Krolik killed rabbits. Someone must have killed bears, for *Pol* Kolpak made bearskin caps. *Rus* Soboleff trapped sables for their furs, as did *CS* Zabel and *Pol* Sobel (with its many variant spellings). *CS* Kunka trapped martens, *Pol* Wydra otters. *Pol* Boba or Bobak trapped marmots, animals resembling hedgehogs; the Czechs thought that Jeschek was in some way like a hedgehog. Mysliwiec was a general name for the hunter in Poland. *Pol* Konopka caught the little birds called linnets, and Skowronek caught larks. *Pol* Lesnick was a gamekeeper.

As was true elsewhere for centuries, the smith was an important part of a Slavic community. In Russia he might be Koval(sky), Kowal(sky), Kuznetsov, or some variant. In Czechoslovakia he was Kovar. The Poles had several names for him, of which Kowalski was most common. (Telephone directories in large American cities are still likely to have a column or more of Kowals and Kowalskis; Chicago's has several columns.) *Uk* Kowalchuk was the smith's son, and Kowalyszyn was his stepson. *Rus* Mednick was a coppersmith, as were *Pol* Koprowski and perhaps Kotlarz, who might also be a brazier. Goldsmiths included *CS, Rus,* and *Pol* Slotnick.

Other people provided other services. *Rus* Lopatin was available for shoveling, and *Pol* or *Uk* Lopat(a) would work with a spade; specifically, *Pol* Kopan(ski) dug ditches or trenches. *Uk* Kolodenko was the son of a logger. *Uk* Kolody made wheels and perhaps the vehicles that they supported and moved; so did *Pol* Kolodziej; Kolasa made two-wheeled vehicles, chaises. *Pol* Swiderski had a specialized occupation —drilling holes; Trzaska split wood to make it suitable for fireplaces that all houses used for heat; *CS* Uhlir mined coal; so did *Pol* Rudnick and Gorniak; Weglarz sold it.

Pol Gwozdz made nails, Igielski needles, *CS* or *Pol* Filc felt cloth, *Uk* Fiala goblets, and *Pol* Flaska little flasks and bottles. Among the potters were *CS* Hrncir and *Pol* Gonciarz; *Pol* Gancarz used either clay or metal in making his utensils. *CS* or *Uk* Sklar was a glazier, who made and sold glass; *Rus* Skloff was a glass merchant; Sklaroff was his son. *Pol* Koschnitzki or Koszyk was a maker and seller of baskets. Krzemien cut stone. *Uk, Rus,* or *Pol* Kadow was a cooper, who made wooden barrels, casks, and tubs; the Czechs and Poles also called him Becvar or Bednar or a variant, and to both Ukrainians and Poles he could be Bodnar(chuk). *Pol* Tokarz or Tokarski, a turner, used the lathe, and Wiercinski used either a lathe or a drill.

When most persons owned but a single pair of shoes, the role of the shoemaker or cobbler was important. In the Ukraine he was called Shvetz or Svec or Sevenko, in Russia Sapoznik, in Czechoslovakia Sevcik, and in Poland Szewc. *Pol* or *Uk* Cholewa made boots.

CS Tesar or Truhlar was a carpenter, known as Tesla or Stolar in Yugoslavia. The Poles called him Ciesla(k) or Stolarz. In Russia he was Plotnick. *CS* Sindelar specialized in making shingles. *Pol* Cegielski helped to make bricks or at least lived near the kilns; *CS* Cihlar also made bricks and perhaps built with them.

As always, there were wars and rumors of wars during the name-giving period. Pushkin, later the name of a great Russian poet, was originally a man who fired a cannon or a giant sling. *Uk* Wojeck was a soldier, *Sl* Haduch an armor bearer. *Uk* Cusack or Kozak and *Pol* Kossa(c)k celebrate the virile warriors we call Cossacks. *Pol* Korda fought with a sabre, Kordek with a small sword, and Luczak with bow and arrows. *Pol* and *Uk* Valosky were shieldbearers. *Pol* Kapral was a corporal. *Pol* Szablewski made swords.

When the Slavs of the period did not make their own clothing (possibly with thread purchased from *Pol* Nitka), they employed the services of a tailor, since obviously there was no mass production. *Pol, CS,* and *Uk* Kravitz and *Cz* Krajci seem to have been generalists, but others specialized. Thus *YS* Kotula made shirts, but in a neighboring house Klobucar made hats. *Pol* Micek and *Uk* Shapowal or his son Shapowalenko made caps. *Pol* Kabat tailored overcoats, and Gunia was a dressmaker. The cloth that all of them used might be woven by *CS* Kadlec. *CS* and *Pol* Sarzynski, catering to the very rich, dealt in silk. *Pol* Skora treated the hides of animals, and *CS, Uk,* or *Pol* Kushner or Kushmar made fur coats of them.

Merchants included *Rus* Polzin, *Pol* Kupsik or Kramarczyk (related to German Kramer?), and *Pol* or *Uk* Zysk. The parson, priest, or rabbi might be *Pol* Kleban, *Ys* or *Uk* Popovich, *YS, Pol, CS, Uk,* or *Rus* Rabinowitz or Rabinovich ‹son of the rabbi›, *Rus* Kogan or Popov, or *Uk* Popenko. Scribes like *Pol* Kupczyk or Pisarek were also learned men.

Few of the occupational names refer to amusements. However, Kuklinski made not only images of holy figures but also dolls for little girls to play with. *Rus* Kukla (a name revived for a puppet in the early days of American television) was a puppeteer; perhaps he glued his puppets together with glue made by his countrymen Lapoff and Lapofsky. *Pol* Kwiecinski and *Uk* Kwitek brightened the landscape with flowers. *Pol* Pianka smoked a meerschaum pipe or perhaps mined the material; Taback or Tabachnick maybe indulged in the snuff that he prepared and sold. (These names presumably originated in the sixteenth century when tobacco was first introduced to Europe.)

And there was music. *Pol* or *Cz* Dudek played a bagpipe, and *Pol* Dudak some sort of pipe. Grajek was a violinist.

The pearl dealers *Pol* Kanak and *Rus* Perloff sometimes cheered up the wealthy, and the barber, such as *CS* Holich, could cut their hair.

If we were still in a name-giving period, the list of occupational names, Slavic or otherwise, would be many times as long. The absence of names pertaining to medicine in the medieval period (except for Spitalny, who worked in one of the crude hospitals of the time) is noticeable. Obviously too the people in the naming period had no knowledge of automobiles, television, plastics; their knowledge of science was gained just from their own observation; they were unsophisticated in the arts; history was mainly word of mouth about what grandpa did. Their occupations, as reflected in their names and many of ours, were almost entirely those that were essential for personal and community survival.

24

THE EASTERN AND SOUTHERN SLAVS:

Russians, Yugoslavians, and Bulgarians

SCHOLARS of American Indian history believe that the ancestors of all American Indians on both continents came originally across the Bering Strait during the last Ice Age, when it was above sea level. Thus in a sense our "native Americans" are "Russians," although clearly there was during the Ice Age no group actually called Russians. "The most feasible route," says A. S. Coon, "considering the climate during the Ice Age, would have been along the eastern Asian coast, from lands occupied by Mongoloids and possibly by ancestors of the Ainu."

After the ice melted, the route was forgotten. In the early part of the eighteenth century neither the Russians nor anyone else knew whether Asia and North America were connected somewhere in the far north. Wanting to find out, Peter the Great sent a series of three expeditions, two of them headed by the Danish Vitus Jonassen Bering, for whom the strait was later named. On the third expedition, in 1741, Bering sailed into the Gulf of Alaska, explored parts of the southwestern coast, saw spectacular Mt. St. Elias, and peered through fog at the Aleutians.

The Russians hoped for a foothold in North America, partly because of prospective riches in Alaskan furs, partly because they hoped to make the north Pacific a Russian lake, and partly because they suspected endless possibilities of development in the coastal areas as far south as California. Fur hunters and traders added to geographical understanding by making frequent trips across the Bering Strait, and a number of small Russian settlements sprang up in coastal or near-coastal Alaska.

One of the most ambitious Alaskan colonies was the one started by Gregory Ivanovich Shelikov, aided by his energetic wife, Natalya Alekseyevna, the first Russian woman known to have visited the Aleutians. The British had earlier been exploring coastal Alaska, but Shelikov went to the places where they had been and buried copper plates saying "Lands of the Russians."

Other Russians moved on southward and started a colony in what is now Sacramento—a colony that included what in a few years would be Gold Rush land. Because it was populated mainly by serfs and convicts and was not well led, it folded in 1841. Indications of the Russian presence in California remain even today, however—a Russian Hill in San Francisco, a Russian river, and a town called Sebastopol.

By 1867 most of the sea otters had been killed, so Alaska seemed less valuable than before to the Russians. Besides, they reasoned, since England still maintained an interest in the area, perhaps Anglo-American relations could be worsened if the huge land mass were in the hands of the United States. The upshot was that they sold Alaska to us for the bargain price of $7,200,000.

Most of the Russian settlers then returned to their homeland. A no doubt incomplete census taken in 1870 showed Alaska's population as 26,843 natives, 350 Americans and other non-Russian whites, only 483 Russians, and 1,421 half-breeds. The explanation of the last group is largely that Russian men, with gifts or by force, had frequently mated with native women. On one occasion the natives were so resentful that they almost wiped out a Russian settlement.

Early in the nineteenth century a Russian group led by a German named Dr. George Anton Schaefer attempted to conquer Hawaii, ruled at the time by the aging King Kamehamaha the Great. They built three harbors and three fortresses and renamed in Russian the places and the people in the areas they controlled. Schaefer was moving toward the overthrow of Kamehamaha when word arrived from Tsar Alexander I that, for reasons of European politics, the attempt should be abandoned.

Until the 1880s very few people emigrated from Russia to the United States. The autocratic Russian leaders did not want to lose any of their subjects. Further, the general illiteracy and poverty and isolation kept most of the inhabitants from realizing that somewhere in the world there might be greener pastures.

There was some easing of the restrictions during the eighties. Jewish people, many of whom were forced to live in sections of Russia's western area known as the Pale of Settlement, were subjected increasingly to devastating pogroms, senseless orgies of destruction and killing. As a result many of them began to emigrate, with or without passports. A much smaller number of Russian peasants, Slavs who also were desperately poor, began to leave, too, although there was no considerable movement among them until the few years starting with 1910 and ending with the outbreak of World War I. As a consequence, the total number of Russian Slavs in this country is relatively small (estimated at 400,000 a few decades ago by Louis Adamic), but when Jews are included the number of immigrants from Russia is several times as large. I treat Jewish names in a separate chapter.

Like other immigrants, Russian Slavs have contributed variously to the United States. Here are a few examples.

- Charles Thiel, known also as Charles Cist, in Philadelphia in 1769 tried to sell anthracite coal as fuel. The shiny black stuff was at the time considered useless. Thiel was treated as a swindler and threatened with imprisonment.

- Agapy Goncharenko late in the 1860s was one of Alaska's first journalists. His *Liberty* was intended mainly to criticize the tsar, but he saved some of his vitriolic language for the American government.
- Peter Demyenov, who became Peter Demens, was a cofounder of St. Petersburg, Florida, named for his city of birth. (Adamic in 1944 counted fifteen American St. Petersburgs or Petersburgs, ten Moscows, nine Odessas, and two Kremlins.)
- Architect Vladimir Stoleshnikov helped to plan Carnegie Hall.
- After the Russian Revolution in 1917 about 40,000 Russian Slavs escaped to the United States, many of them penniless nobles who sometimes began working as doormen, glove sellers, waiters, or cooks. A few made a profession of marrying money. But one who came was Igor Sikorsky, a pioneer in aeronautical engineering, whose Clippers led the way in transoceanic flying and whose helicopters flew countless missions in both war and peace. Another aeronautical engineer who fled the Reds was the one-legged Alexander De Seversky, who developed the prototype of the P-47 fighter plane and wrote the influential 1942 book *Victory Through Air Power.*
- American musicians and dancers from Russian backgrounds are numerous. They include, for instance, Igor Stravinsky, André Kostelanetz, Vladimir Horowitz, Jascha Heifetz, Leopold Godowsky, George Balanchine, and Mikhail Baryshnikov.

The Ukrainians need special mention, since during part of the past century immigrants from the Ukraine were recorded separately from the Russians. According to Wasyl Halich, in *Ukrainians in the United States,* in 1937 there were 700,000 Americans from the Ukraine or of Ukrainian ancestry. Most of the early immigrants, about 70 percent of whom were totally illiterate, worked here as farm laborers, miners, or factory hands, especially in Pennsylvania and the Midwest. Their lives were often difficult, as Halich shows in this generalized portrait of a miner's wife:

During the last two decades of the nineteenth century and the first decade of the twentieth, the life of a Ukrainian miner's wife was almost always one of continuous toil and hardship. When she came to America and a mining village, she was, as a rule, young, healthy, and not infrequently good looking. After several years' residence in her adopted environment, her health was depleted, and she was, in some cases, aged beyond recognition. She cared not only for her husband and from three to ten, or even more, children, but often for roomers and boarders also. From six to twelve of these crowded all the available space of the dwelling. The house was usually rented from the mining company, the rent averaging seven dollars per month, unfurnished. This was deducted from the worker's pay. The miner's wife alone had to do all the housework—washing, cleaning, and cooking for ten to twenty people. In most cases she had to bring all the grocery supplies from the company store, from which employees were obliged to buy. Twice each month the miner's wife had to contend with the anxieties incident to payday—days of drunkenness, singing, arguments, and occasional fighting.

A couple of misconceptions about Soviet languages and names need to be eliminated. One is that everybody in the Soviet Union speaks Russian and therefore has a Russian name. Actually there are at least thirty-three languages used in the USSR. Some of these, like Ukrainian and Byelorussian, may be considered only Russian dialects, although their alphabets contain letters not found in Russian, and many of their words, word forms, and idioms are different. Some of the Soviet languages, however, use alphabets other than the Cyrillic, belong to non-Indo-European language families, and are completely incomprehensible to most residents of Moscow or Leningrad.

A second possible misconception is that all languages and peoples of central, southern, and eastern Europe are Slavic. Romanian, as the name suggests, is a Romance language, not Slavic. Hungarian belongs to what is called the Finno-Ugric family, which includes Finnish as well as Estonian and some other languages of the USSR; it has no known relationship to any of the Indo-European languages. Latvian and Lithuanian are closely related members of the Baltic branch of the

Indo-European family and are therefore only cousins of the Slavic languages.

The languages that are indeed Slavic, like Russian, Polish, and the somewhat differing languages of the Yugoslavs, are all descended from an older form of Slavic, just as the Romance languages descended from Latin. As a result many of their words and names have a family resemblance and are sometimes identical. I have illustrated this point with occupational names in the preceding chapter, and will add more examples at the end of this one.

The name Yugoslavia means ‹land of the south Slavs›. The nation's major population groups are Serbians (42 percent), Croatians (23 percent), and Slovenes (9 percent). Some of the others are Montenegrins and Macedonians. The people of Bulgaria are also counted among the south Slavs.

In the United States a total of 485,000 Croatian and Slovenian immigrants were recorded between 1899 and 1924. During the same years only a third as many Serbians, Montenegrins, and Bulgarians reached these shores, and 53,000 others came from the subgroups called Dalmatians, Bosnians, and Hercegovinians.

The bulk of the southern Slav immigrants were poor peasants, usually driven from their native land by poverty. Many families had attempted unsuccessfully to live on one and a half acres of rocky land per person, when an estimated twelve and a half acres were needed.

At the time when Columbus came to America (reportedly with several Dalmatian sailors among his crew), the coastal city of Ragusa (now Dubrovnik) was a maritime power. Our word *argosy* is derived from *Ragusa*. Shakespeare referred to "Argosies with portly saile" which fly by "with their woven wings." Ragusa traded with England and with Spain. As early as 1530 a Dominican monk from there, Vicko Paletin, carried Christianity to parts of the New World.

According to a record of a seamen's guild in Dalmatia, in about 1540 several Dalmatian ships left Ragusa for America, intending to colonize and thus escape unwanted attentions from the Turks. A story of uncertain accuracy says that one or more of these ships foundered off the coast of what we call North Carolina, and that a number of sailors managed to swim to an island, probably Roanoke. There they are said to have mated with natives, and the resulting mixed breed became known as the Croatan Indians.

South Slav missionaries in the seventeenth century started missions in Mexico and Baja California, thus contributing toward early ventures into California itself. Fernando Consag, S.J., mapped lower California, demonstrating that it is not an island—an event that historian H. H. Bancroft called the most important of that period. Ragusans in the same century rejected opportunities to make large sums of money by engaging in the slave trade from Africa.

In the 1700s and early 1800s more and more Croatians, and smaller numbers of other southern Slavs, came to California and to the southeastern United States. Parts of the California coast reminded them of their own picturesque Dalmatian shores, so they called California "New Dalmatia." Later their descendants would corner most of the apple and fig markets of the state, and would own hundreds of fishing boats in San Pedro.

Fishermen and small shipbuilders appeared also in Tampa Bay, Florida; Mobile Bay, Alabama; and Brownsville and Galveston, Texas. One sizable group of Croats and Slovenes early in the eighteenth century had gone to Prussia to take refuge from troubles with Turks or others, and went from there to establish homes in Georgia.

Louisiana attracted them, too, as George J. Prpic explains in *South Slavic Immigration in America:*

> The mild climate of New Orleans and adjacent regions, the big wide river—the Mississippi—as well as the cosmopolitan atmosphere of the city appealed to the Adriatic sailors. Jobs were available to them, as fishermen, artisans, and traders. Many simply left their ships and stayed, quite a few of them unregistered, a practice that has survived in our ports to this day. Around 1830 these men were finding their way up the Mississippi. . . . Some married in New Orleans and settled there. A few scattered along the seacoast

on both sides of the Delta. Some moved inland. A few sailed to Saint Louis and settled there.

Marko Maranovich built a lovely mansion in north central Louisiana. His French neighbors had trouble with his last name, so he and his house became known only as Marko and *la maison de Marko*. A little town called Marco was later built on the site. In coastal Louisiana today, the descendants of oyster farmers from Dalmatia, most of their names ending in *-ich,* still work at the ancestral tasks.

Unlike most immigrant groups, the south Slavs in general sided with the Confederates in the Civil War—as was natural, since their homes were mainly in the South. The names of several hundred Croatians may be found on the rolls of the gray-clad army, and others, usually called "Slavonians" after one section of Croatia, served with the Confederate navy. The name of George Petrovich ‹son of Peter›, along with several other Slavic names, is on the list of Southerners killed at Gettysburg. Petrovich and his fellows had nicknamed themselves "Johnny Reboviches."

Before and especially after the Civil War the West attracted more and more of the southern Slavs. Prpic says:

> By their nature enterprising and business-minded, some were doing a thriving business during the 1850's on the old Davis Street near the waterfront [of San Francisco], later known as Embarcadero. They owned bars and saloons, grocery stores, restaurants, fruit and vegetable stands, and a variety of other businesses. Operating restaurants and taverns became a Croatian specialty in the West.

There was once also an interesting Dalmatian connection with Hawaii. A sea captain named John Dominis ‹the Lord's day› married in Boston a well-to-do young woman of Puritan stock. They moved to the West, where the captain engaged in trade with the Orient. They built a mansion, Washington Place, in Honolulu. Their son, also named John, in 1862 married Princess Lydia Kamehaha Kapaakea, known also as Liliu Kamakeaha. Young John became governor of Oahu and adviser and secretary to four kings of Hawaii, as well as commander of the armed forces. On the death of the king in 1891, John's wife became the famous Queen Liliuokalani, who unsuccessfully fought Hawaii's annexation by the United States. She is today best remembered as the composer of "Aloha Oe."

An early governor of the territory of Alaska was Mike Stepovich ‹son of Stepan, "Stephen"›, whose father was a Croatian immigrant who was successful in mining, real estate, and business.

The major influx of southern Slavs came between the 1890s and 1914. Most of the reasons for "American fever" are familiar to us from earlier groups: lack of land, high taxes, military conscription, oppression by foreign powers, and the favorable report received from friends and relatives already in America. One unique reason was a disease of grape vines, called phyloxera, which ruined the livelihoods of many. One of those driven out by phyloxera was Croatian Peter Divizich, who put his knowledge of viticulture to use in the central San Joaquin valley by establishing what became the largest vineyard in the United States—one that supplied thousands of tons of raisins, figs, and other fruit products to American armed forces during World War II.

It was not always easy for the Slavs to get out of their country, so many left illegally. Prpic says that often they traveled partly on foot, slipped across a border, and eventually reached France or some other country on the Atlantic. "All along the route the agents and confidants placed them in an 'underground emigrant railroad' until the group reached the America-bound ship." In America earlier immigrants helped them to find lodging and work. Unlike many of their predecessors, most of these immigrants stayed in the North, where they usually worked in factories, mines, or mills. One may find their descendants today not only in the large cities but also the smaller ones such as Joliet, Illinois; Gary, Indiana; and Calumet, Michigan.

World War II, as may be expected, had plenty of American heroes with names ending in *-ic* or *-ich*. One of the first of these was Peter Tomich ‹descendant of Toma, "Thomas"›, a water tender on the *Utah* during the attack on Pearl Harbor.

He got his men out of the sinking ship, secured the boilers, and went down with the ship. He was one of the war's earliest winners of the Congressional Medal of Honor, and in 1943 a destroyer, the U.S.S. *Tomich,* was named for him.

Numerous south Slavs have become at least modestly famous in other ways. One of my favorites is Louis Adamic ‹descendant of Adam›, who wrote some of the most fascinating books about European immigrants in America. Then there was sculptor Ivan Mestrovic ‹son of the master›, whose favorite medium was wood but who worked also in granite, marble, and stone. Nicholas Tesla ‹carpenter›, a Serb, came here at age twenty-eight and worked for Thomas Edison. Tesla disagreed with Edison about the relative merits of direct and alternating current, with Tesla favoring the latter. His research made possible the wide distribution of AC electric power on which so much of the work of our nation now depends. In all he was responsible for some seven hundred inventions, and he was foresighted enough that over a half-century ago he said that solar power must and someday would be harnessed.

The story of another inventor, Michael Pupin, has a moment of drama. He was almost not admitted by immigration officials. As a boy he was traveling to Prague by train, but overslept and had to go on to Vienna. An elderly American couple befriended him and took him to their first-class compartment. They talked with him about Franklin, Lincoln, America in general, and advised him to come here. At age fifteen he did so, but arrived with no relatives, no friends, and only five cents in his pocket. The admission authorities were about to send him back. But he talked with them about Franklin, Lincoln, and Harriet Beecher Stowe, and they decided to let him in.

Twenty-two years later Michael Pupin produced the first X-ray photograph in the United States, shortly afterward he turned to work on radio transmission, and in 1923 he wrote his Pulitzer Prize autobiography, *From Immigrant to Inventor.*

Sometimes one of the *Amerikanci* would return to his native land. At the turn of this century, as Adamic tells us, he was likely to be dressed in

> a blue serge suit, buttoned shoes, with india rubber heels, a derby, a celluloid collar, and a loud necktie, made even louder by a dazzling horsehoe pin, while his two suitcases of imitation leather bulged with gifts from America for his relatives and friends. . . . Thus in my boyhood the idea that the United States was a sort of paradise on earth—the Golden Country, the Land of Promise—was kept vigorously alive by the *Amerikanci* in our village, and, of course, by tens of thousands of returned emigrants in other villages and towns in Eastern, Central, and Southern Europe.

As I did with occupational names in the chapter before this, here I'll illustrate patronyms, place names, and descriptive names from the various Slavic countries.

Patronyms in any language may be of three basic kinds. The first is the Johnson type (Ivanov or Ivanovich in Russian), in which the father's name is used with an affix (such as *-ov, -ovic,* or English *-son* or Irish *O'*) to show that the person named is the son or the more distant descendant of John or Ivan or whomever. The second does not use the ancestor's specific name but identifies him by occupation or in some other way; thus English Smithson and *Uk* Kowalchuk are both ‹son of the smith›. Third, a patronym may be, with or without an affix, the name of some renowned person such as Alexander or one of the early church fathers.

The Slavs used all three kinds of patronyms. We have already noticed a number of the second variety. They were especially fond, however, of the third sort, with countless names echoing those of favorite saints or other (usually) religious figures.

The forms of a name like Peter or John vary from language to language. Also, in a given language one or more pet forms of the name may exist and may not look much like the original name. Thus, in English, Hank for Henry, Dick for Richard, and Bill for William differ considerably from the original. In consequence of the various possibilities, the

Slavic languages may have two or three dozen variants for some of the common names. The list that follows is not nearly exhaustive. Your telephone directory may show you others.

Aaron	*Rus* Aronoff
Abraham	*YS* Abramic, Abramovitz; *Rus* Abramovich, Avramovich; *Pol* Abramovicz, Abramowitz
Adam	*Pol* Adamczyk, Adamowicz, Adamski; *CS* Adamek
Alexander	*Uk* Lesko, Oleksandrenko; *Sl* Sandor
Andrew	*YS* Andrejevic; *Uk* Andrijenko; *Pol* Andrzejewski, Jedrysiak, Jendrzejewski; *CS* Ondrus
Anthony	*Pol* Antzak, Antosz; *YS, Rus* Antonovych, Antonovich
Bartholomew	*CS* Barta; *Pol* Barkowiak, Bartkiewicz, Bartkowski, Bartos; *Rus* Bartkowitz
Basil	*Pol* Vasely, Wasielewski; *Rus, CS* Vasaly; *Rus* Vasilevich
Charles	*CS, Rus* Karlic; *Pol* Karlowicz, Karol; *Rus* Karlov(sky)
Clement	*CS, Uk, Pol* Klima; *Uk* Klemchuk; *Pol* Klimczek; *CS, Pol* Klimek
Constantine	*Pol* Konstanty, Kosciuszko; *Rus* Kost; *Uk* Kostenko; *Bulg, Rus* Kostoff
Demetrius	*Bulg* Dimitrov
Francis, Frank	*Pol* Franczak, Franckowiak, Fronczak; *Rus* Frankovich; *Uk* Frystak
Gabriel	*Pol* Gabrys, Gabrysiak; *CS, Uk* Havlik, Havlicek; *Uk* Gavrick, Hawryluk
George	*YS* Djordevic; *Sl* Djuric; *Bulg* Georgieff; *Pol* Jerz, Jurzak, Jurek, Jurewicz, Jurkiewicz
Gregory	*CS* Grega; *YS* Gregorich; *Rus* Grisin, Hrynko; *Uk* Hryhorczak; *Pol* Grzedorzak

Isaac	*Bulg* Isakov; *Pol* Zisook
Jacob	*Pol* Jakubczak, Jaszkowski, Kubiak; *Uk* Jaskowiak; *Rus* Kubik
John	*Rus* Evanoff, Ivancich, Ivanov(ich), Jankovich, Yanofsky; *CS* Hanik, Hanzel, Jana, Vanik; *Pol* Iwan, Janczak, Jasinski; *Bulg, Uk* Ivanov; *Uk* Iwatiw; *YS* Jovanovic(h)
Joseph	*Pol* Josefowicz, Jozwiak
Lawrence	*Pol* Wawrzyniak
Luke	*Uk* Lucenko; *Pol* Lukas; *Rus* Lukoff
Matthew	*Pol* Mackiewicz, Matus, Matusczek; *YS* Matkovic; *Rus* Matkovich, Matusoff; *CS* Matusow
Michael	*CS* Mical; *Pol* Michalek; *Rus* Mihailovich, Mishkin
Patrick	*Pol* Paderewski
Paul	*CS* Pafko; *Bulg, Rus* Pavel; *Uk* Pavlenko, Pavluk, Pawlyszyn, "son of Paul's wife"; *Pol* Pawlicki
Peter	*Pol* Bieschke, Pietrowicz, Pietrzak; *Bulg* Petrov; *Rus* Petroff; *Uk* Petrenko, Petryshyn, "son of Peter's wife"
Simon	*Rus, Pol* Sienkiewicz; *Pol* Sienko, Simek, Szymanski
Stanislaw	*Pol* Stach, Stanczak, Stankiewicz, Stasiak; *Rus* Stanko
Stephen	*Uk* Stec; *Pol* Stefaniewicz, Stenzel, Stepanek, Szczepaniak; *Sl* Stefanik
Theodore	*Pol, Rus* Feddor; *Uk* Federenko; *Bulg, Rus, Uk, Pol* Fodor; *YS* Todorovic
Thomas	*Pol* Tomaszewski, Tomczak; *YS* Tomich
Timothy	*Pol* Tyminski, *Uk* Tymoszenko

From the place names that became surnames we can learn something of the varied countryside of the Slavic areas. *Pol* Yaworski reminds us, for instance, that sycamore trees grew there, Grabinski lived close to elms, Topol(ski) near poplars, Lipski where the lindens grew; Lozowski or *CS* Vrba shows that willows abounded, *Pol* Swierczynski or Jedlowski or a variant that fir trees were plentiful, Olozewski and Osinski that alders and aspens grew there, Bykowski and Bobka that the beech and the laurel could be found; Javorski and Klonowski called attention to the maples, and *Pol* Sosna and several other names, as well as *YS* Sosnovek, to the pine forests. *Uk* Piddubnyj lived among the oaks, as did *CS* Doubek or Dub and *Pol* Dombrowski or Dubski. *Pol* Beza(r)k was close to the alders, and *CS* Figus refers to a fig tree. *CS* Brezina and *Pol* Brzezinski lived close to the birches.

Many Slavs were identified by their living in or near a forest. Among them were *Uk* Kolodenko ‹son of the woodsman›, *Pol* Borowski, whose wood was small, *Pol* Dolasinski, Kajewski, Lasko(wski) or Lesniak, or the Przyborski who lived beside the great forest. *Uk, CS,* or *Pol* Dubiel was strong as the oaks that were so prominent in his region. Yalowitz was named for the large stands of evergreen trees. *Pol* Zaleski and *Uk* Zaleskyj lived far away, beyond the forest. *Pol* Kierzek and *Uk* Korcyk lived in shrubby, bushy areas.

Pol Blonski's home was on level ground, but many others lived on or near a mountain: *Pol* and *Rus* Gora, *CS* and *Rus* Horwitz or Horvitz, *Uk* Hursky, and *Uk* and *Pol* Komaniecky, among others. *Pol* Zavorski lived in a mountain pass, and *Rus* or *Pol* Podgorny lived at the foot of a mountain. Among the residents of hill country were *Pol* Gura(k) and *YS* Hribar. *Pol* Glazewski's home was in a rocky place, Dubicki's on cloddy land, and Glinka's or Glinski's on clay.

A frequently used way to indicate a place of residence, especially among the Russians and the Poles, was to add *-sky* or *-ski* after the name of the place, although that ending is not restricted to place names. Thus someone who had come from, or perhaps had merely visited, the Russian town called Minsk was named Minsky, and one from Pinsk was Pinsky to the Russians, Pinski to the Poles. A Pole who left his country might be named Polsky in his new land, and if he returned the name Polski might stick with him. In Russia or Czechoslovakia he might be called Polak or Polack, and in the Ukraine Polischuk or Poljak. A "little Pole" among the

Czechs was Polacek, *Rus* Polakoff meant ‹son of the Pole›, and *Rus* or *Uk* Polka was a descendant of a Polish woman.

Someone from Prussia was called Pruski by the Poles, Prusa by the Slovaks. A man from Rome was Rimsky to the Russians, Romansky or Romanenko to the Ukrainians, and Romanowski or Rzymski to the Poles. The person from Cracow was Krakowski or just Krakow to his Polish countrymen. The Lithuanian in Poland was Litvin. A person from Posen was Poznanski. To the Pole a man from Moscow was Moskwa; to his fellow Russians who met him, perhaps, in Siberia, he might be Moskvin or Moskovsky.

Many Slavic place names derive from pictorial business names. It is generally impossible, as I indicated earlier, to say that a person with a name meaning, say, ‹billy goat› (*Rus* Kosloff) got his name because he lived close to a sign depicting a billy goat, or because he resembled a goat, or because his occupation was selling billy goats. That is, is Kosloff a place name, a descriptor, or an occupational name? Regardless of which it is, the name itself shows that goats were well known in the naming period.

Pictures of birds often appeared on the signs. We have *CS* Pav to celebrate the peacock, *Rus* Orloff for the eagle, *Uk* Horobenko for the sparrow, *Pol* Sowa for the owl, and *Rus* or *Pol* Golub or a variant for the pigeon or dove. *CS* Cermak was from the sign of the robin or perhaps hopped about like a robin, *Uk* or *Pol* Kania got his name from the hawk, as did *Pol* Kopczyk, and *CS* or *Pol* Sokol or Sokolowski was named for either a hawk or a falcon. *CS* Kavka also owed his name to the hawk, as did *Pol* Galecki and *Rus* Vorona.

CS Capek had long legs like a stork. *Pol* Kukulka sounds somewhat like his namesake, the cuckoo. The wagtail, which keeps jerking its long tail up and down, apparently decorated the sign that gave *Pol* Pliszka his name. *Pol* Slowik or Slovick is associated with the nightingale, Ziemba with the grosbeak, Sikora with the titmouse, Sroka with the magpie, Szpak with the starling. A general name for ‹bird› is *Pol* Pta(c)k. *CS* Ptacek means ‹small bird›.

Animal names, which also may be either sign names or descriptors or sometimes occupational names, are fairly numerous. Perhaps the original *Pol* Zbik lived near a sign with the picture of a wildcat, or perhaps he was swift, graceful, but fierce. One wonders about the zebra—not a European animal—that gave *Pol* Zebrowski his name. Szczurek was associated with a small rat, Siwek with a gray horse. *Pol* Wilczak or a variant was a young wolf; *CS* Welk or the vowelless Vlk was a wolf, as was *Uk* Vovcenko. *CS* Liska or Lisak lived at the sign of the fox or possessed the proverbial craftiness of the fox; the same is true of *Pol* Liss or Lisicki. *Pol* Kozica or Kozicki honors the chamois, a goatlike antelope. *YS* Kunc, *CS* Zajicek, and *Pol* Zajac or Zajic memorialize long-defunct hares or rabbits. Perhaps *CS* Mroz or Mrosek had a mustache like that of the walrus whose name was given him. There was something reptilian about *Pol* Gadzinski. *Rus* Zablin and *Pol* Zabinski were named for the frog. *Pol* Pajak owed his name to the spider, *Pol* Biedrzycki to the ladybug. *Rus* Khrushchev was named for a large beetle, called *cockchafer* in English, which feeds on leaves and flowers.

The Slavic languages have hundreds of names that may describe physical qualities of their original holders or that may comment on their characters, personalities, or idiosyncrasies. Sometimes small peculiarities are singled out, as with *Uk* Hrajnoha, who kept time with the music by tapping his feet, or *Pol* Sebdza, who broke wind frequently and publicly enough to merit a name that focused on the characteristic. *Cz* Riha was renowned for belching. *Uk* Zyla had prominent veins, and *Rus* Skulsky was notable for high cheekbones.

Slavic people of the naming era were not at all reluctant to call attention to qualities generally considered less than desirable. *Pol* or *CS* Burda and *Pol* Warchol were characterized as pugnacious brawlers. *CS* Klimala habitually overslept. *Rus* Durkee was stupid, and *YS* Durkovic was the son of a stupid man. Several names described people as small and insignificant. Thus *Rus* Bloxin and *CS* Blecha were like fleas, and *Pol, Uk, Cz,* and *Rus* Mucha or Muchnick were as little and unimportant as flies. *Uk* Komarek was like a gnat. *Pol* or *Uk* Krych and *Pol* Kapka were nonentities. *Pol* Golik, Golinski, Liszewski, and Niszczak were once extremely poor and wretched, often dressed in rags. *Pol* Gnojek was considered filthy and nasty by those who named him. *Pol* Podraza was an agitator. *Pol* Baba (with many variant spellings) and *Rus* Babusch were considered old-womanish, lacking in masculinity. (A *babushka* is a scarf traditionally worn by elderly women.) We do not know whether *Pol* Babiarz and Gach, *Sl* Bobiar, and *YS* Babich, all of whom were extremely fond of the sexual favors of women, were regarded approvingly; perhaps approbation varied with the beholder.

Good qualities were also singled out, though. *CS* Hrdlicka was gentle and dovelike, and Hruby had a pleasantly low voice. *CS* and *Rus* Ruml was perhaps applauded as a teetotaler, a sober person, *CS* Radick was charitable, and Smyrl loved peace, as did *Pol* Godzicki, the conciliator. *Pol* Geniusz, as the name suggests even in English, was talented, and Glombicki and Madura were wise and learned (in contrast to the simpleton Plocharski). Spiewak or Spivack could sing well. *CS* Blaha and Stastny were happy or lucky or both. *Pol* Cnota was virtuous, *Uk* Lepchuk handsome. *YS* Bozic(k) served God.

Descriptors of coloration include names like *Pol* Czarnicki and *CS* Crnich, signifying ‹dark›, ‹brown›, ‹black›, ‹brunette›, and the like. People with light complexions or blond hair might be called Belofsky or Belofski in Russia or Poland, Bilek or Bilko or Bily in Czechoslovakia, Belinsky in Russia. *Pol* Czerwonka and sometimes Rudzinski had red hair and often a ruddy complexion; so did *Rus* Rudin.

Pol Drobny and *Rus* or *Pol* Malec, Malik, or Malenki was a small or thin person; *Rus* Malenkov means ‹son of the little man›. Among the names for fat people are *CS* Hladik and Masny, *Uk* Hlad(ko) or Waskey, and *Pol* Banasiak and Bobo(wski). The Polish name Krasner or Krasny suggests that avoirdupois was somewhat admired, since it may mean both ‹fat› and ‹handsome›.

Rus Lapin had big feet, *Pol* Homolka long legs, Kluka a big nose, Gembala a big mouth, and Glowa or *CS* Kotrba a big head. *Pol* Garb and *CS* Hrbacek were hunchbacks, *Pol* Kulinski was bent over, there was something unusual about *Pol* Noga's feet or legs, Kostka was crippled, Kolanko and

YS Koleno had bad knees. *Pol* Jakala stammered, and *Rus* or *Uk* Slipakoff was the son of the blind man. But *Sl* Krska had broad shoulders, *Pol* Figurski a handsome body. *Rus* Zelinsky favored green clothing, but Krashnoshtanoff was the son of a man who wore red pants.

In the United States all or nearly all these names exist, although sometimes in barely recognizable or imperfectly identifiable form. The great numbers of Slavic names depict life as it was in the Middle Ages in the Slavic countries, and today they add unusual variety and color to the long roll call of Americans.

25

THE LITHUANIANS AND THE LATVIANS:

From Persecution and from Famine

AN ANCIENT and proud people, the Lithuanians. Their land may be the ancestral home of the Indo-European language, which was the forerunner of most European and some Asian languages. Kenneth Katzner says, "It has been said that the speech of a Lithuanian peasant is the closest thing existing today to the speech of original Indo-Europeans."

In the Middle Ages the Grand Duchy of Lithuania reached from the Baltic Sea some six hundred miles south to the Black Sea and stretched eastward almost to Moscow. A Lithuanian king once occupied also the Polish throne.

The history of both Lithuania and Latvia, however, is as scrambled as that of the Balkans to the south. At various times Lithuania has been united with Poland, shared by the Prussians and Russians, occupied by Germany, and independent. The less populous Latvia has been controlled wholly or in part by Germany, Poland, Lithuania, Sweden, and Russia, and has been independent.

The hungry Russian bear gobbled up Lithuania late in the

eighteenth century. Not until the Russian internal struggles of 1918 could Lithuania again become independent. Independence did not last long. In 1940 the Soviets moved in and made the country—and Latvia and Estonia—Soviet Socialist Republics. The Germans occupied those countries from 1941 to 1944, killing most of the Jews—about 7 percent of Lithuania's population. Then the Russians took charge again.

As is true of so much of eastern Europe, shifts in rule and in boundaries make it impossible to be precise in citing immigration figures from Lithuania and Latvia, but we do know that comparatively few Latvians came to America. Lithuanians came in much greater numbers. One estimate has it that in 1929 there were 650,000 Americans of Lithuanian birth or descent. Chicago had the largest number, 100,000; New York, 30,000; Philadelphia, Pittsburgh, Detroit, and Boston-Cambridge, 12,000 to 15,000 each. For 1969, A. M. Budrelkis in *The Lithuanians in America* estimated the total at 1,650,000, most of them in the third to fifth generations, but that estimate is considerably higher than others.

A few Lithuanians came early. One of them, Dr. Alexander Cursier, taught Latin in New Amsterdam from 1659 to 1661. He is said to have been the first secondary-school-level teacher in America. A number of Lithuanian Protestants came to New Amsterdam in 1662, and in 1690 some Lithuanian Mennonites settled near Philadelphia.

For the most part, though, Lithuanian immigrants arrived in the late nineteenth century and early twentieth. However, in 1834 some 234 Lithuanians and Poles who had been engaging in one of their frequent and usually futile insurrections against the Russians were brought to America on an Austrian man-of-war. The Americans received hospitably and sympathetically people with odd, long names like Ablamavicius, Putramentas, Skorupsis, the Reverend Jezykowicz, called "the first Catholic priest to come from Lithuania," and all the others. They were granted land in Illinois.

Mid-century, a famine period in the Baltic area, found Petras Svotelis, a former priest, bringing a large group of Lithuanians to America, some to move onto New England farms, others into Shamokin and other places in Pennsylvania. In 1871 Danville, Pennsylvania, about fifty miles north of Harrisburg, had the largest Lithuanian colony in the United States. Lithuanian Lowlanders and some Letts began coming about 1880, especially to the coal fields of West Virginia and to the industrial plants of Boston and Philadelphia. The Chicago-area steel mills and the stockyards attracted many. By 1884 there were about fifteen thousand Lithuanians in the United States, and perhaps a thousand or so Letts. Lithuanian Jews began immigrating about 1885, usually to big cities.

Buffalo Bill Cody attempted unsuccessfully to persuade a number of Lithuanians to settle on his land in Wyoming in 1890. In general they preferred the East, but there are reports from 1906 that a small colony had been established in Los Angeles.

The work that they did was often strenuous and dangerous. One writer estimates that early in the century, when thousands were pouring in, fifty thousand of them were laboring in the anthracite regions of Pennsylvania, another twenty-five thousand in the soft coal mines of Pennsylvania and West Virginia.

Upton Sinclair, in his famous novel *The Jungle* (which led to the passing of a long-delayed, bitterly opposed Pure Food and Drug Act and a strengthened Beef Inspection Act), centered the story on Lithuanian Jurgis Rudkus, employed in Chicago's Packingtown. The descriptions of the work and the working conditions are not for the squeamish:

> [The boss] led him to the "killing beds." The work Jurgis was to do was very simple, and it took him but a few minutes to learn it. He was provided with a stiff besom, such as is used by street sweepers, and it was his place to follow down the line the man who drew out the smoking entrails from the carcass of the steer; this mass was to be swept into a trap, which was then closed, so that no one might slip into it. As Jurgis came in, the first cattle of the morning were just making their appearance, and so . . . he fell to work. It was a sweltering day in July, and the place ran with steaming hot blood—one waded in it on the floor. The stench was almost overpowering, but to Jurgis it was nothing. His whole soul

was dancing with joy—he was at work at last! He was paid the fabulous sum of seventeen and a half cents an hour. . . .

Many Lithuanians in America have shortened their names by chopping off the long tails. So Aleksandravicius has joined the many Alexanders from other backgrounds, Danilevicius has often become Daniel(s), and Markevicius is now probably Mark(s). As these examples suggest, *-vicius* is a frequent patronymic ending. Lithuanian names also often end in *-auskas* or *-aitis* or *-unas,* which may or may not be preserved in the United States. Kavalauskas (sometimes Kavaliauskas or Kavaliunas) was a smith, and Kalvaitis was the son of the smith. Kubilunas was a tub maker or cooper or his son; so was Kubilius. Krachaunas was a tailor. Katauskas raised cats. Koclanes was a tiler or roofer.

The name *John* appears in many Lithuanian patronymics, making the equivalent of Johnson one of the most common Lithuanian names. Ivanauskas means ‹son of John›, and so, approximately, do Janis, Jankauskas, Jankus, Janulis, Jonaitis, Jonas (which may also be Hebrew, Welsh, or English), Jonikas, Jonynas, Yanaitis, and Unitas (the name of one of professional football's all-time best quarterbacks). Simon is another Lithuanian favorite, and is represented by Shimkonas, Shimkus, Simaitis, and Simakaitis.

Other patronyms include Matulevicius or Maciulis (Matthew), Mickus (Demetrius), Ralis (Lawrence), Povilaitis (Paul), Petraitis or Petrauskas (Peter), Tumas or Tumasonis (Thomas), Vasilauskas (Basil), Grigaitis or Grigonis (Gregory), Adamaitis (Adam), Antanaitis (Anthony), and Balchunas, Balciunas, or Bartkus (Bartholomew).

Place names and descriptors are less frequent in Lithuanian than in many other languages. Examples include Svedas ‹someone from Sweden›, Lazauskas ‹one from the willow-place›, Dudas ‹trumpeter›, Kishkunas ‹like a hare›, and Gedraitis ‹calm, unflappable›.

Lettish surnames in general lack distinctive marks, although they frequently end in *s.* Thus Kaspars and Labrencis are patronyms for descendants of Kaspar and Lawrence, and the place name Kokinis (Kokinos, Kokkines) first meant ‹a person from the woods›. Among the slightly more than two million residents of modern Latvia, almost a third have Russian names.

After the Russians took over Lithuania in 1940, President Antanas Smetona fled to the United States, where he was welcomed cordially, especially by Mayor Edward Kelly, whose Chicago claimed more Lithuanians than any other city in the world except in Lithuania itself. After World War II about sixty thousand Lithuanians were classed as displaced persons, and approximately half of them came to the United States.

In 1970 the American people once more showed their friendship to Lithuanians. A seaman, Simas Kudirka, whose mother was American-born, defected from a Soviet trawler off Martha's Vineyard. Picked up by the U. S. Coast Guard *Vigilant,* he asked for political asylum. The Coast Guard consulted the State Department, which ordered him returned to the Soviets.

An eyewitness, Latvian-American Roberts M. Brieze, called the attention of the press, and public clamor followed, with mass demonstrations. As a result of the incident two Coast Guard officials were retired from service, and the United States formulated more precise regulations about political asylum.

As for Kudirka, the USSR sentenced him to ten years at hard labor. Lithuanian Americans and others kept up their efforts to free him. Finally in July 1974 United States courts ruled that because of his mother's place of birth Kudirka was an American citizen. The Soviets released him. A news story in 1980 said that he was living in the United States, hoping and working for a renewal of Lithuanian independence.

26

THE HUNGARIANS:

The Pedestal of the Statue of Liberty

IN PROPORTION to their numbers in this country, probably no nationality has contributed more to American civilization than the Hungarians.

A man named Tyrker may have been the first, although the name was more likely Turkish or possibly Slavic or German rather than Hungarian. He was foster father to Leif Eriksson and is described in the *Heimskringla* (a collection of Norse sagas) as "small in stature and ugly" but "dexterous in all feats." It was he who is reported to have first found grapes on the North American continent, leading to the name attached to it by Eriksson and his men—Vinland.

Hungarians, or Magyars as many would rather be called, were in some of the French and other contingents that fought on the revolutionary side in the American War of Independence. One Hungarian in that war, who became an officer, was Michael Kovats (perhaps an altered spelling of Kovacs ‹smith›). He had fought in the army of Frederick the Great in Prussia, was captured by Queen Maria Theresa's Austrian soldiers, somehow talked himself out of captivity, and hurried to America to fight for its freedom. Pulaski liked Kovats and made him a colonel. He was killed in 1779 in a battle with the British.

Two nineteenth-century Hungarian books, each with the same title, *Journey in North America,* really called the United States to the attention of the Hungarians, who throughout history have spent much of their time defending their land against unneighborly neighbors, and many of whom have longed for a more peaceful and prosperous existence. One of the books, published in 1831, was by Sandor Farkas ‹descendant of the wolf›.

In the other book (1844) Agoston Haraszthy wrote enthusiastically, "The boundless energy and self-assurance characterizing the American above all other nationals are truly breath-taking." He himself showed self-assurance by buying ten thousand acres of land in Wisconsin Territory, naming it Szeptaj ‹Belleview› but then changing that forbidding combination of letters to Haraszthy, not much better. Later it became Westfield and is now Sauk City, long regarded as a domicile for freethinkers and freethinking. (Two nationally prominent non-Hungarian novelists from Sauk City, Mark Schorer and August Derleth, have written about early days in that area.) Haraszthy opened a ferry, built a steamboat, started a restaurant and a school. His son went to California in 1850, where he introduced the Muscat Alexandrian grape and the Zinfandel, founded Buena Vista, extended the grape-growing industry to Napa and Alameda counties, and became state commissioner of viticulture and wrote a book about his specialty.

The books by Farkas and the elder Haraszthy opened America to Hungarians. By the Civil War, about four thousand of them were in the United States. Approximately eight hundred volunteered for war service, and of those about one hundred became officers, including two major generals and five brigadier generals.

After the Civil War, and especially after 1880, immigration increased further. "Meat, plenty of meat in America," returning Hungarians reported. In Hungary there was little meat, sometimes not even enough potatoes. The numbers of immigrants from Hungary are uncertain because Austria and Hungary were at that time united (to the distress of most Hungarians, who were treated as inferior partners), and the figures we have do not differentiate between Austrians and Hungarians. Emil Lengyel, who studied the matter, estimated that by World War I a total of 1.6 or 1.7 million had come here from Hungary but that many of these considered themselves Slovaks, Serbians, Croats, or something else rather than Hungarians. (A Slovak exclaimed, "The Magyars say we are Magyars, the Czechs that we are Czechs. But we are Slovaks!") Three-fourths of all these "Hungarians" were male, and two-thirds had been farmers. Here, however, they often got jobs in mines or tending blast furnaces, especially in Ohio, New York, New Jersey, and Pennsylvania, with smaller numbers in Illinois, Indiana, and West Virginia. By 1920 New York City claimed 76,000 Hungarians, Cleveland 42,000, and Chicago and Detroit not quite 15,000 each.

In a revealing paragraph Lengyel explains how the Hungarian (like other immigrants) learned to cope with an unfamiliar language:

> Gradually, the former Hungarian farmhand became an American miner. He began to pick up enough English—or the language that passed for English in that neighborhood—not to be dependent upon the sign language in his weekly expeditions to town. He talked quite glibly about the coming *pedá,* payday which he sometimes called *tajm,* time. One of his buddies was thinking of a *cséncs,* change to a *fektri,* factory job where he would join the *juni,* union. Another *damflo,* damned fellow was talking big about a *dzsamp,* jump to San Francisco. That *bodi,* body from *Makkishpot,* McKeesport said that he was working on an *incsáj,* engine of the *fanesz,* furnace for *bigárny* pig iron. He mixed his Hungarian with English words, using English terms with Hungarian endings. When he wanted to change cars, he said *"Cséncsolom a karét,"* and when he wanted to go upstairs he said: *"Muffolok optiszba."* He was understood and he understood others speaking the same language.

Americans did not yet know very much about adult education and teaching English as a second language (we still have much to learn). *The New Immigration* (1912), by Peter

Roberts, pictures a young Hungarian who went to school to learn to read English:

> In a New England town, a Hungarian, six feet tall and weighing two hundred pounds, was put in a combination desk, suitable for a child of twelve years, and the first primer given him to read. When a friend of mine visited that school, he saw the son of Hungary bending over his lesson, with his finger on the sentence, "Sophia had a little doll."

The names that the Hungarians brought with them often seemed strange to American ears. A number of them started with *Sz,* as did some Polish names. The original Szabo was a tailor, Szarek was an impoverished nobleman, Szewc a shoemaker (as was the Szewc from Poland), and Szucs a furrier. Szigeti—the name of a violinist famous in America, Josef Szigeti—originally came from one of the numerous places in Hungary with names ending in *-sziget* ‹island of›. Often the *Sz* beginnings were later altered in America to *S* or *Sh: Szasz* ‹one from Saxony›, for example, sometimes became Sass or Sacks.

Some sixteen thousand Americans now on Social Security rolls bear the name Nagy, Hungarian for ‹large, husky›, and nineteen thousand are named Horvath or Horvat ‹Croatian›. A number of Hungarian surnames are recognizable as patronyms, especially those derived from saints or other churchly figures: Andras is obviously Andrew, Endre less clearly so; Bartos is Bartholomew; Ferenc, Francis; Fodor, Theodore; Fulop, Philip; Gabor (a well-known family of Hungarian-American actresses), Gabriel; Gyorgi, George; Istvan, Stephen; Janosfi, Joseph; Karoly(i), Charles; Lorenc, Lawrence; Lukacs, Luke; Matyas, Matthew; Miklos or Mikulas, Nicholas; Mihaly, Michael; and Sandor, Alexander. Balint is barely identifiable as the beloved St. Valentine.

A few Hungarian names faintly resemble those in the cousin languages of Estonia and Finland, although differences are usually greater than the similarities. Hungarian Hegy ‹mountain› is reminiscent of Estonian Magi, Finnish Maki; Halasz ‹fisherman› is probably related to Estonian Kala. Many Hungarians, Finns, and Estonians are apparently aware of their linguistic relationship. Finnish-American Lillian Lahti has written me,

> Grace and I met an immigrant lady at the small church we attended. To make small talk, I asked her the name of her homeland. It was Hungary, and when I announced that my parents had emigrated from Finland, she threw her arms around me and said, "Cousin!" Before we left, Grace and I had an invitation to this lady's home for high tea. I believe she really saw me as kin, just because of this language relationship.

Some Hungarians have German names. Here the explanation is the centuries-old relations, sometimes friendly and sometimes not, with the German-speaking states, particularly Prussia and Austria.

Hungarian Kiss ‹small› is unrelated to English *kiss* but sometimes causes unwarranted amusement when it appears in an American newspaper or classroom. Zukor, the name of a movie producer who worked his way up from showing penny peep shows to making the first American full-length feature film, means ‹sugar›. The name Bartók, held by one of the world's leading composers, is, like Bartos, a variant of Bartholomew.

George Szell, a prominent American conductor, was born in Budapest. So was Leo Szilard, a pioneer in nuclear fission. Nobel Prize-winning Albert Szent-Györgi, biochemist who discovered the muscle protein called actin, pronounced his name sent-dyer-dee; he was a Budapest native originally named Albert Szent-Györgi von Nagyrapolt. In Hungary the surname is not the last name but the middle one. However, on moving to America almost all Hungarians make the necessary changes so that the surname is at the end. Szent-Györgi managed the change by merely dropping his final name.

Other famous Hungarian-American scientists include physicist Theodor von Karman, developer of a theory of turbulence; atomic physicist Edward Teller; and mathematician John Van Neumann. David Lilienthal successively chaired the Tennessee Valley Authority and the Atomic Energy Commission.

Music lovers know the names of Eugene Ormandy, Fritz Reiner, Sigmund Romberg, Zoltan Kodaly.

Jozsef Galamb helped Henry Ford on his early cars, and Twadar Puskas was a collaborator of Edison.

Among Hungarian-American artists are Zoltan Sepeshy, Laszlo Moholy-Nagy, and Willy Pogany.

Novelist Edna Ferber's parents were Hungarian immigrants. Hungarian but sometimes American Max Reinhardt became a leading stage director, and George Cukor directed movies. Paul Lukas was an actor, and the Dolly Sisters (born Rozsika and Jancsika Deutsch) were once adored by American theater audiences.

Lengyel devotes several pages to one of the most famous Hungarian Americans. He begins his account in this way:

> The town of Makó is famous for the grain and onions of the surrounding fertile Hungarian plains. Fulöp Politzer, known to the neighbors as "Red" Politzer because of his red hair, was famous for his success in the grain and onion trade. It was to Fulöp Politzer and Lujza Berger that Providence presented Jozsef who, under the name of Joseph Pulitzer, was destined to make history in the newspaper world of the United States.

Because of his frail body, Pulitzer was rejected for military service in Europe, but when he reached the United States in 1864 the recruiters did not hesitate to sign him up for the First New York Cavalry Regiment, which already had a number of Hungarians. He served under Generals Sheridan and Custer. On leaving service he went to St. Louis, studied day and night in the public library, and got a job on a German newspaper, *Westliche Post.* With the little money he had, he bought the newspaper to use as an agent of reform. At age twenty-two he was elected to the Missouri legislature, but his conservative colleagues were seldom sympathetic toward his reformist zeal.

In 1878 he purchased the financially ailing *St. Louis Dispatch* for one thousand dollars and a little later bought the *Post* and merged the two. He brought life and human interest to the *Post-Dispatch,* trying to dramatize ideas by depicting personalities. He insisted on what he called "active" headlines, and required of his writers the inverted pyramid organization so that readers could get the gist of a story in the first short paragraph. The motto displayed throughout the offices was "Accuracy, Terseness, Accuracy."

He had no fondness for most politicians, and they reciprocated his dislike. He bought the *New York World* from Jay Gould for $346,000, but he antagonized other rich men by advocating a tax on high incomes, attacking monopolies and high tariffs, and urging civil service reforms. But the people liked him, even electing him to a term in Congress, where he again found that he could not endure politicians.

In his will he left two million dollars for the founding of the Columbia University School of Journalism. His will also established the Pulitzer Prizes, which are still being awarded for essentially the original purpose: "the encouragement of public service, public morals, American literature, and the advancement of education."

He performed one other service, which in a way symbolizes what he and many of his countrymen and many other immigrants have done for America: he raised $280,000 to pay for the pedestal on which the Statue of Liberty still stands.

After World War II Russia took over Hungary, making a Communist country of a nation that had been sturdily non-Communist. The Hungarians revolted in 1956 but in bloody fighting were overcome by Soviet tanks and guns. Over 150,000 refugees managed to escape the country, a large number of them to the United States, where, it was reported, some wept when they saw a statue in the New York harbor.

27

THE GREEKS:

Mamma Pappas and Spiro T. Anagnostopoulos

IN *The Rise of the Unmeltable Ethnics,* Michael Novak counts most Greeks among the unmeltables but makes an exception of one of them:

> His father made the move from Anagnostopoulos to Agnew, and he himself went from Spiro to Ted, from Greek Orthodox to Episcopalian, from struggling young lawyer to builders' protegé, from a Greek neighborhood to suburban Loch Raven, from Democrat to Republican. Paul Sarbanes, the young Greek congressman [later a senator] from Baltimore, is partisan: "Agnew never did anything for the Greek community in Baltimore except leave it at the earliest opportunity."

He left it for the governorship of Maryland and then for the vice-presidency of the United States. Regardless of what one may think of Spiro T. Agnew, and despite a fall caused by reaching too far too fast, he typifies Greek ambition, independence, opportunism.

The Greeks of Atlanta in the 1920s, presumably, shared those same qualities. About half of them, breaking free from *padroni* much faster than most Italians did, unwilling to work for others, bought their own businesses there, even though they had first walked down the gangplank, some of them penniless, only five or ten years earlier.

And the Greeks of Tarpon Springs, Florida, owned the boats in a fishing fleet that, before hard times struck, may have brought in more sponges each year than any others in America's coastal waters. In Tarpon Springs, too, stood that symbol of so many hundreds of small business successes, the family-owned Greek restaurant. About twenty thousand Americans have the Greek name Pappas. One of them in Tarpon Springs was a woman whose restaurant—a leading one there—was long called Mamma Pappas'.

According to *Natives and Strangers,* edited by Dinnerstein, Nichols, and Reimers,

> By the 1920s [American Greeks] owned 2,000 restaurants, 150 grocery stores, several hundred shoe-shining and hat-cleaning parlors, and numerous flower shops. They dominated the manufacturing and sale of candy in Chicago, and were well represented in the sweets business throughout America.

Success didn't come easily to all. One group of 150 men in 1888 had been taken to eastern Quebec by *padroni.* But the company that employed them failed after a week, and they were stranded without food, without money, and with no language that could be understood by speakers of either French or English. They walked all the way to Maine, through deep woods. Maine people took up a collection for them and sent them on to Boston, where they established a Greek colony.

Others did manual labor in various American cities, carrying hods, cleaning streets, working on assembly lines. Only on very rare occasions did someone strike it very rich. Men named Lekas and Drivas in 1895 established an import firm, making use of acquaintances still in Greece. They imported black olives, olive oil, Greek cheese, liqueurs, dried fish, figs. In a few years they were grossing three million dollars annually. And some brothers named Stephanos in 1898 sent free cigarettes to officers in the Spanish-American War. The quality was so high that word soon spread, demand for the cigarettes was good, and the brothers, Greek peasants, became millionaires.

Only 77 Greeks came here between 1847 and 1864. But in 1891 a trend started, with 1,105 leaving Greece for economic reasons. The numbers grew. The biggest year was 1907, when 46,283 checked in at Ellis Island. Over the years some half million persons have come to this country from Greece, some of them since 1960. And in the past twenty years or so a hundred thousand men have left the isles of Greece to travel as seamen farther than Ulysses ever sailed. There are said to be more Greek sailors than of any other nation.

Some of the Greek immigrants, like many from elsewhere, say Dinnerstein and his coeditors, "looked outlandish with their [identification] tags, carrying bundles or straw suitcases," and with "their families' pool of silver coins sewed to their rough goatskin underclothing." But, "once in America they worked with the fervor of zealots." Because of natural increases, some two million Americans are now of Greek descent. Chicago alone has about one hundred thousand.

The reasons for so many departures from the historic islands have continued to be mainly but not exclusively economic. Only a quarter of Greece's 51,000 square miles (about equal to Florida's 54,000) can be tilled, and that small amount of arable land must feed a population that is relatively dense—currently about 170 persons per square mile. Except for bauxite and coal, Greece has few mineral resources. Most roads in the countryside are rough and narrow. The majority of the people are poor. Small changes in the economic policy of other nations can considerably affect a country with a marginal economy. For example, a new French tariff in the 1890s ended the market for Greek currants, and hundreds of currant growers in the Sparta and Tripolis areas had to move out.

In addition, wars and rumors of wars are almost constant in Greece. A feud with Turkey goes back for centuries and flares up intermittently. Civil disorders, even a savage civil war after World War II, and a frequently unstable government cause special pain to the many Greeks who love peace.

No American immigrants have ever brought with them a prouder heritage than the Greeks. To the ancient Athenians the Western world owes the genesis of a democratic tradition, the superb literature of Homer and the ancient dramatists, sculpture that is still unsurpassed, some of the world's most renowned architectural styles, many early contributions to the Christian faith, and philosophical creeds that are still widely studied in the world's universities.

Only now and then do modern Greek names reflect this past glory. Alexopoulos does recall the all-conquering Alexander the Great, now and then a modern Hermes brings to mind the messenger of the gods, and here and there Greek parents name a son Aristotle or Sophocles or recall the ancient goddess of harvest with the forename Dimitrious.

Patronyms abound among modern Greek surnames, often but not always signaled by the ending *-opoulos* ‹descendant of› or a variant. Here is a list of some of the patronyms, which are often church related.

Anagnos	‹descendant of the acolyte›
Anastos	‹descendant of Anastasius, "resurrection"›
Andros or Andrulis	‹Andrew's descendant›
Antonopoulos or Antos	‹Anthony's descendant›
Apostol (several variants)	‹descendant of an apostle›
Athanas (several variants)	‹descendant of Athanasius, "immortal"›
Demos or Demopoulos	‹son of Demosthenes or of Demetrius›
Diakoumis	‹descendant of little Jacob›
Eleftherios or Theodoropoulos (variants)	‹son of Theodore›
Fotopoulos	‹son of Photes, "light"›
Frangos	‹descendant of Frank›
Gavril (several variants)	‹descendant of Gabriel›

Georgakopoulos (variants)	‹descendant of George›
Gianakis (variants), Gianaras, Ioannides	‹John's descendant›
Karadimos, Karageorgis, Karagiannis, Karahalios	‹dark Demetrius, George, John, or Michael›
Konstantopoulos, Kostakes (variants), Kotsos	‹Constantine's descendant›
Marangopoulos	‹the carpenter's descendant›
Markopoulos	‹Mark's descendant›
Mikos	‹Michael's descendant›
Mitropoulos, Mitros	‹descendant of Demetrius›
Nicolopoulos	‹descendant of Nicholas›
Panos	‹descendant of Peter or of Panayotis, "of our Lady"›
Pavlatos	‹Paul's descendant›
Stavropoulos, Stephanos	‹Stephen's descendant›
Vasilakis	‹Basil's descendant›

Priests of the Greek Orthodox church, in which clerical celibacy is not required, during the naming period must have been very much revered or very fecund, as the many occurrences of Pappadopoulos or Pappas or other variants attest. Often the priest-father is honored by name. In one recent telephone directory I find Papachristopoulos, Papadimitriou, Papageorge, Papagiannis and Papagiannopoulos and Papaiannou (all three referring to John), Papakonstantinou, Papamichelis, Papandreu, Papanicoliaou, Papantoniou, Papanos, Papastefan, Papasthenasiou, Papavasiliou, and occasional variants.

Place names are rare among Greek surnames. One example is Kritikos ‹a person from Crete›. Occupational names are also infrequent, although Vla(c)hos, a fairly common name, was originally a shepherd, Poulakidas raised chickens, Korbas raised black goats, Argiris dealt in silver or worked with it, Daskal was a teacher, and a remote name-ancestor of the late singer Maria Callas coated the interior of pots and pans for a living. The name of Metaxas, who was the dictator of Greece from 1936 to 1941, means ‹silk dealer›.

Descriptives are somewhat more common. The name of the late shipping magnate Onassis means ‹useful›, Argos was light in coloration or perhaps had silver hair, Haritos was gracious and charming, Hondros was fat, Kara or Karras or Mavros was dark, Kontos was small, Kotsiakos was a brave man, Livanos had gray hair, Makris was tall, Rigas seemed regal, Xanthos had yellow hair, and Xenos or Xenakes (sometimes spelled with a Z in this country) was foreign born. Koulogeorge was one-armed George, and the ancestor of Koutsogiannis was lame John.

One of the great success stories in American business and entertainment is that of Spyros Panagiotes Skouras (1893–1971). Born in Greece. Emigrated to St. Louis (1910). Busboy. With brother George, bought a share in a theater, made it prosper. Served in World War I. By 1926 the Skouras brothers operated thirty-seven theaters in St. Louis, Indianapolis, Kansas City. Warner Brothers, then Paramount, put Spyros in charge of their operations. He helped form Twentieth Century-Fox, and became its president. Films of the studio include *Ox-Bow Incident, Miracle on 34th Street, All About Eve, South Pacific, The Diary of Anne Frank, The Robe,* hundreds more. The Greeks must have a word for such a man.

Part IV

FROM THE REST

OF THE WORLD

28

THE JEWS:

Toward the Promised Land

IN 1655 New Amsterdam's governor, Peter Stuyvesant, refused to allow Jews to serve in the community's small military force, despite the ordinarily open attitudes of the colony. He explained that in Holland

> . . . the said nation [the Jewish people] was not admitted or counted among the citizens, as regards trainbands [militia] or common citizens' guards, neither in the illustrious city of Amsterdam nor (to our knowledge) in any city in Netherland. But in order that the said nation may honestly be taxed for their freedom in that respect, it is directed by the director general and the Council, to prevent further discontent, that the aforesaid nation shall . . . remain exempt from the general training and guard duty, on condition that each male person over sixteen and under sixty years contribute sixty-five stivers [$1.30] every month.

Stuyvesant may have regretted his decision to reduce his garrison in this way. A few days after the proclamation, there was an Indian attack and several citizens were killed because the guard was not numerous and strong enough to protect the settlement.

Some Sephardic Jews who had been exiled from Spain in 1492 had fled to Holland. It may have been a few of their descendants who mingled with the Dutch, French, and other settlers of the short-lived New Amsterdam in the early seventeenth century. Other Jews, some Sephardic and some the usually less dark ones from farther north in Europe, soon crossed the ocean. Some came from Brazil, where they had gone from Spain and Portugal but had again been forced out by Portuguese who were settling numerously in Brazil. By the time of the American Revolution there were Jews in all thirteen of the colonies. Some had become very successful. Aaron Lopez (most Sephardic Jews had Spanish or Portuguese surnames) was a prominent merchant; his father-in-law, Jacob Rivera, reportedly manufactured the first whale-oil candles in America. Judah Monis, who in 1720 was the first Jew to receive a Harvard degree, later became a Harvard professor and the author of what seems to have been the first Hebrew grammar written in this country. Myer Myers (a German name rather than Sephardic) became prominent enough as a silversmith to become president of the Silversmiths' Society when Paul Revere was just learning the craft. Many Jews owned small businesses, and some had become wealthy enough to own ships used in international commerce. They established a synagogue in Newport, Rhode Island, in 1763, and other synagogues in large cities in about the same period. The 1790 census listed 139 Cohens or close variants plus a much larger number of Cains and others, some of whom were also probably Cohens. Today, some 118,000 Americans use the spelling Cohen, and another 25,000 Cohn or Kohn.

In general, Jewish people, so grievously persecuted elsewhere, were accorded full civil rights in America. For a while Maryland was an exception, denying Jews admission to the bar or to political office. Judge Henry M. Brackenridge (the name is Scottish for ‹one from the fenny ridge›) struck an eloquent blow for the repeal of this law in 1819, and it was finally taken from the books in 1825.

Sir, I have had the honor of being acquainted with a number of American Jews and do not hesitate to say that I have found at least an equal proportion of estimable individuals to that which might be expected in any other class of men. None, sir, appeared to me more zealously attached to the interests and happiness of our common country; the more so as it is the only one on earth they can call by that endearing name. None have more gallantly espoused its cause both in the late [War of 1812] and Revolutionary War; none feel a livelier sense of gratitude and affection for the mild and liberal institutions of this country, which not only allow them, publicly and freely, the enjoyment and exercise of their religion but also, with the exception of Maryland, have done away with all those odious civil and political discriminations by which they are elsewhere thrown into an inferior and degraded caste.

Many Jews were in the influx of Germans who came over during the nineteenth century. By 1880 there were eighty thousand Jews in New York City alone, a fair number of them already successful in business or the professions. About that time spokesmen for the Russian tsar expressed the wish to kill a third of that nation's Jews, drive out another third, and "convert the rest." A series of horrible pogroms followed, and families or even whole villages fled from the guns, the knives, and the arsonists' torches. Between 1881 and 1914 one and a half million Russian Jews reached America, along with half a million from Romania and what was then Austria-Hungary. "By the 1920s," says J. C. Furnas,

7 of 8 Jews in America were of Eastern European birth or immediate descent, and the proportion of Jews to Gentiles had risen . . . to some 3 in 100, mostly in large Northeastern cities, particularly New York City.

By 1924, about two million of New York City's population were Jewish. Since that time Sephardic Jews have arrived from Greece and Turkey, thousands of other Jews—including intellectuals like Albert Einstein in the dawn of Hitler's power—came here to escape the Nazis, and other displaced Jews arrived from other lands in the 1940s and later decades. Today between one-fifth and one-fourth of New York's residents are Jews—some 40 percent of the total Jews in the country. Add in the New York suburban areas and the portion rises to 50 percent. New York has a numerically larger Jewish population than any other city in the world has ever had. In contrast some parts of the nation have almost no Jews: a single rabbi serves most of southern South Dakota and even crosses the line into Minnesota.

Among the Jewish intellectuals who fled Hitler's threat was novelist Thomas Mann. I remember hearing him lecture —brilliantly—a tall, mustached, serious-looking man, wearing rimless eyeglasses, looking like a formal portrait of Woodrow Wilson. At the time I did not know of the drama involved in his flight. He had gone on vacation shortly after Hitler came into power. Knowing that his criticism of the Nazis endangered him, he stayed in Switzerland until 1937. The manuscript of the third volume of what is perhaps his most distinguished work, the tetralogy about the biblical Joseph, was left behind in Munich. His daugher Erika slipped back and in the dark of one night "stole" the manuscript and brought it to him. He finished it, *Joseph in Egypt,* in Switzerland, and it was published in Stockholm in 1936. In the United States after that (he became a U.S. citizen in 1944), he started *Joseph the Provider* while a lecturer at Princeton, finishing it and two more novels later.

Although both German and Eastern Jews have had distinguished careers in many fields, "Around the world," says Nathan Glazer,

> the Jews of Eastern Europe became in large proportions businessmen. Too, wherever they went, they showed a fierce passion to have their children educated and become professional. . . . Arriving with no money and few skills, beginning as workers or tiny tradesmen, they have achieved remarkable success.

Most of New York's major department stores, as well as spin-offs in other major and minor cities, bear Jewish names, the garment industry has long been controlled by Jews, and the proportion of blue-collar workers has steadily dwindled as more and more have moved into trade or the professions.

Once crowded a dozen people to a room in some of the worst American ghettoes, the Jewish people on the average have become more affluent than most Americans because of their hard work and their devotion to learning. Many have made reputations in music, the arts, philosophy, science, medicine, law, entertainment. Their competitiveness has helped some to develop physical averageness into athletic supremacy, but they are most likely to be found in intellectual pursuits. Half or more of New York City's teachers and about the same proportion of school administrators are now Jewish; the ratio of Jews in other professions, in New York and many other places, is much higher than one would expect from a mere 3 percent of the total American population.

According to tables compiled by Elsdon Smith and published in 1969, Smith was New York City's most common surname, but Cohen was in second place, with Schwartz in seventh, Levine in eighth, Friedman in tenth, Goldstein in eleventh, Levy in fifteenth, and Goldberg in sixteenth. In Boston, of the names from the same list only Cohen—in sixth place—made the top twenty, and in Chicago, Milwaukee, Minneapolis,and San Francisco no name commonly regarded as Jewish was in the first twenty. Today's Los Angeles phone book has only a page of Cohens, a half page of Levines.

For several reasons, though, it is difficult to make definitive classification of a name as Jewish:

1. The names of Sephardic Jews are usually the same as Spanish or Portuguese names. I have already mentioned the eighteenth-century merchant named Aaron Lopez. Another example is Benjamin Cardozo (the name of a place in Spain), who became a Supreme Court justice. In fact, if one traces the ancestry of a hundred holders of almost any Spanish or Portuguese surname, one may find from one to five who go back to Jewish forebears.
2. Some of America's early Jewish settlers and many who established themselves here in the nineteenth century came from Germany, where most of them had taken or been given German names not many years earlier. Although some of these names (Rosenblum, for instance, or Blumenthal, or Goldstein) are almost always Jewish, others

may not be. There are many German Schwartzes, for example, as well as many Jewish Schwartzes. Sometimes a Jewish family would take a name already used by thousands of Germans; Schmidt, for instance, is generally German but occasionally Jewish.

3. Names from eastern Europe pose special problems. Many of these are Slavic names. Some are versions of Old Testament names that may or may not be roughly the same as Slavic forms. Some are German or Yiddish names acquired in western Europe before the move to eastern Europe, or taken in America to make their holders seem more like the Meyers or Friedmans or Sachses who had already become successful. It is often impossible to tell for sure whether a person with a seemingly Jewish name—if he or she is Jewish at all—is from eastern or western Europe.
4. Some Jews from Greece, Turkey, or various parts of the Middle East may have names indistinguishable from those of their non-Jewish former countrymen. Lazar or a close variant, for instance, may be Hebrew or Syrian, as well as Russian, Ukrainian, or French.
5. A few Jewish names are actually acronyms. Thus Brock (which can also be an English name) stands for *B*en *R*abbi *K*alman; Brk, with a vowel sound added, becomes Brock. Zak, which sometimes is confused with Sack or Sachs, stands for *z*era *k*edoshim ‹the seed of martyrs›. Bran, when it is not a shortening of the English name Brand, may be an acronym of *B*en *R*abbi *N*achman. *Ben* is the equivalent of Arabic *Ibn* or English *-son*. For instance, Polish-born David Gruen moved to the Middle East and took the old Hebrew name David Ben-Gurion ‹David, son of Gurion›; he eventually became the first prime minister of the new nation Israel. Ben Rabbi Nachman should be understood as ‹son of Rabbi Nachman›.
6. Some genuine Hebrew names still exist among American Jews. Cohen, the most common Jewish name, means ‹priest›. Ephraim is nominally a descendant of the biblical Ephraim, Ephron means ‹like a fawn›, Halevy is a Levite, Hyman is a descendant of Hyam ‹life›, Joffe is handsome,

Jaffe may be a descendant of Japheth. Itzowitz is nominally descended from Isaac but seems to have wandered through Poland; Levi or Levy is the descendant of Jacob and Leah's son Levi; Odem or Odom—like all the rest of us, supposedly—traces his lineage back to Adam; and Yohana is our familiar friend Johnson.

7. Most confusing of all, large numbers of Jewish people have changed their names, sometimes more than once. I've already mentioned the Jewish-American Rosenheimers who, it is said, in successive generations became Rosenheim, Rosen, Rose, and Ross. Elsdon Smith tells a less probable story of an itinerant Jew born in Lithuania and called Bevelterpisser. In Germany he was Spritzwasser ‹squirtwater›, in France La Fontaine, in England Fountain, in America Waters; his son, inheriting the wealth his father had amassed, decided that Delawaters would sound better. Onomatists say that about half of America's Jews no longer have names that seem Jewish. I'll say more about changes of name in another chapter.

The story of Golda Meir tells us a little about Jewish names, much about Jewish determination. She was born Goldie Mabovitch in what is now Ukrainian USSR. When she was eight, she and her family joined the Russian Jews' great flight from fear to hope. In America she was educated in Milwaukee and married Morris Myerson. She and her husband emigrated to Palestine where, after some years, she helped to found Israel. At age fifty-eight she Hebraized her name to Meir ‹light› or by metaphor ‹scholarly›. At age seventy-one Mrs. Meir, daughter of Ukrainian Jewish peasants, became prime minister of Israel.

The total story of Jewish names is much too complex to be told in a few pages. Rabbi Benzion C. Kaganoff has told it well in a book of 250 pages, *A Dictionary of Jewish Names and Their History*. He explains that the seeds of the surnames may be found in the Bible and the Talmud, where those from places are foreshadowed in names like Uriah the Hittite and Todos of Rome, patronyms in those like Johanan ben

Zakkai, occupational names in those like Samuel the Astronomer, and descriptors in those like Abba Arekha ‹Abba the Tall›.

Kaganoff tells us that in the Middle Ages and up to the eighteenth or early nineteenth century most Jews still did not have official and unchanging surnames. But then most European countries made adoption of surnames compulsory. Part of the motive was humanitarian: to make half-nameless Jews seem less different from two-named Gentiles. But other motives existed, too: "The levying of taxes would be expedited by fixed surnames, and so would the conscription of Jewish soldiers."

In Germany,

> registering of names proved a new way of extorting money from Jews. Fine-sounding names derived from flowers and gems (Rosenthal, Lilienthal, Edelstein, Diamant, Saphir) came at a high price. Those who could not afford to pay were stuck with such German names as Schmalz ("grease"), . . . Ochsenschwantz ("ox tail"), . . . Eselkopf ("donkey's head").

When German Jews were allowed to choose their names freely, one method was to open the Bible at random and select the first name they saw.

> We know of one congregation that assembled in the synagogue at the direction of its rabbi, who then opened a prayer book and assigned the first word on the page to the first family, the following word to the second family, and so on.

Sometimes names were taken from literature, and in some German-dominated areas of Hungary Jews were split into four groups, to be named Weiss ‹white›, Schwartz ‹black›, Gross ‹large›, or Klein ‹small›.

Most often, though, those who could choose took something appropriate to the family heritage. It was generally considered an honor to have a priest (rabbi) in one's family, and so, says Kaganoff,

> Those who were descended from the priestly caste *(kohanim)* became Cohen, Kahn, Barkan ("son of Kahn"), and Katz (the latter an acronym for *kohen tzedek,* "priest of righteousness")—or, in

Slavic countries, where there was no "h" sound, Kogen, Kagan, and Kaplan (the last meaning "descended from priests").

Persons of Levitic heritage might show it by selecting Levy, Levin(e), Levinsky, Levitt, or Segal (from *seg*an *l*eviyyah ‹member of the Levites›).

Patronyms, too, were often selected: German Mendels(s)ohn, Slavic Mendelovitch, for example. Kaganoff's own name, obviously, means ‹son of the priest›. Matronyms, although much more rare, also existed: Sarassohn, Perlessohn ‹Sarah's son, Perl's son›. And, in homage to an adored wife—perhaps one who earned their living while he continued his rabbinical or other studies—a Jew might choose a name like Estermann or Perlmann ‹husband of Esther, husband of Perl›.

Occupational names were often the easiest choice. In that way many Jews became Kramer ‹merchant›, Goldschmidt ‹goldsmith›, Wechsler ‹money changer›, Kantor, Resnick ‹butcher›, Lehrer ‹teacher›, and the like.

Descriptives were not infrequent: Schnell ‹fast›, Gelber or Geller ‹yellow›, Graubart ‹gray beard›. And place names were fairly common: Dresner for the person from Dresden, Ginsberg or Ginzburg for one from a town of that name in Bavaria, Horwitz or Horowitz or Gurowitz for one from a mountain or from Horice or Horitz in Bohemia.

A couple of centuries later the Nazis used names to make Jews more easily identifiable by specifying which names were "officially Jewish." Any Jew whose name was not on that list was required to add Israel or Sarah to his or her name. France and Norway, while under Nazi control, passed similar laws. "Thus," says Kaganoff, "the hands on the clock of history and of civilization were turned back."

I have already suggested a few of the contributions of Jewish people to American life. A full list of the contributors could go on indefinitely. Instead of making even a selective list, I want to recall the kinds of difficult lives that these so often highly successful men and women or their parents or grandparents lived after they reached this "promised land," as Mary Antin, a Russian Jew who became a distinguished writer, called it. The following brief quotations are snippets from an informative, illustrated bookful of articles and news stories collected by Allon Schoener and entitled *Portal to America: The Lower East Side, 1870–1925.*

THE FIRST DAY "A train hurtling and panting along overhead produced a bewildering, a daunting effect on me. The active life of the great city made me feel like one abandoned in the midst of a jungle. Where were we to go? What were we to do?" (Abraham Cahan, *The Rise of David Levinsky*)

THE GHETTO "It is quite unnecessary to go to Europe in order to see a genuine Jewish ghetto. There is one, a large one, the largest in the New World, in fact, right here in New York. . . . The pavements along both sides of Hester Street are lined by a continuous double row of pushcarts." (The *New York Times,* November 14, 1897)

THE STREET "The ash cart comes along and takes what is in sight, and perhaps five minutes later some of these people will empty pail after pail of household ashes and garbage into the middle of the street." (The *New York Times,* July 30, 1893)

ROWDYISM "Orthodox Jews in the observance of the New Year ceremony were assaulted and mocked by gangs of ruffians along the river front." (*New York Tribune,* October 2, 1905)

PLAY IN THE STREET "[Asphalt pavements] add to the park area of that region, serving as they do as playgrounds for the children and breathing spaces for their parents. . . . When it is called to mind that a certain East Side block has 3,700 dwellers, it is easy to believe that these streets are crowded on summer evenings." (*New York Tribune,* July 5, 1896)

RUSH TO BE NATURALIZED "Both lines are made up, for the most part, of Russian Jews and Italians, though an occasional Irishman or German insisted upon his right to have an earlier hearing than an ordinary *dago.*" (*Evening Post,* August 7, 1900)

THE END OF THE SHADCHENS "[The matrimonial agent] is branching out into other ways of making a living. He writes letters for the illiterate, acts as interpreter in business transactions, or does odd jobs around the synagogues. Marriage brokerage used to be one of the best-paying businesses on the East Side, but that day has passed, and the *shadchens* think it will never return." (*New York Tribune,* September 30, 1900)

FRONT NAMES "A long-bearded pushcart man was asked in court recently, 'What is your name?'

" 'Yaikef Rabinowski,' he answered.

"The magistrate evidently thought that was the man's family name and asked, 'What's your Christian name?'

"The man became indignant at being suspected of anything 'Christian' about him, and 'front name' has been the proper expression at that seat of justice ever since." (*New York Tribune,* July 3, 1898)

LEARNING THE LANGUAGE "[After drill on 'I have a piece of chalk,' the teacher], patting the head of a little girl . . . asked her what part of the body it was. With a serious, almost sad, look the child faced the class, and tapping her curly locks she said, 'Dis ist my piece of head.' " (*New York Tribune,* September 16, 1906)

RIOT IN THE SCHOOLS "Rioting women and children by the thousand, swept into a senseless panic by an absurd story that children's throats were being cut by physicians in various East Side schools, swarmed down on those buildings all over the Lower East Side in great mobs yesterday, intent on rescuing their children and companions. Excitable, ignorant Jews, fearing Russian massacres here . . . outdid all previous resistance to vaccination." (*New York Tribune,* June 28, 1906)

THE RED LIGHT DISTRICT ". . . the big tenement houses in Chrystie, Allen, Stanton, and Forsyth Streets shelter crime in its worst form, and the inmates of these apartments contaminate their neighbors and create an atmosphere in which good morals cannot exist. For years these places have been known by the red lamps which shone in the windows or hallways." (*New York Tribune,* November 25, 1900)

WORK IN THE SWEATSHOPS "Miss Minnie Rosen, who is a young woman of the thinking kind, says that all the girls demand are living wages and fifty-nine hours work a week instead of the present system of one hundred eight hours work weekly on salaries ranging from $3 to $6 weekly." (*New York Tribune,* June 18, 1897)

29

THE ARABS AND THE TURKS:

The Man with the Red Fez

PULLED by an old brown horse, the enclosed wagon of the Lebanese peddler visited our midwestern village twice each year. Unlike the shabby wagons from which unbathed uncouths dispensed smelly fish or meat of questionable freshness, it was painted with lovely curving designs in yellow and brown and red and was lovingly wiped clean when the horse grazed. The peddler himself even on our dusty roads kept his face and hands almost immaculate by washing them at the pump in the town square and then rubbing them dry with a huge red bandanna with a yellow floral design.

He was short and dark and clean-shaven. He wore a red fez and blousy blue pantaloons like some I saw in my illustrated (and expurgated) edition of the *Arabian Nights.* His eyes darted but penetrated and were all-seeing. No one of us boys would have dared to try to swipe any of the gorgeously decorated pocketknives he sold from the back of the wagon.

He looked not at all like the sheik that Rudolf Valentino was portraying in those years, but there were rumors that

Ado Annies from neighboring towns found his physical charms no less alluring than the scarves, shawls, lacy underthings, kimonos, and pins and earrings with which he wooed from them their painfully saved half-dollars and dollars. His English was broken and hard to understand, but somehow he communicated easily with the teenaged girls and their slightly older married sisters and even the most impressionable of their mothers or grandmothers.

From my *Arabian Nights* I had learned of what I imagined his background to be. I saw oases set like emeralds on backdrops of endless sand. And I could envision tan cities with rounded mosques and slender minarets and camels and veiled women and turbaned men some of whom bore titles like muezzin or mullah or caliph. I wanted to be a caliph. I wanted to listen enchanted to unending tales told by my personal Scheherazade, who would look much like the dark-haired nine-year-old temptress who sat in front of me in school. Perhaps, I thought, the Lebanese peddler was a caliph in disguise, collecting girls like my Isabella for his harem.

The places of the exotic Near East had names of mystery: Araby. Persia. Samarkand. Baghdad. Damascus. Mecca. Morocco. Aleppo. ("Her husband's to Aleppo gone, master of the Tiger," a witch in *Macbeth* told me later.) The novels of P. C. Wrenn *(Beau Geste, Beau Sabreur, Beau Ideal)* and of Rafael Sabatini *(The Sea Hawk)* brought my fancies a little more up to date.

"The Syrians," Arabic historian Philip Hitti tells us, "discovered America in the latter part of the [eighteen] seventies, but the first Syrian to enter the United States was a Lebanese, Antonius-al-Bishallany, who landed in Boston in 1854." The first Syrian *family* was that of Joseph Arbeely of Damascus in 1878. Years later, when the Arbeely family picture was taken, someone placed beneath it this legend, *Ha ana wa-l-auwlad sa' idna bi-l-hurri-'yyah:* "The children and I have happily found liberty."

Spoken by about 120 million people, Arabic is the official language of Algeria, Bahrain, Egypt, Iraq, Jordan, Kuwait, Lebanon, Libya, Morocco, Oman, Qatar, Saudi Arabia,

Sudan, Syria, Tunisia, and Yemen. It is a Semitic language, closely related to Hebrew.

These facts about Arabs are less well known than they should be:

- Most Iranians are not Arabs. They are Persians and speak an Indo-European language, not Arabic.
- Not all Arabs are Muslims. About nine million of them are Christians, even though Presbyterian missionaries who tried to make converts as early as 1819 had little luck.
- For many centuries most Arab lands were the domains of scores or hundreds of chieftains or sheiks, some of whose descendants still maintain much authority and are often hostile toward one another. National regimes, like that of present-day Saudi Arabia, are often fragile because old tribal arguments have never been resolved.
- The ancient groupings named in the Old Testament or in college courses in ancient history have largely vanished. Hitti, a Syrian, says, "My first day in New York I met a lady who said to me, 'You are the first "Assyrian" I have ever seen.' I explained to her that the kingdom of the Assyrians was destroyed in 606 B.C., and so I could hardly claim any connection with them."

Of the Arabs who have come to the United States, the majority are Christian. They have settled especially in New York City, Detroit, and Boston, and in various smaller places in New York, Massachusetts, Pennsylvania, Ohio, Michigan, and other states—even Alabama and Texas. Detroit, with what may be the largest group, has about seventy thousand Arabic speakers. The Muslims among them settled first in central Detroit and Highland Park, where the earliest mosque in America was built in 1919 (it later became a church), but have since moved to South Dearborn. Chaldeans moved from the same area to north Detroit and Southfield. Arabs from Yemen have moved into Hamtramck, a largely Polish area. Some southern Lebanese and Palestinians are located almost in the shadow of the Ford Rouge plants. Iraqi names in Detroit include Assar, Essa, Hakim, Kory, Kaca, Losia, Orow, and Peter.

Barbara Aswad's *Arabic Speaking Communities in American Cities* contains this snatch of description of one Detroit neighborhood:

> The coffee shops with men standing around the entrances, the Islamic Mosque with Middle Eastern architecture, the many signs in Arabic, and swarthy appearance of the people and the frequency with which Arabic is heard . . .

Of the Christians, many have changed their names to more European-sounding ones. Thus in the Maronite community of Detroit, according to one study, 85 percent have altered the spelling or have translated. So among given names, Najib has become James; Boutros, Peter; and Suleiman, Solomon. A surname starting with *J* is likely to end up Jones, and an Abdoo may become an Abbott.

The Arabs who have maintained the Muslim beliefs—apparently fewer than 100,000 in the United States—tend to keep their Arabic names. Among those that occur with some frequency are these: Ali ‹descendant of Ali, "exalted"›; Fuad ‹descendant of Fuad, "heart"›; Hadjepetris (which can also be Greek) ‹a person named Peter who has made the *hajj* or *hadj* (pilgrimage to Mecca)›; Hajyousif, a similar person named Joseph; Hassan ‹descendant of Hassan, "beautiful"›; Mahdi ‹descendant of Mahdi, "guided by Allah"›; Musa ‹descendant of Moses, "saved from the water"›; Sharif ‹descendant of Moses through Hassan›; Suleiman ‹descendant of Solomon, "peaceful"›; Yahya ‹son of John›; and Yusuf ‹son of Joseph›.

In Arabic countries the prefix Ibn ‹son of› is often found as an indicator of a patronym; thus Musa Ibn Ibrahim is Moses the son of Abraham. In America this indicator is customarily dropped.

Comparatively few common Arabic names are not patronyms. Besides the occupational name for Smith, Had(d)ad, for whom I find two or three dozen listings in the phone books of Chicago, Los Angeles, and Manhattan, there are a less frequent Hakim ‹learned man; medical doctor›; Harrar ‹decorator of silk›; Khoury ‹priest›; Mallah ‹dealer in pepper or other spices›; Naggar ‹carpenter›.

Among descriptors, Habib was beloved, Khalof was an heir, Kahlil (as in Kahlil Gibran, the Syrian poet who spent the last two decades of his life in the United States) attracted true friends, and Maloof was famous. The place name Hammad was bestowed on someone who came from a stony part of the desert, and Jerico obviously hailed from biblical Jericho.

An estimated 75,000 to 100,000 American blacks have exchanged their names for Arabic names. According to Abdo Elkholy, these blacks only "call themselves Muslims." Some "twist [the Muslim] principle of equality to 'black supremacy.' " So Arab Muslims tend to dissociate themselves from Black Muslims and "consider them a great danger," Elkholy declares.

Although about 98 percent of Turks are Muslims, comparatively few of them are Arabs. Turks are basically an Asiatic people, with a language most closely related to Azerbaijani, spoken in parts of the Soviet Union and Iran, and Turkmen, spoken in the Turkmen SSR on the east side of the Caspian Sea. However, a considerable admixture of Arabic and Persian words has filtered into the language, including a number of personal names.

Until 1928 Turkey used the Arabic alphabet, but in that year its president, Kemal Atatürk, who also abolished harems, the veil, and the compulsory fez, dictated a change to the Roman alphabet, minus *q, w,* and *x*. Literacy rapidly increased from about 12 percent to the present 60 percent or more. Kemal also purged from the language as many Arabic and Persian words as he could, and he insisted that every person without a surname adopt one. The Turks thus were among the last people in the civilized world to take surnames. But Lambert and Pei commented that as late as 1960 ". . . the old custom persists [in Turkey] to the extent that a man with a name like Mahmud Kadoglu is seldom known as Mr. Kadoglu, but almost invariably as Mr. Mahmud."

Since Turkey remained chiefly Islamic in religion, and since many of the personal names referred to that religion, inevitably many Turkish names are similar to or identical with Arabic except for the alphabet in which they are written. So Turkish and Arabic Abdullah ‹servant to Allah› are pronounced essentially the same but look quite different because of the entirely dissimilar scripts. In American listings the Turkish and Arabic name would of course be identical. Among other names shared by the two languages are the following:

Aziz	‹descendant of Aziz, "beloved"›
Has(s)im	‹handsome› ‹kind›
Ibrahim	‹descendant of Abraham›
Iqbal	‹well-wisher›
Malik	‹descendant of the king› Also, in some Slavic languages, ‹the little man›
Muhammed	‹descendant of Muhammed›
Mustafa	‹descendant of Mustafa, "chosen"›

A frequent patronymic ending in Turkish is *-oglu*. So Demircloglu means ‹son of the smith›, Harunoglu ‹descendant of Aaron›, Sarkioglu ‹descendant of the singer›, and the variant Mansuroghu ‹son of Mansur, "the one helped by Allah"›.

Among names of occupations the Turks share with the Greeks Kazazis, who was a weaver or a seller of silk. Pas(h)a or Bashaw was a military officer or some other person of high rank, Shah a member of the king's household, and Suk a person who worked in or at least lived near a bazaar or marketplace.

Surnames from places are rather rare in Turkish, but Koprula lived close to a bridge, Deniz near the sea, and Yucel in a high place. Yalman, a name taken by some in the twentieth century, means ‹the very top of the mountain›.

Descriptors are fairly common. Akyuz means ‹a fair complexion›, Hujar ‹an emigrant›, Kadish ‹very religious›, Karambelas ‹dark catastrophe›, Malamud ‹jealous, envious›, and Serad ‹brave›.

About a third of a million Turks have entered the United States in the past century. Slightly more than half of these immigrants came from Turkey in Asia, which is thirty-three times as large as European Turkey. The peak years were

1913 and 1914, when Middle Eastern unrest drove a total of some 45,000 Turks to our shores.

The intensity of religious feeling of the devout Muslim, whether Turk or Arab, is difficult for the lukewarm among Christians to understand. "In 1885," says an elderly Muslim woman quoted by Elkholy,

> my father planned to accompany some Christian friends to America. He bought the ticket and boarded the boat. Shortly before sailing he asked the captain whether America had mosques. Told that it had none, he feared that America was *bilād kufr* [a land of unbelief]. He immediately got off the boat.

Not all, obviously, got off the boats. In Toledo, Ohio, one Syrian Muslim family entered the liquor business despite the Muslim ban on spirituous beverages. (It's apparently all right to sell but not to drink them.) The business prospered, and the family brought in relatives and friends who had settled in other states. In less than twenty years Muslims owned 127 of Toledo's 420 bars, besides liquor stores, carry-out stores, and restaurants with liquor licenses.

The Catholic Chaldeans in Detroit have specialized in grocery stores. Many other Detroit Arabs help to build automobiles. The father of Michael De Bakey ran a drugstore. Michael invented equipment and developed procedures used in open-heart surgery, and in 1963 first implanted a mechanical device into a person's chest to assist the heart's work.

Ralph Nader, son of Lebanese immigrants, graduated cum laude from Princeton's Woodrow Wilson School of Public Affairs and from Harvard Law School. He has made a career of protecting consumers against questionable practices of big business, big labor, and big government. A controversial figure often attacked in the press, Nader nevertheless has been given credit for effecting legislation designed to increase safety of automobiles, gas pipelines, coal mines, nuclear installations, pesticides, and food additives, among other things.

Elia Kazanjoglous was born in Constantinople (now Istanbul) to Greek parents in 1909. In the United States he shortened his name to Kazan and got into the theater, first as an actor, then as a director. Among his directorial successes on stage have been *The Skin of Our Teeth, One Touch of Venus, Deep Are the Roots, Death of a Salesman,* and a series of Tennessee Williams plays including *A Streetcar Named Desire*. He also won Oscars for film direction with *Gentleman's Agreement* and *On the Waterfront*.

Thousands of Arabs, especially from Syria and Lebanon, got their business starts in the United States with little conveyances like the one-horse wagon I knew in my boyhood. One of these became a well-known Arab-American author, Salom Rizk, an orphan from Ain Arab, who began as a peddler in a Model T Ford, selling rugs and tapestries.

Another Arab of less fame but no less merit was Michael A. Shadid, who by peddling in the 1890s saved up five thousand dollars to pay for his medical education. Near the end of his life he wrote,

> When I was peddling jewelry from door to door those first years in America, I saw a lot of America. And the more I saw of it, the more I loved it. But some things disturbed me. Here and there were injustice, oppression, and discrimination.

Dr. Shadid practiced medicine successfully and continued to save his money. Finally he had enough to set up the first cooperative hospital in the United States, in Elk City, Oklahoma, to provide inexpensive medical care. He said,

> I owed a debt to America for the opportunities she had given me, and I felt I ought to repay it in some concrete way. This hospital is part of my payment.

30

THE ARMENIANS:

My Name Is Aram Garoghlanian

WILLIAM SAROYAN, an Armenian-American writer with special pride in his heritage, had this to say in a prefatory note to his collection of short stories called *My Name Is Aram* (1937):

As far as I am able to tell, what this book is is the story of an Armenian boy named Aram Garoghlanian. I do not pretend that this story has any plot, and I hereby give fair warning that nothing extraordinary is going to happen in it.

The way to pronounce that name is to say *Gar,* pause, *oghlan,* slight pause, *ian.* The name is an Armenian name made of two Turkish words, *gar,* meaning dark or possibly black, and *oghlan,* meaning, unmistakably and without qualification, son; *ian,* meaning, naturally, of that tribe. In short Garoghlanian Aram, meaning Aram of the dark or black sons. Which may not be a matter of the very greatest importance to anybody this year, but may take on an appropriately modest importance later on. As to whether or not the writer himself is Aram Garoghlanian, the writer cannot very well say. He will, however, say that he is not, certainly, not Aram Garoghlanian.

With borders once extending from the Caspian Sea to the Black Sea and touching the Mediterranean, Armenia is a region perched perilously on the crossroads between Asia and Europe. As a result its boundaries have changed often as its neighbors fought over one piece and then another. At various times it has been ruled by Egyptians, other Arabs, Persians, Greeks, Turks, Mongols, and Russians. The Assyrians and Medes as well as the Persians of Old Testament times battled over it, it was on Alexander the Great's route of conquests, and it was occupied for a few years by the hordes of the legendarily cruel Tamerlaine.

Presently the highly progressive Armenian SSR occupies part of old eastern Armenia, and most of the rest of what was once Armenia lies in Turkey in Asia. Before World War I, conquering Turks massacred thousands of Armenians, and during the war they herded most of the others into the desert lands of Syria, where hundreds of thousands died. Some survived unbelievably arduous journeys and reached havens in Romania, Poland, France, the United States, or other countries.

In consequence of their troubles, the remaining Armenians are almost as scattered as the Jewish people. There are still an estimated 50,000 speakers of the language in Turkey, 3,500,000 in the Soviet Union, 150,000 each in Syria and Lebanon, 100,000 in Iran, and a small number in Iraq.

The Armenian language is a branch of Indo-European, but only a trained linguist can spot any similarities between it and such cousin-languages as English or Italian. Its alphabet, most of whose thirty-eight characters to the uninitiated look like peculiar *m*'s, *n*'s, *u*'s, *y*'s, and *h*'s, is not shared by any other people. It dates back to A.D. 400.

In the United States the Armenians have largely discarded their language and have learned that of their new home. It is estimated that about a quarter of a million of them are in this country, most prominently active in the selling of fine rugs, but also often successful in a variety of other businesses, in various crafts, and in banking. The struggles of their people have made some of them intensely competitive and therefore successful in athletics and coaching.

Perhaps, though, the two best-known Armenian Americans have been writer William Saroyan, whose "The Daring Young Man on the Flying Trapeze" first introduced his eccentric style in 1934 and who prolifically produced Armenianized stories, plays, articles, and movie scripts until his death in 1981; and abstract expressionist painter Arshile Gorky, born Vosdanig Manoog Adoian, whose paintings—those that survived a catastrophic fire in his studio—are displayed in leading museums of modern art.

Armenian surnames, after being changed to our Roman alphabet, are among the easiest to recognize, since with few exceptions they end in *-ian* ‹of the tribe of› or ‹descendant of›. In Saroyan and a few other names *y* is used instead of *i*. Most of the names are patronyms, but the ending is the same for other kinds of names.

Worshipers in the Eastern Orthodox faith, the Armenians have adopted some of the same names of church figures as the Slavs and most western European nations, although the spellings and their transliterations do of course differ. We can readily recognize Armenian Andreassian as Andrew, Grigorian and Kirkorian as Gregory, Simonian as Simon, and Stephanian as Stephen. Good guessers may equate Apelian with Abel, Atamian with Adam, Giragosian with George, Hagopian with Jacob, Hovsepian with Joseph, and Smulyan with Samuel. Boghosian or Bogosian is unrecognizable for Paul. Papazian ‹son of the priest› corresponds to the Greek Pappadopoulos. Kasparian, named for the Kaspar or Gaspar who was one of the Three Wise Men, is equated with Latvian Kaspars and Polish Kasperski, Kasprowicz, or several other variants.

Among the few Armenian names based on occupations, Nalbandian was the son of the man who shod horses—about like Smithson. Boyajian dyed cloth. Kazarian, a name similar to Greek and Turkish Kazazis, worked with silk.

Aram Khachaturian is frequently thought of as a Russian composer but was actually an Armenian trained in Moscow. His name, which has several other spellings, can be either a place name or a descriptive. The original holder of the name either lived near a cross or believed in the cross of Jesus.

Other place names include Kassabian, who lived in town; Izmirlian, from the Turkish town of Izmir; Zoolalian, who lived close to the clear water; and perhaps Tashjian, who may have lived near a large stone or been the son of Tash ‹stone›. Saroyan is a variation of Saro Khan ‹mountain prince›.

Armenians, some of them say, were born to trouble. But, to quote Aram Garoghlanian again, "One of these days, my uncle said, you'll see the loveliest garden in the world in this desert."

31

THE AFRICANS:

They Chose Their Own Names

1498 Pedro Alonzo Nino, called "el Negro" and believed by most historians to have been black, was one of the navigators for Christopher Columbus on his third voyage, and was associated with Christobal Guerra in the first successful commercial voyage a year later.

1513 Thirty blacks helped Balboa's expedition push across the Isthmus of Panama to the Pacific.

1540 A black left Hernando de Soto's expedition in Alabama and settled among the Indians—only the second non-Indian settler in that area.

1619 A Dutch ship brought a cargo of "twenty Negras" to Jamestown—the beginning of Negro history in English America.

1624 William Tucker was the first black child to be born and baptized in English-speaking America.

1645 Year of infamy. The *Rainbowe,* the first American slave ship, made its first voyage.

How did a young Negro feel when he or she was abducted from home and sold into slavery? Olaudah Equiano, subsequently named Gustavus Vasa after a Swedish king, late in the eighteenth century was captured by other blacks when he was eleven years old, sent on a long overland journey in which his "masters" changed repeatedly, and after six or seven months reached the seacoast. Years later he told the story:

> The first object which saluted my eyes when I arrived on the coast was the sea, and a slave ship, which was then riding at anchor and waiting for its cargo. These filled me with astonishment, which was soon converted into terror when I was carried on board. I was immediately handled and tossed up to see if I were sound by some of the crew; and I was now persuaded that I had gotten into a world of bad spirits, and that they were going to kill me. Their complexions, too, differing so much from ours, their long hair, and the language they spoke (which was very different from any I had ever heard) united to confirm me in this belief. Indeed, such were the horrors of my views and fears at the moment that, if 10,000 worlds had been my own, I would have freely parted with them all to have exchanged my condition with that of the meanest slave in my own country. When I looked around the ship, too, and saw a large furnace of copper boiling, and a multitude of black people of every description chained together, every one of their countenances expressing dejection and sorrow, I no longer doubted of my fate; and quite overpowered with horror and anguish, I fell motionless on the deck and fainted.

In Mexico the Spanish attempted with slight success to enslave Indians, some of whom were themselves slaveholders. The importation of blacks as slaves into Virginia did not proceed rapidly after the initial appearance in 1619. In the 1680s Virginia still had three times as many indentured servants as slaves.

With the increased popularity of tobacco, however, slave labor became more advantageous to planters, and the total in the colonies grew to 59,000 in 1714 and 263,000 in 1754. The invention of the cotton gin in 1793 widened the worldwide market for cotton, and by 1860 the number of slaves used in planting, picking, and other labor had passed 4 million. Most worked on southern plantations, but they were also present in a number of cities, and in the Narragansett region of Rhode Island, where they worked on the cattle-raising and horse-raising estates of the Hazards, the Updikes, and the Champlins. The southern owners included men like Virginia's Robert Carter, who owned a thousand slaves and 300,000 acres of land, and William Byrd, who founded Richmond and needed many slaves to till and care for his 179,000 acres. In general the plantation owners held relatively common English names, like Mason, Lee, Beverly, Harrison, or the aristocratic-sounding Fitzhugh.

Their black slaves were usually people who in Africa had been so unfortunate as to be captured by other blacks and sold to white slave traders. They came from many tribes, with many languages, and therefore often could not converse with one another. Neither in Africa nor in the United States until the Civil War did they ordinarily have surnames, but some of their one-word African names were shared by several tribes. Lorenzo Turner and others have shown, for instance, that Sambo was such a name, sometimes signifying ‹second son›, sometimes ‹disgrace›, sometimes something else. Some of the transported names indicated the day of the week on which the child was born (although certainly not all or many African tribes had a seven-day "week").

	MALE	FEMALE
Sunday	Quashee	Quasheba
Monday	Cudjo	Juba
Tuesday	Cubbenah	Beneba
Wednesday	Quaco, Kwaco	Cuba
Thursday	Quao	Abba
Friday	Cuffee, Cuffy	Pheba, Phibba
Saturday	Quami, Kwame	Mimba

Of these names, apparently Cudjo and Cuffee were used especially often on the plantations. According to William A. Stewart, Cuffee survives as an occasional surname today, but in the form Coffee, "referring to the color of the skin."

Elsdon Smith, however, says that Coffey or Coffee is an Irish name meaning ‹grandson of Cobhthach, "victorious"›.

1661 The first petition by a slave for his freedom, addressed to the governing body of New Netherland, was granted.

1668 Settlers in Germantown, Pennsylvania, made the first formal protest against slavery in this hemisphere.

1704 Elias Nau, a Frenchman, started the first school for blacks in New York City.

1712 Pennsylvania forebade the importation of slaves.

1720 Jupiter Hammon, who would be described as the first Negro American writer, was born in Africa.

1731 Benjamin Banneker, who would become a leading mathematician, astronomer, and compiler of more-accurate-than-normal almanacs, was born a free Negro near Baltimore.

1733 Samuel Sewall published the colonies' first antislavery tract, "The Selling of Joseph."

1745 Jean Baptiste Pointe Du Saible (or Du Sable), a Negro who would establish the trading post from which Chicago grew, was born in Haiti, of French and African parentage. (His wife would be an Indian of the Potawatomi tribe.)

1761 Phillis Wheatley, age eight, was brought to Boston on a slave ship. Her mistress, Mrs. John Wheatley, helped her to learn English, Latin, and Greek, and encouraged her writing of poetry; her first book appeared when she was twenty.

1770 (March 5). In Boston British soldiers shot into a crowd of taunting colonists. One of those killed was a black, Crispus Attucks, who was perhaps a runaway slave. He thus became one of the first, maybe the first, to die for American independence. Augustus St. Gaudens' statue of him stands in Boston Common.

No other group of newcomers to American shores ever so completely lost their native names as did the Africans. Many

Americans of Italian, German, Scandinavian, Chinese, or Japanese descent, among others, still reveal their heritage by their names, but very few blacks do. And when an Italian or a German has changed his or her name, the action has ordinarily been voluntary. But the black slave had no option.

Africans of the slavenapping era generally had but a single name. It tended to be based on something in the African environment, such as a kind of bird, animal, tree, or food, but sometimes it might be based on a common verb, such as Kea, which in the Bini language might mean ‹to remain›, ‹to open›, ‹to tie›, or ‹to look for fruit at the base of a tree›. Or the African name might be based on an adjective: the same Kea in Kongo meant ‹very small›, and Jola in Menda could mean ‹very tall›.

African names were generally not hereditary. Thus the son of Kanko (Hausa for ‹thyself›) would not be Kanko or the equivalent of Kanko-son, but might be called almost anything else.

What appears to be the same name usually had different meanings in various parts of Africa, and within the same language might carry several definitions (as of course is also true of some European names). As one example of varied African meanings consider Banna, a feminine name:

LANGUAGE	MEANINGS
Hausa	‹anything; this year; decay, destruction›
Efik	‹to dress, adorn; an ornament›
Kongo	‹that, those›

As another example, note the masculine name Cata:

LANGUAGE	MEANINGS
Mende	‹nut; a connecting wall; to confine; catfish›
Kongo	‹penis; to stretch or straighten out›
Hausa	‹anything; in daylight; a calabash, gourd; a salty cake›
Bangi	‹to grasp or hold›
Swahili	‹to carve, cut, cut down›
Ngombe	‹lizard›

On a single large plantation there could be a babel of tongues. Had all black slaves spoken a common language (other than the English they learned little by little), many more African words and African names might have survived in this country.

As it was, the captains and the crews of the slave ships did not want to bother to learn the names of any individuals within the masses huddled or sometimes shackled in the hold or on the deck. And once in their new homelands the slaves did not find their owners or overseers very eager to twist their tongues around strange-sounding names, some of which used phonemes not employed at all by the speakers of English, Dutch, Spanish, or French. And there was not much in common linguistically between the Mende to whom Cata might mean ‹nut› or ‹catfish› and the Ngombe to whom a similar-sounding name meant ‹lizard›. So Banna or Cata was likely to be called something else, and so were Cumba (Mende for ‹short skirt›), Foi (Efik for ‹strike›), Ketto (Hausa for ‹to make fire with a flint›), and all the rest.

One name was usually regarded as enough for a slave, although when two or more shared a name a distinguisher such as Big or Old or the name of a former owner or the place of purchase might be added. The names that the whites bestowed on "their" blacks were usually much the same as white given names. In a sample of 972 names of male black slaves collected from records extending from 1619 to 1799, Newbell Niles Puckett found that the following were most common:

Jack	(57)	Frank	(16)	Daniel	(8)	Cof	(6)
Tom	(47)	Charles	(15)	Simon	(8)	Francis	(6)
Harry	(34)	Joe	(14)	Abram	(7)	Joseph	(6)
Sam	(30)	Prince	(14)	Jacob	(7)	Pompey	(6)
Will	(23)	Ben	(12)	Lew	(7)	Isaac	(5)
Caesar	(21)	George	(12)	Sambo	(7)	Jupiter	(5)
Dick	(20)	Tam	(12)	Stephen	(7)	Ned	(5)
Peter	(20)	James	(11)	Thom	(7)	York	(5)
John	(18)	Piet	(9)	Andrew	(6)		
Robin	(18)	Cato	(8)	Bob	(6)		

Obviously, common English given names and nicknames predominate in this list, but with an admixture of possibly ironically used classical names (Caesar, Pompey, Jupiter). Cato is perhaps also classical, but may be a slightly altered version of the African Cata. Piet may be Dutch, Tam can be Dutch or Scottish, and Thom seems Scottish. The only almost unquestionably African names surviving in this list from the first 180 years of black slavery are Sambo and Cof.

When we look further down the list of 972 names, however, some additional but less-used names appear that are probably of African origin, among them these:

> Anque, Bamba, Batt, Bendo, Boomy, Boyyas, Bumbo, Burrah, Ciah, Commenie, Cub(b)ah, Cudah, Demmee, Ducko, Ebo Roben, Fait, Gato, Gumba, Jobah, Joo, Kinck, Lando, Mingo, Nease, Pinna, Qua, Quack, Quaco, Quam, Quamana, Quamina, Quamno, Quas, Quashoo, Quay, Roos, Sackoe, Sawney, Sem, Simbo, Sive, Tanoe, Taynay, Temba, Tomma, Wann, Warrah, Yamboo, Yaumah, and Yearie.

Common black female slave names from the same period also show scanty African survival. These are the most frequently used names in a group of 603:

Bet	(38)	Phillis	(14)	Dien	(8)	Jenny	(7)
Mary	(22)	Nan	(13)	Isabel	(8)	Maria	(6)
Jane	(18)	Peg	(12)	Judy	(8)	Nancy	(6)
Hanna	(16)	Sary	(12)	Lucy	(8)	Amy	(5)
Betty	(15)	Gin	(10)	Susan	(8)	Dine	(5)
Sarah	(15)	Gen	(9)	Grace	(7)		

The only ones of these that may conceivably be of African origin are Gin, Gen, and Dien, and even these are more than likely only variant spellings of Ginny (Virginia), Jennie, and Dinah, although there are a Swahili Ginci, a Bobanga Gena, and several Hausa or Mende feminine names from which Dien may have come. (Dien could also be Dutch.)

Later in the same list of black female names come the

following of African origin, most with only a single holder of the name:

> Abah, Abanna, Abb, Alyema, Ambo, Annika, Bat, Battah, Bayna, Be(c)k, Bilah, Binah, Comba, Cumba, Demeca, Dibb, Durah, Farih, Farry, Fassiah, Janna, Juba, Kauchee, Kea, Kouba, Libe, Loos, Mally, Mila, Mima, Minda, Roos, Sena, Simboh, Sooh, Tiller

In *American Negro: His History and Literature* (1855) William C. Nell preserved a list of Free Black Patriots, a group whose names appeared in Revolutionary War days on the payroll of the 4th Connecticut Regiment. This is one of the first extended lists of black surnames in America, and presumably represents names chosen voluntarily by these eighteenth-century former slaves. Among the 117 names only these appear two or more times:

Freeman	(7)	Rogers	(3)	Jackson	(2)	Rhodes	(2)
Johnson	(4)	Ball	(2)	Liberty	(2)	Vassall	(2)
Brown	(3)	Caesar	(2)	Phillips	(2)	Williams	(2)
Greene	(3)						

The reason for the high regard for Freeman and Liberty is obvious, but Vassall is puzzling. Caesar, a name frequently bestowed by slaveholders, survived (and is still found occasionally among both blacks and whites, for instance the comedian who works as Sid Caesar). The other names in this group are common English surnames.

In the total Revolutionary War Connecticut list the African name Cuff appears once, and the interesting derivative Mc Cuff is also included. Surviving first names that are probably African are Cuff (3), and Juba, Juber, Congo, and Mingo, all of which since that time have become very rare in America.

1775 (June 17). Negro soldiers were among those who fought in the battle of Bunker Hill. Peter Salem is remembered especially, because he mortally wounded Major John Pitcairn, in command of the British troops.

(November 7). Lord Dunmore, the royal governor of Virginia, offered freedom to all male slaves who became British soldiers. This action forced Washington to request a change in a resolution of the Continental Congress to bar blacks from the revolutionary forces.

1776 (February 28). Washington invited Phillis Wheatley to visit his headquarters to receive thanks for her poetry.

(July 4). The Declaration of Independence failed to denounce the slave trade, although that had been one of the original grievances against the crown.

(December 25). Prince Whipple and Oliver Cromwell, Negroes, were with Washington in the historic crossing of the Delaware.

1778 Four hundred Negroes withstood a British force of fifteen hundred in the Battle of Rhode Island. (In all, over three thousand black soldiers fought in the Revolutionary War.)

1779 Spying by Pompey, a black soldier, contributed to Anthony Wayne's victory at Stony Point.

1797? Sojourner Truth (legally Isabella Van Wagener, after one of her owners) was born. She would become a leading abolitionist and advocate of female suffrage. President Lincoln made her a counselor to freedmen in Washington.

1806 Norbert Rillieux was born in New Orleans. His invention of a vacuum pan would revolutionize the manufacture of sugar.

1807 Ira F. Aldridge, who in Europe would become the best-known Shakespearean actor of his time, was born in New York City.

1834 Henry Blair patented a corn harvester—the first black known to have received a patent.

1844 James Beckwourth discovered Beckwourth Pass through the coast range to the Pacific.

1847 William Leidesdorff launched the first steamboat in San Francisco Bay. Later he built the town's first hotel.

1856 Booker T. Washington, who would found Tuskegee Institute, was born. In 1896 he would tell a white audience at Harvard, "No member of your race in any part of our country can harm the meanest member of mine, without the proudest and bluest blood in Massachusetts being degraded. . . . There is no escape—man drags man down, or man lifts man up."

1861 (April 10). Robert Smalls, a Negro pilot, watching preparations for the attack on Fort Sumter, said, "This, boys, is the dawn of freedom for our race." A year later he seized an armed Confederate steamer, the *Planter,* sailed her out of the Charleston harbor, and presented her to the United States Navy.

Some 3 percent of male blacks in the South retained, or perhaps readopted, African forenames after obtaining their freedom. A list of 645 names of freedmen, mostly from the 1790 census, includes 5 persons named Mingo, 3 named Cuff, and 1 each Caffee, Cock, Coffee, Congo, Cuffee, Cuffy, Goffe, Hamutt, Kitt, Mial, Nace, Quash, Razin, and Samboe. A corresponding group of 406 free female Southern blacks shows 3 persons named Binah, 2 Siller, and 1 each Affee, Becae, Bek, Conney, Conny, Ege, Ibby, Manzey, Murriah, Sibb, Tene, and Tinah. Most of these probably look back to Africa, although Conn(e)y, Murriah, and Tinah are dubious. None of these African names compare in popularity with Sarah (24), Hannah (19), Rach(a)el (19), or Mary (12).

In areas of America where French or Spanish was the usual language, names from that language were for obvious reasons given to the slaves. Thus among 106 Louisiana slave names before 1800, there were 6 persons named Francisco, 5 named Francis, 5 Jean, 4 Manon, 3 each Maria, Naneta, Pedro, and Pierre, and 2 each Antonio, Arsene, Charlot, Delphine, Isabella, Juana, Junon, Leon, Magdalena, Mariana, Marie Louise, Nicholas, and Rosette, with single instances of many such names as Alphonse, Angelique, Calais, Carlos, Celeste, Eugenie, Gil La Rose, Helene, Jacques, Modeste, Petit Jean, Pierrot, Reynaldo, and Therese.

In the United States of the nineteenth century the number of freed slaves or their descendants steadily increased, and so, of course, did the number of their surnames, since probably every freed person was eager to adopt a second name as one of the symbols of his or her new status. In addition, forenames were often more formal than the nicknames widely used by owners and overseers. Ben tended to change his name to Benjamin, Will to William, Dick to Richard, Tom to Thomas, and so on. Jack, the most common slave name in the eighteenth century, was not in the top ten among nineteenth-century freedmen, nor did the short forms Tom, Sam, Will, or Dick (all in the top seven before 1800) appear in the top ten on the freedmen's list.

Among women's given names, Elizabeth gained most noticeably from freedom, rising from thirty-eighth place to seventh, far outstripping the once popular Bet. Nancy and Mary were the new first and second-place names among black women. Betsy and Eliza also grew in popularity, as did Sally and Polly and Patsy. Maria, Harriet, Matilda, Louise, and Caroline fell decidedly, as did Dinah.

In choosing surnames, freed blacks tended to be very conservative and to adopt a name held by many whites. In consequence, Jones emerged as the most common name for blacks before the Civil War. In order, the top twenty-five names were as follows:

1. Jones	(1)	10. Williams	(3)	18. Moore	(5)
2. Scott	(60)	11. Evans	(20)	19. Morris	(67)
3. Johnson	(9)	12. Mitchell	(19)	20. Lewis	(33)
4. Smith	(2)	13. Freeman	(100+)	21. Green	(40)
5. Brown	(7)	14. Hill	(6)	22. James	(77)
6. Jackson	(26)	15. White	(23)	23. Stewart	(47)
7. Harris	(11)	16. Collins	(60)	24. David	(4)
8. Wilson	(24)	17. Anderson	(51)	25. Martin	(16)
9. Carter	(10)				

The numbers in parentheses in the preceding list show the rank of the same name among the white surnames of the period, according to Puckett's statistics. The similarity between the white names and those voluntarily chosen by the freed blacks is of particular interest but is not surprising. By the time freedom came to substantial numbers of blacks, they had lost most of their African language, had forgotten most of its names, and had learned to a considerable extent the language, names, and customs of America. It was customary for Americans to bear such unremarkable names as Jones, Smith, or Harris, so the freed blacks, wanting to conform and to be assimilated to the greatest degree possible, frequently chose the names most conventional in what to them was their new home. In a study that Puckett made of still another group of freed blacks—a list compiled in 1830—not one of the 600 most common names was of African origin.

The practice of taking Ol' Massa's name as one's own did exist, but perhaps not to the extent that is generally believed. Before freedom, a black belonging, say, to Mitchell, might be identified as Mitchell's Jack and sometimes as Jack Mitchell to differentiate him from Moore's Jack or Jack Moore. Puckett adds these examples:

> Thus Matilda Davis was the slave of Thomas Davis (Kentucky, 1855), William Isaac Rawlings (Tennessee, 1837) was the son of his master Isaac Rawlings by a slave mother, and Isaac of Cowling (Virginia, 1800) belonged to Thomas Cowling. In the cases of Jane Harper, owned by a Mr. Wallis, and of Mary Harry, owned by the McCants, the surname was probably that of a former owner. In some instances, a double name may have been amalgamated into a single one by an owner or overseer. Thus Jimboon (Mississippi, 1840) might originally have been Jim Boone.

However, since masters were by no means universally loved or even admired or respected, many newly freed slaves preferred almost any other name to that of the former owner. On one plantation, owned by a man named Jones, only one freed slave chose that name. The others, whatever their individual reasons, took the names Brown, Jackson, Quinton, Nellicliff, Thompson, Wallace, Marshall, Howard, Verdier, Golphine, Ash, Yeomans, Baker, Goodwin, and Pinckney.

Following the Emancipation Proclamation (1863) some four million ex-slaves adopted surnames. A number of lists are available to show what names they chose, and most of them show the same names, although the rank orders vary somewhat. As the decades passed, the names remained much the same, and never differed greatly from those of the whites, as these records (based on several of Puckett's tables for Augusta, Georgia) show:

Surnames in Augusta, Georgia

	AUGUSTA'S BLACK SURNAMES				**AUGUSTA'S WHITE SURNAMES**	
	1877	**1899**	**1919**	**1937**	**1877**	**1937**
1.	Williams	Williams	Williams	Williams	Smith	Smith
2.	Jones	Johnson	Jones	Jones	Williams	Johnson
3.	Johnson	Jones	Johnson	Johnson	Johnson	Jones
4.	Smith	Brown	Brown	Brown	Jones	Williams
5.	Jackson	Smith	Jackson	Smith	Brown	Davis
6.	Thomas	Jackson	Smith	Jackson	Davis	Brown
7.	Brown	Thomas	Thomas	Thomas	Moore	Thompson
8.	Walker	Walker	Walker	Walker	Thompson	Anderson
9.	Davis	Davis	Harris	Green	Miller	Clark
10.	Green	Harris	Davis	Davis	Hill	Wilson
11.	Robinson	Robinson	Robinson	Harris	Walker	Hall
12.	Scott	Green	Green	White	Baker	Moore
13.	Harris	Scott	Scott	Scott	Clark	Howard
14.	Turner	Wright	Glover	Washington	Wilson	Adams
15.	Anderson	White	Butler	Evans	Parker	Walker

It is remarkable that all ten of the top black surnames of Augusta were the same in 1937 as in 1877, although the order differs slightly. Six of the top ten white surnames are also among the top ten black names.

Names of Montgomery, Alabama, blacks in 1933 and of Pine Bluff, Arkansas, blacks in 1936 repeat most of the Augusta surnames, although Taylor—inexplicably missing in

Augusta's top twenty-five—ranks high in both, and there are a few other minor differences.

1872 Poet Paul Laurence Dunbar was born.

1873 The "father of the blues," W. C. Handy, was born.

1876 E. M. Bannister, a black painter, won first prize at the Philadelphia Centennial Exposition.

1883 Jan E. Matzeliger invented a shoe-lasting machine that completely changed the process of shoe manufacturing.

1893 A black surgeon, Dr. Daniel Hale Williams, performed the world's first successful heart operation in Chicago.

1904 Charles R. Drew was born. He would develop an efficient way to store blood plasma in blood banks. He thus saved countless lives in World War II, Korea, and Vietnam.

1914 George Washington Carver led in revising and reviving southern agriculture through finding new uses and markets for peanuts, sweet potatoes, and soybeans and growing those instead of further exhausting the land by relying on cotton.

1929 Martin Luther King was born. Before his assassination in 1968 he would lead his people in nonviolent yet strong opposition to injustice.

1941 (December 7). Dorie Miller, a messman on the USS *Arizona,* during the attack on Pearl Harbor manned a machine gun and shot down four attacking Japanese planes. He typifies the heroism of numberless black service personnel in America's twentieth-century wars.

1954–1964 A series of court decisions and legislative acts brought about the greatest progress yet toward assuring civil rights for black Americans and other minority groups.

1961 Henry Lewis became the conductor of the Los Angeles Philharmonic Orchestra, the first black to be the regular conductor of a major symphony orchestra.

Soprano Leontyne Price was the first black to open the season of New York's Metropolitan Opera in the leading role.

In the 1930s Puckett collected from the directories of twenty-seven predominantly black colleges the names of their students, wanting to see whether the names of these more highly educated blacks differed greatly from the rest. The list of most common black college surnames looks like a replay of the Augusta list and many others that Puckett collected. The first ten spots were held, in order, by Johnson, Williams, Jones, Smith, Brown, Jackson, Davis, Robinson, Harris, and Taylor.

In World War II many blacks advanced to positions of military leadership, and thousands more served honorably as both privates and NCOs. The war expanded black horizons, and positive improvements in black education and a large amount of federal, state, and local legislation led toward greater equality. In business and industry, and most conspicuously in entertainment and professional athletics, blacks gained prominence and financial success.

Blacks steadily became more outspoken, and many were more openly resentful of the treatment that their ancestors (and to a smaller extent they themselves) had received from people with white skins. A minority of blacks wanted to divorce themselves as fully as possible from anything that suggested a resemblance to Whitey. Names like Williams, Johnson, or Smith were, to those few at least, constant reminders of a heritage they did not consider their own.

A privately printed pamphlet, copyrighted in 1972 by the Pan African Students Organization, was called *What Is Your African Name?* It was written by persons identifying themselves as Kamuyu-wa-Kangéthe and Maina-wa-Kinyatti. In a foreword Odinga Odinga said:

> My slave-master's name was Allen. To be proud of this name is to be proud of the traditions and culture through which it was received. To honor this name is to honor the rapes of my mothers and the beastly lynchings of my fathers. . . .

In my case, I forsake the name "Allen." In one sense this is hard—for thusly I have been called, and I am proud of the people who have borne this name for the past three generations. In another sense it is easy, for the name was never mine in the first place.

The pamphlet lists some three hundred to four hundred names from various parts of Africa, with their meanings. A few examples:

Ethiopia	*Men*	Tesfay "hope"; Haile "strength, powerful"
	Women	Netfa "free woman"; Almaz "beautiful free diamond"
United Arab Republic	*Men*	Amir "prince"; Asifa "storm"; Kamal "a together man"
	Women	Amir "princess"; Hana "happiness"; Amal "hopeful"
West Africa	*Men*	Sele "elephant"; Ola "noble man"; Nyagwa "ruler"
	Women	Menjuiwe "the trustworthy"; Jawole "clear water"
East Africa	*Men*	Magaidi "guerrilla fighter"; Jomo "burning spear"
	Women	Kirabo "gift"; Amina "the peaceful one"
South Africa	*Men*	Soma "king"; Sawandi "the founder"
	Women	Bukẹka "the pretty one"; Sonesu "what wrong have we done"

The pamphlet authors urge, "Claim your Africanity and ancestry by taking two names. Do the same with your entire family." There is no hint as to whether one of the names should be a surname and thus hereditary. For a strict return to earlier African customs it should not. For preservation of a family's heritage and a nation's records, it should.

A small but often conspicuous group of blacks have indeed changed their names to African ones, although few of them have been able to discover what names their ancestors were known by before they arrived in America. One well-known exception is Alex Haley, whose *Roots* was a publishing and television sensation of the 1970s, and who recounted in detail his successful search for his own slave and African ancestors. Haley probably did more to arouse interest in genealogy—among whites as well as blacks—than anyone else has ever done. He did not, however, take an African name, but stuck with Haley, an English name meaning ‹one who lives along the way to the manor house or hall›.

Among prominent blacks who did change their names were such athletes as Cassius Clay, a heavyweight champion boxer, and Lew Alcindor, a star college and professional basketball player. Clay became Muhammad Ali, and Alcindor chose the name Kareem Abdul-Jabbar. Jackie Robinson, however, who broke the color line in big-league baseball, did not change his name, nor did Wilt Chamberlain or Bill Russell, black basketball players of Alcindor's caliber. Neither did most other black athletes. Members of the Black Muslim religious sect often adopted Arabic names.

One of the women who adopted an African name was Paulette Williams, daughter of an American surgeon and a professor of early-childhood development; she became a black-nationalist advocate and, after she changed her name to Ntozake Shange, author of and actress in the long-running Broadway play *For Colored Girls Who Have Considered Suicide —When the Rainbow Is Enuf,* "made up of poetry, music, dancing, and light," the *New Yorker* said.

Probably not many blacks even contemplate a name change, and those who do may adduce arguments on both sides. An African name would give a black a sense of identity with others of his or her race and—if one's accomplishment was considerable—would call attention to what a black had done. But the multiplicity of African languages might make it difficult to ascertain a name that would be authentic for one's own use. Also, by accentuating differences between blacks and whites, African names in large numbers in America might contribute to increased tensions and retard progress toward harmony and true integration. Name barriers, like all language barriers, can cause friction, as English- and French-speaking Canadians illustrate each day. In a society in which whites outnumber blacks five to one, an odd-sounding name can add to a black person's handicap. Many Poles, once faced with opposition because of their own odd-sounding names, chose those that the majority of Americans could pronounce and feel at home with. For a black, the choice between a name like Henry Jones and one like Lango Miak can be a difficult one.

32

THE CHINESE AND THE INDOCHINESE:

"On to Kum Shan!"

WHEN the United States Bureau of Immigration began its reports in 1820, it recorded the first Chinese immigrant—just one for the whole year. Five years later there was another, and there were no more than seven in any other year until gold was discovered in California.

Word of the strike reached China early and caused much excitement. "On to Kum Shan!" became the cry, especially in Kwangtung province in southeast China, of which Canton is the chief city and the capital. A Hong Kong ticket broker circulated widely in Kwangtung a leaflet for those who could read. It said in part,

> Americans are very rich people. They want the Chinaman to come and will make him welcome. There will be big pay, large houses, and food and clothing of the finest description. . . . It is a nice country, without mandarins or soldiers. All alike, big man no larger than little man. There are a great many Chinamen there now. . . .

Forty smallish vessels left Hong Kong for California in 1850. By some estimates 25,000 Chinese immigrants had reached there by the end of 1851. Most of them expected to return to their families in China, and many indeed did so; half or more were married.

Alexander McLeod, in *Pigtails and Gold Dust,* has described how these small men looked to the often burly white prospectors:

> [The Chinese man] was usually seen hurrying along in a funny kind of dog trot, bending his knees very much under enormous loads which he usually carried in two baskets at each end of a pole over his shoulder. . . . The skin of his head seemed always to be pulled so tight by his queue that he could hardly wink his eyes.

The Hong Kong broker's circular, the Chinese found, had not been truthful. Not nearly all Americans were rich. The "big pay" was only whatever a person could scrounge to get. The "large house" was often only a dingy little room, frequently shared with several other Chinese men. There were almost no earlier Chinese settlers who could smooth the way. The Chinese immigrant continued to wear the simple, drab garment he had worn at home.

And—emphatically—Chinese were not made welcome. After 18,400 of them arrived in 1852, whites became afraid that they themselves would soon be outnumbered, and that much hard-to-find gold would go to China with these yellow-skinned hoarders. The whites were often less methodical and thorough and assiduous than the Chinese in their work. One miner complained, "When a Chinaman gets through goin' over the diggin's with a comb, there ain't enough gold left to fill a bedbug's tooth."

Most of the Chinese, though, soon gave up prospecting and went into other and more dependable income-producing work: gardening, fishing, cigar making, lumbering, labor in factories or paper or powder or woolen mills, brick making, salt condensing, shoemaking.

A decade or so later, Chinese, along with—more often separately from—Irishmen, supplied much of the manual labor for the building of the first transcontinental railroad. The monumental feat was completed between 1864 and 1869; with today's work habits and labor-saving machinery and computers it would take much longer. General Grenville M. Dodge, chief engineer for the project, wrote a book about it, *How We Built the Union Pacific Railway*. Here he comments on labor problems involving two of the major groups of immigrant laborers:

> Between Ogden and Promontory each company graded a line, running side by side, and in some places one line was right above the other. The laborers upon the Central Pacific were Chinamen, while ours were Irishmen, and there was much ill-feeling between them. Our Irishmen were in the habit of firing their blasts in the cuts without giving warning to the Chinese of the Central Pacific working right above them. From this cause several Chinamen were severely hurt. Complaint was made to me by the Central Pacific people, and I endeavored to have the contractors bring all hostilities to a close, but, for some reason or other, they failed to do so.
>
> One day the Chinamen, appreciating the situation, put in what is called a "grave" in their work, and when the Irishmen right under them were all at work let go their blast and buried several of our men. This brought about a truce at once. From that time the Irish laborers showed due respect for the Chinamen, and there was no further trouble.

Maybe there was no further trouble, but the rivalry did not stop. To celebrate the finish of the huge construction job, a special wooden tie, made of California laurel and highly polished, was inscribed with a silver plate that read "The last tie laid on the completion of the Pacific Railroad, May 10, 1869." It was to be nailed into place with a spike made from California and Nevada gold and a second spike made from Montana and Idaho silver. The dignitaries were in place and the ceremony was about to begin. But the polished tie was missing. The Irish searched frantically for it, because they had anticipated the honor of carrying it in. But then, as one account says, four "meek and mild Celestials" came marching in, the tie shining on their shoulders.

As California's population grew, so did the Chinese component. Whenever there was a shortage of jobs among whites, the Chinese were blamed. Hostility increased and was often bitter. Congressmen Edwin R. Meade, for instance, told the Social Science Association in 1877 that a Chinese was

> a mere animal machine, performing the duties in his accepted sphere, punctually and patiently, but utterly incapable of any improvement. . . . Coolie labor means to white labor starvation, almshouses, prisons filled, and, lastly, capital wasting itself.

The coolie, Meade went on, is "devoid of conscience," inveterately untruthful and dishonest and unreliable, and comparable to "the wild African fresh from his native jungle."

As I write I have before me a small book published in 1882. Its title is *History of the Capture of California and Oregon by the Chinese, A.D., 1899*. Its author is named as "Robert Woltor, a survivor." It explains that there were so many Chinese in China that they could overrun the United States, and depicts in sometimes hideous detail the use of poisons and other vile means by which hordes of Chinese captured the West Coast.

Partly because of alarmists like Meade and Woltor, Congress passed in 1882 a Chinese Exclusion Act which effectively put an end to Chinese immigration for decades to come. Only occasionally since that time have we received in one year more than two thousand Chinese immigrants.

Chinese Americans have as a rule refuted and by example rebuked those who opposed them a century ago. Although there have been internecine tong wars and some addiction to narcotics, in general the Chinese have had remarkably low crime rates, have often been successful as small shopkeepers, and in some instances have distinguished themselves in the biological and physical sciences. For example, Tsung-Dao Lee and Chen Ning Yang, at ages thirty-one and thirty-five, won a Nobel Prize in physics in 1957. A look at the catalog of any major American university is very likely to reveal professors with Chinese names in departments of science and mathematics and in other departments as well.

Most Chinese Americans now congregate mainly in the Chinatowns of large cities, and tend to remain aloof from other ethnic groups. There are a page and a half of Wongs in the Manhattan telephone directory, most with addresses on Mott street and other southern streets of the borough. Los Angeles lists almost two pages of Wongs, but Indianapolis has barely a dozen entries for that name. Among all San Francisco surnames, Wong is the fifth most common, and Lee, which may be either Oriental or Caucasian, ranks third although in the nation it is only thirty-fifth.

Most of the surnames of Chinese Americans are of Cantonese origin, mainly because Hong Kong, the usual port of embarkation for emigrants, is far from northern or western or even central China but close to Canton.

Although variations in the Chinese language are so great that generalizations are unsafe, it does consist primarily of monosyllables and makes considerable use of tonal differentiation. A Chinese written character consists basically of a semantic (meaning) component and a phonetic (pronunciation) component, neither of which shows up very well in our transliterations. Surnames, of course, are also single syllables. The total number of Chinese surnames is not large—perhaps a thousand—so in an American Chinatown hundreds of persons named Chew or Ling or Won or Wu or Toy have no family relationship but share the name only by chance.

The Western classification of surnames as patronyms, place names, and so on breaks down with Oriental names. Chinese names are often translatable as adjectives and hence perhaps could be called descriptives, but even these do not refer to personal skin coloration or other physical attributes so commonly named in the West. A few names seem in their origin to have referred to places, very few to occupations.

Here are the meanings of some common and representative Chinese names as usually spelled in America:

Chan	‹old›
Chang	‹open›, ‹a mountain›, ‹a bow (weapon)›
Chew	‹hill›
Chou, Chow	‹everywhere›
Eng	(a place)
Fu	‹teacher›
Han	‹a fence›
Ho	‹what›, ‹to congratulate›
Hung	‹very›
Kwan	‹to shut›
Le	‹pear tree›
Lee, Li	‹plums›
Lin, Ling	‹forest›
Ming	‹bright›
Ng	‹crow›, ‹person from Kiangsu›
Song	‹to dwell›
Soo	‹to revive›
Teng	‹a mound›
Toy	‹tortoise›
Wang	‹prince›, ‹yellow›
Wong	‹wide (body of water)›

As the name Lee suggests, some names of Chinese origin are identical with those from English sources, but only because of coincidence. Elsdon Smith points out as examples Chew (Chinese ‹hill› but a river in Somerset), Chin (‹increase› or ‹tree› in Chinese but a part of your face), and Wing (‹warm› in Chinese but from the name of towns in England).

Few Indochinese immigrated to the United States until the 1970s. Then, in the aftermath of the Vietnamese War, some 700,000 fled from Vietnam, Laos, and Cambodia between 1975 and 1979, including about 135,000 South Vietnamese who left with the Americans when Saigon fell. Most of the others did not come to the United States; for instance, many who fled from North Vietnam were ethnic Chinese who returned to their ancestral homeland. A total of some 200,000 Indochinese, mostly from Vietnam, did come to the United States.

Many of them came with tales of horror and tragedy. Some had barely escaped from Vietnam with their lives, often leaving behind all their belongings and sometimes their close relatives. Many had spent weeks, even months, on crowded, leaking small boats, not permitted to remain in

Malaysia or other relatively nearby lands, sometimes not even permitted to disembark. Often they had seen friends or relatives drown or die of hunger and thirst. Some were picked up by American or other ships and eventually found a way to our shores.

In 1975 we set up temporary refugee centers for them at military bases in California, Arkansas, Florida, and Pennsylvania, and helped them to find work and housing, and taught them the rudiments of English. Their neighbors, some of whom I know in Pennsylvania, reported that the refugees had a few strange customs and dietary habits and that many of them were unpredictable drivers. But they also reported that the Vietnamese there were pleasant and eager to work. The owner of a shoe factory asserted that production went up noticeably after he began hiring them.

The two states that most often became the new homes of the refugees were California and Texas, with 47,000 and 16,000, respectively, by 1978. Others that "adopted" 4,000 or more each were Louisiana, Virginia, Washington, Florida, Illinois, New York, Minnesota, and Oregon, but every state became home for at least a few of them.

The names brought in by the Vietnamese seemed to their new neighbors to be somewhat like Chinese names—not surprising, since about half of the Vietnamese vocabulary is of Chinese origin. There were some problems in pronouncing some of the names, like Nguyen ‹cause, origin›, Xuan ‹silly›, and Nghi ‹to doubt; to rest; to think; to decree›.

Each component in Vietnamese names is likely to be a word rather ordinary in meaning, so it seems fairly easy to translate them. A complication arises from the fact that many words in Vietnamese are written with one or more diacritical marks over or under the vowels, and that the presence or absence of a mark reveals different pronunciations, tones, and meanings. Ho, for instance, may mean either ‹to cough›, ‹to shout›, or ‹a surname›. (The question "What is your surname?" is written "Họ ngaì lā gì?") To complicate matters further, the context may make a word mean something quite unrelated. An onomatist, then, seeing "Ho Chi Minh" in a newspaper, cannot translate those words without knowing what the original markings and context were.

Here are parts of the possible meanings of a few names of Vietnamese as you may find them, for instance, in the Los Angeles telephone directory:

Ba	‹three; grandmother; poison; residue›
Chi	‹lead (lĕd); mind; to show; elder sister›
Dong	‹copper; a pile; to move›
Hong	‹flank, side; red, rosy›
Khiem	‹humble; to need›
Ky	‹to sign; strange; to abstain from, to fear; carefully›
Minh	‹the body›
Pham	‹greedy; to commit›
Thien	‹heaven; to geld; expert; narrow-minded›
Thieu	‹be short, be missing; the minority›
Tho	‹poem; fiber; to breathe; workman›
Tran	‹to overflow; forehead›
Van	‹literature; short; striped tiger; to twist›

The Vietnamese, as well as the much smaller numbers of Laotians and Cambodians, have adapted themselves with unusual quickness to this country, although often their work is different from what they formerly did (former Prime Minister Nguyen Cao Ky, for instance, bought a liquor store in California). Sometimes, too, they have run into conflicts with citizens who felt that their own prerogatives or territories were being invaded—in fishing rights, for example. But often their stories are success stories, as is this one reported in *Newsweek* on July 2, 1979:

> Tran Van Hung, 60, an air conditioner and refrigerator repairman at Emory Hospital in Atlanta, proudly displays his job-performance sheet. It rates him "excellent" in four categories: attendance, cooperation, dependability and initiative. . . . Hung's wife, Minh, 55, sits next to him in her starched uniform. . . . Their five children are in high school or college and are "A" students. The Tran family left Saigon aboard a fishing boat in October, 1977, and recently they celebrated the first anniversary of their

arrival in the U.S. In halting but poetic English, Hung declares, "We are shrubs, planted in a new place, needing care and water to grow again."

President Jimmy Carter had said the same thing less poetically a year earlier:

> Refugees are the living, homeless casualties of our world's failure to live by the principles of peace and human rights. To help them is a simple human duty. As Americans, as a people made up largely of the descendants of refugees, we feel that duty with special keenness. . . . I hope we will always stand ready to welcome more than our fair share of those who flee from their homelands because of racial, religious, or political oppression.

33

THE JAPANESE AND THE KOREANS:

Meetings of East and West

DURING World War II Pearl Buck wrote a short story, "The Enemy," that attracted some unfavorable attention because its central character did not conform to the current and then-understandable stereotype of Japanese as vile little yellow devils with buck teeth, malevolent grins, and no redeeming features.

The story takes place in Japan during the war. Dr. Sadao Hoki, who received his medical education in the United States, saves the life of an American soldier, an escaped prisoner of war, at considerable risk to himself and his family. At one stage in the story the young American says, "I guess if all the Japs were like you there wouldn't have been a war." The story ends with the doctor looking out into the darkness into which the soldier has gone.

And into his mind, although without reason, there came other white faces he had known—the professor at whose house he had met [his future wife] Hana, a dull man, and his wife had been a silly talkative woman, in spite of her wish to be kind. He remembered his old teacher of anatomy, who had been so insistent on mercy with the knife, and then he remembered the face of his fat and slatternly landlady. He had had great difficulty in finding a place to live in America because he was a Japanese. The Americans were full of prejudice and it had been bitter to live in it, knowing himself their superior. How he had despised the ignorant and dirty old woman who had at last consented to house him in her miserable home! He had once tried to be grateful to her because she had in his last year nursed him through influenza, but it was difficult, for she was no less repulsive to him in her kindness. But then, white people were repulsive of course. It was a relief to be openly at war with them at last. Now he remembered the youthful, haggard face of his prisoner—white and repulsive.

"Strange," he thought. "I wonder why I could not kill him."

Perhaps Pearl Buck was saying only that kindness begets kindness. Or maybe she was dramatizing, through the doctor's feeling of revulsion toward the man he was saving, the human tendency to distrust and dislike whoever seems very different from oneself. Or maybe she was saying that spending even a few years in the United States may permanently influence a person.

The tendency to distrust and dislike those who are "different" has shown itself repeatedly in American immigration statutes, with laws written expressly to exclude Chinese or Japanese or some other group, or to reduce the proportion of Italians or eastern Europeans or someone else.

There is no official record of Japanese immigrants' coming to America before 1861, mainly because until 1866 any Japanese who tried to leave his native land could be executed. One Japanese did arrive somehow in 1861, and 596 passports were issued between 1868 and 1875. By 1884 a few thousand Japanese were sailing to Hawaii to work on the pineapple plantations. When Hawaii became an American territory in 1898, the 60,000 Japanese who were there could leave for the American mainland without a passport if they wished.

In 1900, some twelve thousand of them did just that, and Californians were alarmed. Murmurings about the "yellow peril" became shouts on the front pages of the Hearst papers and some others.

Perhaps few people noticed another news story that same

year, to the effect that one Zintara Yamada was so completely revolutionizing truck gardening in California that each acre of land was tripling or quadrupling the amount of food grown on it.

And perhaps two years earlier, at the beginning of the Spanish-American War, few noticed that seven Japanese crewmen were among those killed when the battleship *Maine* was sunk in Manila harbor. They were the first of many Japanese who would someday die for their adopted country.

Even including the losses of white civilians and service personnel at Pearl Harbor on the day of Japan's unforgivably treacherous attack in 1941, 80 percent of Hawaii's World War II dead and 88 percent of the wounded were Japanese Americans: Issei (first generation), Nisei (second), or Sansei (third). In that war the most decorated of all American service units was a Nisei group, the 442nd Regimental Combat Team.

The Japanese language has more than 100 million speakers, mostly in Japan. It appears unrelated to any other language with the possible exception of Korean. It uses Chinese pictograph characters and distinguishes the *kanji,* the nouns, verbs, and adjectives that carry most of the meaning, from the *kana,* which indicate suffixes, connectives, and the like. Each *kana* represents a syllable rather than a word; therefore Japanese may be said to have a syllabary rather than an alphabet. Each syllable ends in a vowel sound.

Most Japanese surnames consist of two parts, not necessarily related in meaning, that were combined centuries ago by people who happened to like the sound or the connotations of the combination. The same component may be used in many names. For example, a character transliterated *ta* or *da* means ‹rice field› and appears in these names as well as many others:

Arita	‹have, rice field›	Iwata	‹rock, rice field›
Fujita	‹wisteria, rice field›	Kuroda	‹black, rice field›
Fukuda	‹good fortune, rice field›	Morita	‹forest, rice field›

Furuta	‹old, rice field›	Tagawa	‹rice field, river›
Hirata	‹flat, rice field›	Tanabe	‹rice field, side›
Honda	‹base, rice field›	Tanaka	‹rice field, middle›

As those examples show, a given component, like *ta,* may appear in either the first or the second position.

Here is a do-it-yourself list of the meanings of some other frequent components of Japanese names:

fuji *or* tō	‹wisteria›	mura	‹village›
gawa *or* kawa	‹river›	naka	‹middle›
hara *or* no	‹field›	o	‹little›; ō ‹large›
hashi	‹bridge›	oka	‹hill›
hoshi	‹star›	saka	‹slope›
iwa	‹rock›	saki	‹headland, cape›
kami *or* ue	‹upper›	shima	‹island›
ki	‹tree›	shita	‹below›
kita	‹north›	suzu	‹bell›
kuchi *or* guchi	‹mouth›	ta *or* da	‹rice field›
marui	‹round›	toyo	‹plentiful›
matsu	‹pine›	wa	‹peace›
moto	‹origin›	yama	‹mountain›

Using some of these components you find, for instance, that Suzuki means ‹bell, tree›, that Toyota means ‹plentiful, rice field›, or that the place name Fujiyama means ‹wisteria, mountain›. The language has, of course, hundreds of other such components.

At various times China, Russia, and Japan have all tried to control Korea. From 1894 until the end of World War II, Japan held the reins. Its rule was harsh, extending so far as to attempt to impose the Shinto religion, to prevent the study of Korean history, and to force the adoption of Japanese names. Following the war the United States and Russia agreed in effect to the division of the nation into the present independent South Korea and the Communist-dominated North Korea.

A few Koreans managed to get to Hawaii in the nineteenth century, and a few more to the American mainland. But numbers were seldom large despite a desire to escape continued oppression. Mexico attracted some Koreans at about the turn of this century, and a Korean Cuban, Hai-Young-Yi of Havana, imported 288 of his former countrymen to work the sugarcane.

Korean students began coming to the United States between 1899 and 1909. About half of them found ways to remain after they got their education. The numbers increased from 1910 on. Students who asserted that they were fleeing the Japanese were allowed to enter without passports.

Warren Kim, in *Koreans in America,* published in Seoul in 1971, says that the immigrants were almost always poor:

> The Koreans who came to the United States early in the twentieth century as immigrants or students landed with a pair of empty hands [and] had to work for a living as laborers on the farms, railroads, fisheries and mines. Those in the cities worked as cooks, kitchen helpers, waiters, house-boys, and janitors. Some had small businesses such as restaurants, vegetable stands, barber shops, second-hand furniture stores, rooming houses, groceries, but none had sufficient capital.

They did not have sufficient female companionship, either. The solution, which other Orientals and some white groups found, too, was picture brides. The first of these whose name we know was Sara Choi, who came to Honolulu in 1910 to become Mrs. Nai-Soo Yi. They had never met, but Yi had paid a go-between to secure pictures and other information concerning possible Korean brides, had liked Sara's picture, and sent her the money to join him. In the next few years, in Hawaii and on the mainland, there were about a thousand Korean picture brides. For some reason, unclear to me, the Hearst papers and large segments of the American public thought that such an approach to the altar was so shameful that it should be legally banned.

By 1948 there were still only about 10,000 Koreans in the

United States. The pace picked up during and after the Korean War in the 1950s. Some American service personnel married Koreans, and America also showed considerable willingness to accept Korean expatriates, several thousand of whom have come over each year. Some cities, especially on the West Coast, have fairly large Korean enclaves; Los Angeles, which has about 1,300 Kims in its phone book, has a small, young college, called California International University, many of whose faculty and students are Korean.

The Korean language may be distantly related to Japanese, but not to Chinese, even though it makes use of Chinese characters as well as its own twenty-five-letter alphabet. Because of its proximity to China it has borrowed many Chinese words, including surnames.

Kim is the most common Korean name. "Every other Korean is named Kim," an American serviceman said not quite accurately. It means ‹gold›. Among names that are both Chinese and Korean are the following:

Chang	‹constantly›	Ko	‹yellow›
Chin	‹to grasp›	Kong	‹hole›
Cho	‹draw a bow›	Kwak	‹rampart›
Hwang	‹yellow›	Kwan	‹to shut›
Kang	‹one from a river or bay›	Li	‹black›

The war news from Korea in the 1950s was filled with such names and with other monosyllables like Rhee, Ahn, Shin, Yu, Yun, Ser, Park, and Pak. And when the war finally droned to a close in seemingly interminable negotiations, a bright comic drama called *M. A. S. H.* filled the theaters and then, starring Alan Alda, became one of television's finest series. Although concentrating on the troubled lives of American medical personnel in a war they could not understand, it brought to the American public occasional compassionate glimpses of the Korean people in a war that most had never wanted. The Koreans in *M. A. S. H.* were ridiculed as "gooks" by a few, and there was occasionally a girl willing to exchange her body for a bowl of soup for her ailing child. But mainly the American viewers saw a gentle people, dreadfully poor, usually uneducated, not knowing how to escape from one of the dozen corners that the rest of the world too often tramps across.

Part V

CHANGING NAMES IN AMERICA

34

Names Don't Stay the Same

LOUIS ADAMIC, born in the Slovenian section of what was the Austro-Hungarian Empire but is now in part Yugoslavia, once wrote a factually based story, "The Importance of Being Kobotchnik," about Mr. Kobotchnik and his dog. The dog, which formerly had belonged to a Finn, was named after a famous Finnish runner, Nurmi, but Mrs. Kobotchnik insisted that it be called Buster.

> Well, in a couple of months he looked like he was going to pieces. I'm not exaggerating. I sure am not. His tail was down most of the time. He was nervous and jumpy. His nose was warm. It was summertime, but he shivered like he was cold. He let out little squeals. He was afraid to bark. What kind of dog's life was that? I ask you!

Eventually Buster ran away, back to his first owner, where he again was Nurmi and became his old rabbit-chasing self. Kobotchnik, pressed by his wife and daughter who were ashamed of his old-country name, changed it to Cabot.

Thirty-seven years later his wife was dead and he legally changed his name back to Kobotchnik.

I asked him what difference it made whether one was called Cabot or Kobotchnik.

For a moment he looked at me in helpless silence. Then:

"What difference it makes! To me it makes this difference: now I am happy! . . . I feel like I was before I changed my name to Cabot, only maybe more so. . . .

"What difference it makes! As Cabot, I was not happy. How could I be? I'm not Cabot. . . .

"I was born a Russian. I came from the Carpathian mountains. If that's not the best place to come from, I'm sorry, I can't help it, but that's where I come from, so my name is Kobotchnik. I feel good now. When I was a Cabot, I felt awful—like a dog I once had."

Many immigrants and some of their children have been as fond of their names as Mr. Kobotchnik was of his, but many others changed names and never changed back. Writing about Ukrainian names in western Pennsylvania, Stephen P. Holutiak-Hallich says that 76 percent were changed to some degree by no later than the third American generation. Thus the odds were better than three to one that a Ukrainian's surname would not be exactly like his grandfather's. The changes were less than systematic and must sometimes have been confusing. "In western Pennsylvania, father, son, and brother often have different American English spellings of the same surname."

Although this 76 percent is much higher than we are likely to find among most immigrant groups, change of name is by no means uncommon. Sometimes the immigrants themselves have made an alteration or have had to accept it willy-nilly because a customs officer misspelled the name at Ellis Island or because an employer insisted that he couldn't hire someone named Szefczyk but might hire a Sheppard or even a Sefchik. Sometimes, however, immigrants resisted change, but their children or grandchildren considered it a desirable or even imperative part of the Americanization process. Infrequently there was a backlash against change, as when the son of novelist Irving Wallace changed his own name back pler and more common spelling Comstock, and Fergueson or Fergusson also each dropped a letter as they became Ferguson. A Finn named Starkku changed his name to Stark so that he wouldn't be considered "some kind of foreigner" when he enlisted in the army in 1917. Today, with the complications caused by Social Security registration, telephone listings, tax records, armed forces records, real estate and stock purchases, and other advantages of civilization, such informal changes, even when minor, can cause problems, so that a petition to a court is generally desirable.

Several types of name change, besides dropping of accent marks and moderate simplifying of spelling, are common. One of them is translation. So German Braun (which Americans generally mispronounce) changes the spelling but not the original pronunciation by the easy translation to Brown. German Freund becomes Friend, and Schwartz becomes Black. But a judge is likely to advise Herr Schwartzkopf not to switch to the literal translation Blackhead.

Partial translation is also frequent. Wasservogel, literally ‹waterbird›, may appear as Waters or possibly as Bird. Koenigsberger ‹a person from Königsberg "King's hill"› may become King or Hill.

Shortening by amputation of the tail often occurs. The same Koenigsberger might choose to be known simply as Koenig. Kocolowski, the Pole whose ancestor worked at a caldron, becomes Kocol. Lukasiewicz becomes Lukas, Lucas, or Luke.

Beheading is common, too. Our Koenigsberger may select Berger as his name—or Berg, thus chopping off both ends. Many a modern Bach, Baum, Berger, Blum, Feld, or Wald once had Rosen or some other syllable or two at the beginning of his name.

Less frequent is dropping of the middle part, but some Jasons were once Jacobsons, some Linns once Lippmanns.

Some name changers prefer a somewhat phonetic respelling. So Treu ‹true, faithful› becomes Troy, and the Jordan from the South who pronounces his name "Jurden" may

to the earlier form, Wallechinsky. Many Jews who moved into the recently formed nation Israel changed their names to a Hebrew form.

Occasional angry arguments arose between old and young, as this letter to the *Toronto Daily Star* (July 13, 1959) illustrates:

> My father says that my name is just as good as any other surname, and he doesn't want to see me at home if I change it. We argue all the time and this makes my mother cry. I don't want to leave home, but it would be much better for me if I were something like a John Smith. Please tell me what to do.

The reasons for wanting change varied from person to person. If the alphabet used in the immigrant's language was not Roman, obviously some sort of transliteration was necessary. American business and government and the schools simply couldn't cope with names in Chinese characters, or in the Cyrillic alphabet used by many of the Slavs, or in the esthetically beautiful Arabic script used widely in the Middle East, or in any other of the fairly numerous non-Roman alphabets of the world. The solution for these people was to find the combination of letters that came closest to representing the sounds of the immigrant's native language. Often the transliterated name could only approximate the sound of the original. The alphabet we use cannot, for example, represent at all the tonal distinctions so important in Chinese.

With names already in the Roman alphabet there could still be problems with spelling and pronunciation, and it was to avoid such problems that most changes were made. One reason for the above-average proportion of changes in Slavic names is that many of them are spelled with letter combinations not familiar to the older American stock. So Pylypchuk might become Phillips; Derij, Derry; Czop, Chopp or Chepp; Walcsiak, Walsh; Dzeckaeiar, Decker. German names with *sch* were often simplified by a change to *sh* or *s*. Greek names were often cut to a third their original length.

Many early immigrants were illiterate or almost so and simply did not know what the "correct" spelling of a name was. As a result numerous variants might appear in the way they signed, or in official and semiofficial records, and sometimes members of the same family were differently identified. In the abstract for a property that my wife and I own, the name Deere is spelled in half a dozen different ways. These different spellings may be considered unconscious changes. In the 1790 census we find these variants of what may be one name: Swinney, Swainey, Swainy, Swaney, Swany, Sweaney, Sweany, Sweeney, Sweeny, Sweney, Swenney, Swiney, Swinne, Swinny. Twenty-one spellings of Sullivan were recorded in that census, eighteen of Sargent, seventeen of Robertson, twenty of Osborn, twenty-three of Lemmon, twenty-five of Humphrey, twelve of Barkley, and eight of a name as simple as Clark.

Sometimes names were changed out of a desire to break completely with an unhappy past. America represented a new life, new hope, new perspective. Why not enter it with a new name, an "American" name that would have no association with the life forever left behind?

Some immigrants believed, rightly in some instances, that their chances for material success would be improved if their name did not betray their origins. So O'Hallahan might become Hall, or Ghibault, Gibbs. Some of the changes in Jewish names were made for this reason, or for the related reason that a non-Jewish name might reduce the likelihood of unfair treatment or even persecution which many Jews feared even in a land reputed to offer freedom and equal rights.

A few new names were taken because they belonged to earlier arrivals who had become successful in America and whose names were therefore honored and respected. A Frenchman, for instance, might think Lafayette or Fayette "better" than his own name.

Finally, a name might be changed because it was or seemed to be semantically objectionable. Frankenstein might be shortened or altered to something else because of the well-known Frankenstein's monster of Mary Shelley. During the Nazi regime in Germany some Americans named Goebbels or Goebel or something similar made changes to dissociate themselves from the Nazi propagandist. The name Fuchs was sometimes embarrassingly mispronounced. The translation of one Jewish name (cited in an article by Ernest Maass) was "Green Woodpecker"; its owner felt obligated to make a change.

In the United States, legal name changing is relatively easy. It usually requires only a brief court appearance. The judge ascertains the present name, the desired name, and (if he or she is curious) the reasons for change. Denial is rare, and almost never capricious, although if the applicant's choice of a new name seems to be unwise, the judge may say in effect, "Your new name will cause more trouble than the old one. Come back when you have made a better selection."

Apparently the judge did not object when Samuel Gelbfisch petitioned for the almost literal translation Goldfish, but a later judge may have been better pleased when Samuel Goldfish asked for a second change, to Goldwyn. (This man became a prominent movie producer.) A different judge, though, declined to allow a Mr. Lipchovitz to change to the easier-to-spell Lipshitz—perhaps unaware or uncaring that German Lipschitz means ‹one who lives near the linden trees›, and that several dozen Manhattanites have names pronounced like the one that Mr. Lipchovitz wanted.

Some changes require no legal formalities at all. One example is transliteration from a non-Roman alphabet. Another is the dropping of diacritical marks, which are especially common in a number of central European languages but also exist elsewhere. Thus a name like Czech Hořčička, in which the marks indicate an "irregular" pronunciation of the letters, becomes simply Horcicka, which Americans are likely to pronounce in an un-Czech way "hore-sik-a." One justification of such changes is that ordinary typewriters and typesetting machinery are not equipped to set the dozen or more diacritical marks fairly widely used in one country or another. Neither are they equipped for the three extra letters in Scandinavian alphabets, so these need to be substituted for in anglicized spellings.

In the past many people appear to have made slight changes in their surnames without bothering to go to court. Compstock, for instance, may have quietly adopted the sim

sometimes begin spelling it that way. Joseylin or Josslyn may shift to Joslin.

Transpositions sometimes occur. Aron may like Arno better, but Arno may consider Aron preferable.

Occasionally a name may be anglicized in such a way that it still somewhat resembles the original but has a quite different meaning. Thus Mittwoch ‹Wednesday› shows up as Mitford, and Kielbasa ‹sausage maker› may be Keel or Kiel.

Sometimes a person likes his or her given name better than the surname. Ernest Maass mentions a Lutz Rosenthal who became Mr. Lutz, and an Ingeborg Katz who got both a given name and a surname from the first name: Inge Borg.

Names of female relatives, especially the mother's maiden name, are sometimes more appealing than one's own. Maass gives as examples the Cohn who changed to Hahn and the Lemberg who became Bing.

Once in a while an immigrant who made an intermediate stop before coming here was favorably impressed by the stopping place and adopted a name from it. Thus a German Schwartz spent some time in France; once here, he chose the French equivalent of his name, Noir.

British Names

British names in America have undergone fewer changes than any others, mainly because they already conform to the nomenclature common in this country. So there is seldom a feeling that most of these names are odd or difficult.

Nevertheless, some of the British names reported in the 1790 census (a number of which I have listed in chapter 8) have virtually vanished. A few of the families represented by Tripe, Tongue, Savory, etc., may have died out, or almost so, but it seems likely sometimes names seemed so strange or were so subject to ridicule that their holders changed them. Here is an arbitrarily selected list of names from 1790 that have disappeared or become very rare. A few of these, such as Beersticker, may not be of British origin.

1. Anger
2. Beersticker
3. Bloomer
4. Broil
5. Cockledress
6. Coldbath
7. Coldflesh
8. Coldiron
9. Coopernail
10. Cornhouse
11. Crack
12. Diet
13. Drips
14. Duel
15. Empty
16. Hickrynut
17. Hogshead
18. Hunger
19. Huntsucker
20. Lightcap
21. Literal
22. Livergall
23. Mendingall
24. Mush
25. Partneck
26. Peacemaker
27. Pockerpine
28. Quaint
29. Reedhovel
30. Register
31. Salts
32. Scoot
33. Screws
34. Shambark
35. Sharpneck
36. Tallowback
37. Tenpenny
38. Tubes
39. Waistcoat
40. Wallflour
41. Warts
42. Weedingman
43. Willibother
44. Witchwagon

It should not be thought, though, that all odd-sounding names of apparent British origin have vanished. H. L. Mencken encountered the following earlier in this century, although he admitted that some of them may be "clumsy adaptations of non-English names."

1. Mary Admire
2. Oscar R. Apathy
3. Julia C. Barefoot
4. John Bilious
5. Emil E. Buttermilk
6. Keith R. Catchpole
7. E. J. Cheesewright
8. William Dollarhide
9. Christian Girl
10. George Goatleg
11. Irma Halfway
12. Henry Kicklighter
13. James A. Masculine
14. Memory D. Orange
15. Ansen B. Outhouse
16. George Pig
17. Eche Rattles
18. Robert Redheffer
19. Chintz Royalty
20. Julius A. Suck
21. Willy Twitty
22. G. H. Upthegrove

It would be interesting to know whether any of these persons or their descendants changed their surnames. Perhaps they didn't. At any rate the current Manhattan phone book still lists people named Admire, Barefoot, Orange, and Twitty. There are also a Kickliter and a Rattless, which conceivably represent alterations of Kicklighter and Rattles. I've known a Royalty, a Dollarhide, and an Upthegrove.

Hyphenated names, for a couple of centuries common devices in England to indicate an inheritance from the mother's side, are generally changed to single names in this country because of "the ribaldry of the vulgar," as Mencken puts it. He says, "The name of Vice-Admiral the Hon. Sir Reginald Aylmer Ranfurly Plunkett-Ernle-Erle-Drax, K.C.B., D.S.O., R.N. . . . would ruin him in the United States." Even in England, Sir Winston Churchill was seldom referred to as Sir Winston Spencer-Churchill.

Mencken also points out occasional British shortenings or other modifications of pronunciation, citing as examples Callowhill, "sometimes pronounced Carrol"; Norsworthy, Nazary; and (rather unbelievably) Ironmonger, Munger. Also, English and Irish people generally accent the first syllable in names such as Doran, Burnett, Maurice, Moran, Waddell, Bernard, Purcell, Sinclair, and Mahony, but Americans generally move the stress to the second syllable, as they do also with Latino names such as Perez.

Americans also tend to pronounce all the letters in a name, but some Britishers say Bostick for Bostwick and Harrod for Harwood and Crunchell for Crowninshield. Beauchamp, originally French for ‹beautiful plain›, as an English name often comes out something like "beach 'em" in the British Isles but in America causes all sorts of trouble. Some of its owners hold out for the Frenchlike "bo shomp," but others prefer the British version. I've heard persons unfamiliar with the name call it "bo champ," while others, ignorant of French, start it as if they were going to say *beauty*.

Unquestionably many American changes in spellings of English, Scottish, and Irish names arose originally from low literacy and resulted in numerous variations of the same name—some of them imported from the British Isles, others invented here. Many of the altered names have now reverted to a more common form. The 1790 census reported nineteen spellings of O'Bryan, but in the current Manhattan directory I find only O'Brian, O'Brien, Obrien, and O'Bryan—an indication, probably, that most of the variants have moved toward a common denominator. In 1790, sixteen spellings of Olmsted were recorded, but the present Chicago directory gives only three of them: Olmstead, Olmsted, and Onstead. Mencken points out other examples: Leigh and Lea have been largely absorbed by Lee, Davies by Davis, Cowper by Cooper, Baillie by Bailey, Forster by Foster, Colquhoun by Calhoun, and Smyth and Smythe by Smith. Silent final *e*'s tend to fall off in this country, so that Browne, Greene, Graye, Helme, Halle, Goode, and other such names often become one letter shorter.

Irish names with *Mc* are sometimes reduced to Mack. A great manager of a Philadelphia baseball team, born Cornelius McGillicuddy, spent his baseball life as Connie Mack. Other McGillicuddys simply shorten their name to McGill. An occasional McCauley (in its various spellings) becomes McCall ‹son of Cathal, "battle mighty"› or ‹son of Cathmhaoll, "battle chief"›, even though the honored ancestor thus becomes a different man, since the Irish or Scottish ancestor of McCauley was Amhalghaidh or Amlaib. McClenaghan or Monaghan often loses a *g* in America. Many a McMahon or a variant becomes McMann.

In the directories of four major American cities I find only two survivals of the once common Welsh prefix *ap* ‹son of›; in Wales quite a few such names still exist. Both here and there, however, most of the *ap* names have melded, as I said earlier, so that ap Howell, ap Rhys, ap Richard, and so on have become Powell, Price, Prichard, and the like.

Names from the Germanic Languages

A half-century ago Howard F. Barker illustrated with the name Bachman ‹a person from near a brook› what has happened, in greater or lesser degree, to many German names. Bachman was sometimes written Baughman in official immigration records, perhaps by Ulster Scot scribes who tended to spell *ch* as *gh*. Baughman, says Barker, was "promptly misunderstood as *Boughman* (pronounced to rhyme with *ploughman*), and then more easily spelled *Bowman,* which made possible one more shift in pronunciation."

For individual families or family members the name might get stuck in any one of the stages, so that today we find all four spellings. Bowman of course is usually an English name meaning ‹archer› or ‹bow maker›. But today we cannot be sure, without a knowledge of family history, whether a given person named Bowman is of English or German descent or what the "real" meaning of the name is.

The alteration of German names to English or English-sounding forms was frequent. Edgar Allan Poe's paternal ancestors may have been Palatine Germans named Pau. Many a present Green had ancestors named Gruen or Grun or earlier Grün, and some Greenwoods were earlier named Grünewald. Hayman or Haymond, when not descended from an English hedge trimmer, may be derived from Heumann, a German who grew and sold or worked with hay, although the same name can also come from an older German name Hagiman, associated with either hedges or forests.

Mencken names several prominent Americans whose names lost some or all of their earlier Teutonic character: General George Custer, descended from a Hessian soldier named Köster ‹church worker›; General John J. Pershing, whose family name was once Pfoersching, possibly related to German Pferch ‹sheepfold, pen›; and others. The list is greatly extended when we choose people of less renown: Snavely from Schnäbele ‹large nosed›; Pepper and Bloom from their synonyms Pfeffer and Blum; Black or Block from Bloch ‹short› or ‹stupid›; Kline or Cline from Klein ‹little›; Hines from Heintz ‹descendant of Heinrich›; Bower(s) from Bauer ‹farmer›; Young from the synonymous Jung; and so on and on.

I once taught a university student named Knees, who told me that his ancestors had come from a German town called Kneese; he kept the *k* sound in his name: "kuh-neez." A year later I taught another Knees, not a relative, but also from a family who once lived in a place called Kneese; she pronounced her name "neez." The latter illustrated the tendency to simplify rather difficult German words in this country, but the former showed that not every family has gone along with the tendency.

Similarly we have the *oe* that often but not universally changes to *o* or *a:* Schoen to Schon or Shane. Schueller still exists beside Schuler and Schuller and Shuler. The German "broad *a*" almost always gets changed by a family's non-Germanic neighbors to the "short *a*" so common in America; thus Lang, Strang, and Mann change their pronunciations but usually not their spellings. In the name of the Anheuser-Busch brewery commercials the *eu* seems to have lost its German "oy" pronunciation and become "long *i*." Other German vowels have also been changed to sounds more common in American speech, and many *e*'s pronounced at the ends of German words are dropped over here. The umlauted vowels ä, ö, and ü have been regularly replaced by the simpler (for Americans) short vowels or something else. Müller appears as Mueller (first syllable like "mule"), Muller, and Miller.

The name of the Volkswagen car illustrates the problems of the transported *v* (pronounced /f/ in German) and the *w* (pronounced /v/). Few Americans pronounce the word in the German way, "fokes-vah gen," but one may hear "fokes-waggin," "vokes-waggin," and several variants. Similarly German Wagner is everywhere in America pronounced "wag-ner" except by the musically knowledgeable, Vogel ‹birdlike› is pronounced with /v/ unless the family switches to an *f* spelling, and Weis or Weiss is so steadily pronounced with /w/ that many a family has given up and changed the name to Wise or White.

Translations of German names are frequent. Bach becomes Brook(s); Koch, Cook; Bischof, Bishop; König or Koenig, King; Schaefer, Shepherd or Sheppard or a variant; Schneider, Taylor; Jaeger, Hunter; Zimmermann, Carpenter. Perhaps most such translations are occupational names, but some are descriptive, as when Kurtz and Lang become Short and Long, or Fuchs becomes Fox. Sonntag often becomes Sunday.

The Pennsylvania Germans made many changes that were not common elsewhere. Donald Yoder has written of what he calls the "dutchifying" of German names, and has suggested that the spellings they adopted corresponded to their own dialectal pronunciations. Among Yoder's examples are these:

a to *o*	Sp*a*hn to Sp*o*hn
au to *aw*	L*au*ffer to L*aw*ver
au to *o*	St*au*ffer to St*o*ver
e to *a*	Sp*e*ngler to Sp*a*ngler
ei to *oi* or *oy*	M*ei*er to M*oy*er
eu to *ei*	Kr*eu*zer to Kr*ei*tzer
i to *a*	H*i*rsch to H*a*rshbarger
oe to *e*	G*oe*tz to G*e*tz
ue to *e, ie,* or *i*	Z*ue*richer to Z*e*rcher, K*ue*fer to K*ie*ffer, G*ue*ngerich to G*i*ngerich
b to *v*	Ger*b*er to Gar*v*er
g to *k* or *k* to *g*	*G*intner to *K*antner, *K*reider to *G*reider
ig to *ich*	Neid*ig* to Neid*ich*
p to *b* or *b* to *p*	*P*ressler to *B*ressler, *B*itsche to *P*eachy
t to *d*	*T*ressler to *D*ressler

The names of the Amish, a small conservative religious sect originally from southern Germany, provide an interesting footnote to German names—not because they changed but because they often did not. In an article about them, Elmer L. Smith tells of the frustration of a rural mail carrier in southeastern Pennsylvania among whose patrons were 437 named Stoltzfus (which may mean either ‹one who walks with a limp› or ‹one who walks proudly›). In fact, throughout their territory over a fourth of all the Amish are called Stoltzfus, Smith says, and only 14 names make up over 90 percent of the total. One study gives this order for the top 10: Stoltzfus, King, Beiler, Fisher, Lapp, Zook, Esh, Glick, Riehl, and Smucker, although farther west Graber, Schwartzendruber, Troyer, Hershberger, Coblentz, Schwartz, and Burkholder get into the act.

Why so few names among the Amish? They were a small group to begin with, and hence had few surnames. They married only within their own sect, and they did not try to make converts; therefore they added no names from the "outside."

But even in this conservative and self-isolated community, names have not remained constant in spelling and, presumably, pronunciation. King, second most popular, was almost certainly once König; Fisher assuredly had a *c;* Glick must have been Glück ‹lucky›.

Concerning names from the Netherlands, Mencken commented that after the fall of New Amsterdam, some of the

> wealthier and more resolute . . . dug in up the Hudson . . . and in consequence a number of their names survive to this day, along with some of their money—for example, *Van Rensselaer, Stuyvesant, Ten Eyck,* and *Schuyler.* But the lesser folk were helpless, and in a little while most of the *Kuipers* were *Coopers,* nearly all the *Haerlens* were *Harlands,* and many of the *Van Arsdales, Van de Veers,* and *Reigers* were *Vannersdales, Vandivers,* and *Rikers.*

Later a Dutch Prins was likely to bow to his new environment and become Prince, and the more humble Werkman changed a letter to become Workman. Dutch Koning, like its German cognate, became King. Huisman became Houseman, and names that Americans thought unpronounceable, like Nieuwhuis and Christaanse were simplified to forms like Newhouse and Christian(s). The Van Roosevelts, like many other Dutch families, dropped the *Van;* doing so may have helped one or two of them in an election. Bomgaert switched to Bongart or Bogard or a variant, Lammaerts to Lambert, Concklijn to Conklin(g), Boetcher to Butcher.

The Scandinavians, too, brought to this country linguistic features that the dominant British stock could not or, more likely, would not cope with. The barred *o*'s, the occasional ligatures of *a* and *e,* and the diacritical markings of course were not even considered for retention. Various combinations with *j (sj, bj, fj, hj, lilj)* didn't last long in most places, although Minnesota and Wisconsin directories, among others, still reveal an occasional Bjork ‹birch›, Bjorklund ‹birch grove›, Bjornson ‹son of Bjorn, "bear"›, Fjeld ‹hill, mountain›, Fjord, Hjelmstrom ‹helmet, stream›, Liljegren ‹lily, green›, Ljungholm ‹heather, hill or island›, Sjostrom ‹sea, stream›, etc. Most such names have been anglicized, however, perhaps with a change of meaning, to names like Burk, Field, Helm or Helmstrom, Lilly, or Young; sometimes the *j* was merely dropped so that Fjord, for instance, became Ford. Since most Scandinavians had not long had possession of inherited surnames, they may have felt less attachment to them than did some other people.

In fact, many early Scandinavian immigrants had followed the custom, in their homelands, of using the father's given name as a surname: to refer to an earlier example, the son of Lars Olson might be Hans Larson. In the United States such a change every generation was anathema to tax collectors, lawyers who drew up wills and contracts, and record keepers in county courthouses. So Hans Larson was pressured to make sure that all his children bore the name Larson, with not a Hanson in the lot.

Translation of some Scandinavian names also occurred but was relatively unlikely when there were no problems in pronunciation. In Minnesota, for instance, I taught several Eklunds but no Oakgroves or even Oaklands. Dahl ‹valley› and Dahlstrom ‹valley, stream› tended to stay put, although one girl named Doll told me that her family's name had once been Dahl. Nygren sometimes becomes Newbranch but usually is not changed. Actress Anita Ekberg would probably not have seemed any more attractive to anyone as Anita Oakhill.

Among patronyms the frequent *ss* (Lars + son = Larsson) has generally lost an *s:* Svensson is usually Svenson or even more often Swenson in this country, Olsson is Olson, and so on. Some families have changed *-sen* to the more common *-son,* although the reverse has also happened, especially in communities with many Danes.

Knutson has sometimes been altered to Newton. Örnberg may become either Ornberg or Earnberg. Nilson often shifts to the more common Nelson, Karlson to Carlson. And in a small attempt to approximate the Swedish pronunciation, Kilgren is sometimes respelled Chilgren.

Greek and Romance Names

Writing about changes in Greek names, James Alatis commented,

> . . . there are some names which defy classification. How a man named Zikopoulos came to adopt a name like Marion, or Tzitzikos came to be Murton, and Taularides came to be Curtis, is a question the answer to which can only be conjectured.

Many Greek Americans have made no changes at all in their names, except those forced on them by transliteration from the Greek alphabet or by the American insistence upon "flat *a*" or other sounds not customary in Greek. In a metropolitan directory are still hundreds of names like Papagiannis or others starting with *Papa-* or *Pappa-,* hundreds more ending in *-poulos,* and other hundreds scattered among Alexakis, Tsokolas, and others recognizable in modern Athens.

Perhaps even more Greeks, however, have changed their names than have left them intact. When under Turkish rule, many Greeks increased their admiration for the priests who were often political as well as spiritual leaders, and in fond recollection many Greeks in this country wanted to honor or continue honoring the *papa* ‹priest›. So there's a column of people named Pappas in the Chicago directory, a similar number in Manhattan, a quarter of a column in Los Angeles. Most of these persons, or their parents or grandparents, no doubt once had longer names starting with *Papa-;* others may have changed to Pappas from something quite different. When a young man named Lambros A. Pappatorianofillosopoulos was inducted into the army a newswriter commented, ". . . word may get around before he is long in the army that he'd answer if called Pappas or even Mr. Alphabet."

Shortenings include Alex from Alexopoulos, Leon from Leontsines, Anast from Anastopoulos, and Poulos or Polis or Poles from any Greek name ending in *-poulos.* Shortening is sometimes accompanied by an anglicization that completely disguises the name. So Adamontides may become Adams; Skoularinas, Schooley; Filiopoulos, Phillips.

Ts, often pronounced in Greek with a sound like that of English *ch,* sometimes comes to be written in that way, so Tsiriakos may show up as Chirakis, Tsarlitos as Charlitos, Tsikitas as Chikitas.

Translation of sorts also occurs. Alatis gives as examples Peterson from Petrakis (although writer Mark Petrakis has done well without a change), Golding from Chrystoules (from *chryso* ‹golden›), and Brilliant or Bright from Foteinos ‹luminous›. Some people named Masters were once Mastorides; some Diamonds, Diamantides.

Names from the Romance languages have tended to remain largely unchanged except for the inevitable small variations in pronunciation and the equally inevitable loss of diacritical markings, such as the French cedilla, circumflex, and accent indicators.

In places where French people were not numerous, they sometimes did consider it advantageous to change their names. Today some American families with unremarkable names like White or Miller can trace ancestry back to French Le Blanc or Meunier. Mencken gives the examples of Woods for Dubois, Drinkwater for Boileau, Larch for L'Archevêque ‹archbishop›, Larraby for La Rivière ‹the river›, Shampoo for Archambault, Benway for Benoit, Lovewear for Lavoie, Lashaway for La Joie, Goochey for Gauthier, and Shackway for Choquette.

One French name, Bonne Pas ‹good step› was changed to Bon Pas, then to Bumpus, and then to Bump (not much of an improvement). A L'Estrange family became successively Streing, Strange, Strang, and Strong.

Spanish names generally have only two or three syllables and do not have the silent letters and the nasals that often make French names difficult for Americans to pronounce. As a result, changes in the spelling of Spanish names are relatively infrequent. However, the mother's name (the last of the three Spanish names) is almost always dropped in America or switched to the medial position. Thus Manuel Perez y Garcia tends to become Manuel Perez or Manuel Garcia Perez.

Portuguese names are changed more often, mainly because the Portuguese in the United States are fewer in number than the Spanish and often are greatly outnumbered by other national groups wherever they settle. Also, Portuguese pronunciation is harder for most Americans to master than is that of the Spanish. The Portuguese patronymic ending *-es* sometimes causes confusion, as when Lopes (equivalent to Spanish Lopez) is mispronounced to rhyme with *ropes*.

Mencken, expressing his indebtedness to John R. Reinecke, gives the following examples of

> common Portuguese surnames [that sometimes] undergo radical changes in spelling and pronunciation: Roach for Roche, Marks for Marques, Perry for Perreira or Pereida, . . . Martin for Martines, Morey or Morris for Moreira, Cole for Coelho, Sylvia for Silva, Jordan for Jordaõ, and Rogers for Rodrigues. Sometimes a name is translated, as when Silva becomes Wood or Forest, and Reis, King.

Italian names, like Spanish, are not often changed, although long, unwieldy names are exceptions. Francescone may become Frank or Francis, Gianpietro sometimes is shortened to Pietro or anglicized to Peters, Olivieri loses a couple of syllables as Oliver, and Ghilarducci may become Gaylord. Occasionally a spelling is changed to provide a pronunciation hint for the non-Italian: Ameche for Amici, Galliano for Gagliano, Matza for Mazza. The final vowel, characteristic of so many Italian names, may give way to *s* or be dropped: Alberts for Alberti, Martin for Martini or Martino, Richards for Ricardi or Riccardo. The prefatory *de, della, la, li,* or *lo* or the like sometimes disappears, so that Di Paolo may become Paolo or be further Americanized to Paul, De Luca becomes Luca or Luke, and Lo Piccolo emerges as Piccolo or is translated to Small or Little. Vinciguerra is translated directly as Winwar, Chiesa to Church, and Casalegno to Woodhouse.

Romanian names almost instantly lose their diacritical marks, and not much later their un-English letter combinations, including the distinctive patronymic suffix *-escu.* So Antonescu may be Americanized to Anton or Anthony, Samojla to Samuel, Vasilescu to Basil, and Noie to Noah or Noyes.

Slavic Names

Theresita Polzin opens *The Polish Americans* like this:

> "Did you know that Doc Flowers is Polish?"
> "Polish? With that red hair and freckles? I'd take him for an Irishman—like me!"
> "I did, too, until last week I found out his name used to be Kwiacarski."
> "How did you find out?"
> "One of my friends who belongs to Our Lady of Częstochowa Church told me."
> "Huh? You must be Polish, too! Are you?"
> "Sure. How did you guess?"
> "You said those two words as smooth as if they were English—his name, I mean, and the name of that church."
> "Oh! Kwiacarski (kvya-CHAR-ski) and Csęstochowa (tchen-stoh-HOH-vah)? That's right. They are Polish. You see, *kwiat* (kvyat) is the word for 'flower.' So Doc Flowers dropped the ending and translated his father's name. The red hair and freckles are from his Irish mother."

An early high-ranking official in Alaska was a Pole named Krzyzanowski, and other persons have held to their Slavic names in America while attaining positions of leadership in politics, science, business, and the arts. Nevertheless the usual tendency, especially among Poles, has been to change names.

Ordinarily these changes have been intended to simplify, but there is one important exception. The ending *-ski* was regarded by many Polish immigrants as a badge of distinction and also as an indicator of the heritage that many of them were proud of. For that reason, many who did not wear a *-ski* in Poland added it on the ship across the Atlantic. Many a Kowal thus became Kowalski. (Sometimes the Russian Smith, Koval, similarly became Kovalsky.) Kramarz or Kramarczyk ‹shopkeeper› sometimes made the slight change to Kramarski, and sometimes a Koziarz ‹goatherd› preferred Koziarski.

In "The Canadianization of Slavic Surnames" Robert Klymasz lists several reasons why many Slavic immigrants or their descendants decided to change their names. In general the reasons are the familiar ones I have already noted: to avoid ridicule or embarrassment, to gain social prestige, to try to hide one's ethnic origin, to escape hostile attitudes, and to get rid of a name that seemed "lacking in distinction or a handicap in business." But, perhaps more among the Poles than any other group, names were changed to simplify spelling and pronunciation.

Klymasz illustrates richly the types of changes that were especially common. The *sz* and *cz* sibilants were very frequently altered. Adamczyk might become Adamchuk or be shortened a syllable to Adams; Chernisz might become Chernish; Korczak, Korchuk. *J* was often replaced by *y* or *i:* Baj (pronounced "by") changed to Bay, Marjasz to Mariash, Hajny to Hayny, which might be revised to Hayne(s), Haines, or another variant.

Sometimes a letter was added to make a name look "more American." Thus after a vowel a *k* appears rather naked to the American eye, so Cybak might stick in a *c* and come out Cyback, Holyk might become Holick. Smal added an *l* and thus became indistinguishable from Small of English ancestry. Polish has a nasal *a,* sounding somewhat like French *on;* to preserve an approximation of that sound, some Poles respelled their names; thus Drazek might become Dronzek.

Often the change of a letter or two would suffice to "Americanize" a name: Bednarz to Bednard, Bonk to Bond, Dach to Dash, Hordy to Hardy, Danych to Danish, Kilar to Keller (to avoid Killer), Pilips to Phillips, Sutoff to Sutton.

Sometimes, however, the surgery had to be more severe. Raczyka had to make several alterations to become Roscoe. So did Bryczka (Bricker), Kolodziejczuk (Kolodi), Hladij (Halliday), Hnatuk (Knight), Tkachuk (Thatcher), Dobruskin (Ruskin), Yaroslasky (Lasky), Skolazky (Kaye), Cocoroch (Roach), Hryhorushyn (Harrison). Adamic tells of an illiterate man named Evanich who could not tell his boss how to spell his name, so the boss wrote it Evans. Thus did the Croatian Evanich family become the apparently Welsh Evans family. Some *-vic*'s and *-vici*'s and *-ich*'s were chopped off, but other families with those endings changed them to the slightly more familiar *-vich*.

Other shortenings and simplifications are evident in Dobovicsky (Doby), Grabowski (Gray), Kuryk (Kirk), Stankewich (Stanky or Stanwick), Bartoszewski (Barto(n)), Bukachewski (Buck), Rychlich (Rich), Boychuk (Boyd), Smilovitch (Smiley), Basarowich (Barry), and Shcherbanievich (Smith!).

When Pitz changed his spelling to Pitts, the sound also changed, for Pitz was pronounced "peets." And when Baran became Baron, the accent shifted away from the second syllable, where the Slavs put it. Similar shifts of stress occurred when Belous became Bellows and Polak became Pollock. Slovak names, however, accented on the first syllable, often have the accent shifted in this country, as is attested by Ivan J. Kramoris, whose name almost all Americans accent on the *mor* rather than the *Kra*. Kramoris gives as other examples Lednicky, Peterka, and Zemanovic, all of which among the Slavs would have first-syllable stress. Concerning the name Jelačič, Kramoris ruefully comments that the Slovaks say it Yélahchich but that in America it comes out Jelássick—a considerable difference.

In contrast, the prominent Slovene American Louis Adamic would have preferred the Slovene pronunciation "ahdáh-mitch," but found that Americans ignored that one and debated only between "ád-um-ik" and uh-dám-ik." But he said in *What's Your Name?* that he was "willing to let the pronunciation establish itself." Since language tends to go its own way anyhow, that seems like a wise decision.

Translations have been comparatively unimportant in Slavic names, but Czornij or Czerny or a variant has sometimes become Black; Melnik, Miller; Muszka, Fly; Svek, Shoemaker; Kovacs, Smith; Popiel, Ash.

One of the sacrifices of Czech immigrants had to be their diacritical markings. In the Czech script an acute accent(´) indicates a long vowel and a chevron (ˇ) above a *c, s,* or *z* shows the pronunciation to be that of *ch, sh,* or *zh;* and ř sounds like *rzh* (which is why composer Anton Dvořák pronounced his name as he did).

R sometimes serves in Czech as a vowel, as exemplified by Krk ‹neck›, but Americans could only guess at how to pronounce a name like Hrncir, so its holder might translate it to Potter or change it to something related only in sound, like Horner. Some of today's Horlicks were Czech Hrdlickas, although anthropologist Ales Hrdlicka was one of many who did not find a change necessary. Sometimes an *Hr* combination was shortened to *R,* as in Hruby to Ruby. Senator Roman Hruska of Nebraska, however, was one who kept the *H.* Also, a vowel is sometimes inserted before the *r;* some Hrubys have become Horubys, and some people named Vrba have become Verba.

Some Czechs settled in America among Germans or Irish and took German or Irish names. Mencken reports the Krejči ‹tailor› who became a Schneider, the Prujín who was next a Brian and then an O'Brien, the Otřáska who emerged as O'Tracy. Perhaps the humor was intentional when Zajíc ‹rabbit› renamed himself O'Hare, or when Sýr ‹cheese› thought of adopting the German name for the product, Käse, but settled instead for the Irish Casey.

Russian names cause Americans comparatively little trouble (except when the same person in a Russian novel is called by six different names), but for one reason or another some Russians have chosen to obliterate *-vitch, -ov, -off, -sky,* or other endings. Similarly some Lithuanians and Ukrainians have deleted such typical endings as *-aitis, -onis, -unis, -vicius, -auskas,* and *-enko.* The Lithuanian endings *-vicius, -auska(s), -inska(s)* were originally Polish, and during the eighteen years of Lithuanian independence (1922–40) some attempts were made, both in the homeland and in the United States, to change to non-Slavic forms. So Antanavicius might become Antanaitis, Antan, Anton, Antony, etc. "In other cases," says Alfred Senn,

> the change went deeper, e.g., when Dzimidavicius was transformed into Daumantas, with the explanation that this had actually

been the original form. Not only surnames of living persons were changed, but also those of historical personages.

Jewish Names

Perhaps the chief reason for the unusually high proportion of changes in Jewish names is the one cited by R. M. R. and Beatrice L. Hill:

> There was no particular attachment to the family name, which had often been imposed from above and which was not used within the [Jewish] community. The bearer did not really care what form his family name had, as long as it fitted in to the system of his new community.

Since many names borne by Jews are German, some of the changes are similar to those made by Germans. Froehlich, for instance, was sometimes translated to Gay, Hertz to Hart, Schoenbach to Fairbrook, Schwartz to Ebon, Blumenthal to Bloomingdale. Partial translations also exist: Braunschweiger to Brown, Rosenberg to Hill, Reichman to Richman. Some names were shortened: Feuchtwanger to Wanger, Herzberg to either Herz or Berg. Slavic Stolar means ‹carpenter› and was taken over in Yiddish but sometimes appears in the translated form.

Numerous spellings may exist for the same name, such as Levy, Levi, Levin, Levine, Levitt, Levitz, Levitsky, Lever, Lewitt, and many other variations, any of which may be changed by some persons to Lee, Lewis, or something else. As early as 1790, as I noted previously, American Cohens used at least ten different spellings.

H. L. Mencken mentions that Jacobson, Jacobovitch, and Jacobovsky are sometimes mutated into Jackson, and that Yankelevitch also sometimes becomes Jackson, for "Yankel is Yiddish for Jacob." He goes on:

> It has become impossible in America to recognize Jews by their names. There are not only multitudes of Smiths, Browns, and Joneses among them, but also many Adamses, Lincolns, Grants, Lees, Jeffersons, and Harrisons, and even Vanderbilts, Goulds, Schuylers, Cabots, and Lowells.

Some of the names that the Jews gratefully shed were originally bestowed by Germans in ridicule: Küssemich ‹kiss me›, Eselkopf ‹donkey's head›, Saumagen ‹sowbelly›. Others were ordinary Slavic names like Ragowsky or Adamowicz, and the Jews seldom had reason to feel affection for these, either.

At Mencken's request Dr. Solomon Solis Cohen prepared a rationale for the countless name changes by Jewish people:

> Why should any Central European or eastern Jew burden his children with a lot of useless and generally mispronounced syllables, that seem to flaunt a foreign flavor? There is nothing Hebrew, Jewish, or Israelitish about these cognomens. They are German, Polish, Russian, Hungarian, etc. If not changed in spelling, they will inevitably be changed in pronunciation. Why not a rational, deliberate change?

In 1898 the *New York Tribune* noted some examples of such deliberate change: Bochlowitz to Buckley (whose son reduced it further to Buck), Freudenstein to Gladstone, and Neuberger to Newburger to New (by one son) and to Berg (by another). And a teacher, unable to pronounce a "family name which was full of twists and turns, and ended with a 'witch,' " told two little brothers that she would call them Holz. "One day the father called at the school to see me about his boys and introduced himself as Mr. Holz! He seemed to be as much at home with the name as though he had been born with it."

Lee Friedman tells of a Jewish family whose members spelled their name variously as Campanel(l), Campanal(l), and Campernal. Gradually and quietly they all became Campbell. Says Friedman, "Often . . . we find Campbell and Campanel graves [in New England] sharing the same family burial lots."

Part VI

E PLURIBUS

UNUM

35

Melting Pot, Salad Bowl, or Compartments?

MICHEL-GUILLAUME-JEAN DE CRÈVECOEUR ‹sad heart› (1753–1813), known also as Hector Saint-John de Crèvecoeur, was born and educated in France but wandered about in the New World and then became a farmer in Orange County in southern New York. A gentle man, he was caught up in the tangle of opposing political beliefs during the Revolutionary War. His wife was from a Loyalist family, but some of his best friends were Revolutionists. In the middle, maligned and persecuted by both sides, thrown into an English army jail, he fled to London with one of his two sons. There, in 1782, he published what became one of the most highly regarded and influential books about the young nation across the water, *Letters from an American Farmer.*

The book, soon published in four more countries, quickly made him famous. It told much about the emerging nation, told it charmingly and sometimes folksy-philosophically. It described the countryside—de Crèvecoeur was a naturalist of sorts—and characterized people like those the author had known as a young and as a mature man.

The third and most famous letter responds to the question "What is an American?" It says that in America "individuals of all nations are melted into a new race of men, whose labors and posterity will one day cause great change in the world." This new race, the author says, must develop and follow principles unlike those of the long-established and more homogeneous nations of the Old World.

De Crèvecoeur's metaphor of the melting pot governed much of America's thinking about itself for more than the next century and a half and is still not dead. Highly popular plays developing the metaphor include *The Melting Pot* (1908), by a British Zionist leader, Israel Zangwill; Anne Nichols's *Abie's Irish Rose* (1924), with over 2,500 performances in New York and uncounted others elsewhere, which tells of the love of Jewish Abie and Irish Rose, who struggle to overcome parental and community opposition to their marriage; and Leonard Bernstein's *West Side Story* (1957), which moves the Romeo and Juliet theme into the ethnic neighborhoods of the then-contemporary New York City.

More scholarly writers, too, conceived of the United States as a melting pot. Marcus Hansen, for one, in such influential books as *The Immigrant in American History* (1940), stated that every national group eventually becomes "amalgamated into the composite American race"—a clear echo of de Crèvecoeur's "new race of men."

Most of our schools, at the insistence of the established community and many of the newcomers alike, have taught in English and helped immigrants to learn English, required flag salutes and pledges of allegiance, and taught American history but seldom that of foreign lands. Business and industry encouraged uniformity, in the name of efficiency. Uniformity of product and of procedures led often to near-uniformity of thought among leaders of commerce.

Since the mid-1950s, however, the melting pot metaphor has been under fire and seems to be shifting. Now, instead, many think of America as a salad bowl, and some, unfortunately I believe, think of it as a box divided into compartments.

The differences are of major significance, and since human thoughts and actions are to a considerable degree determined or at least guided by metaphors, the differences are worth examining.

In a melting pot all the ethnic groups are stirred around as in a modern blender, becoming increasingly homogenized as time passes. They intermarry: De Crèvecoeur said in 1782, "I could point out to you a man whose grandfather was an Englishman, whose wife was Dutch, whose son married a French woman, and whose present four sons have now four wives of different nations." In a melting pot old-country costumes disappear, and then old-country customs. Foreign-language newspapers exist for a while but fade out. The ethnic church often merges with a faith not quite the same. Sczymczak becomes Simpson, and perhaps O'Donald drops the *O*.

In a salad bowl there is of course a mixing, too, but it is less thorough. The lettuce, the pieces of apple and carrot, the raisins—whatever—are still distinguishable despite a dressing that coats almost everything. When ethnic groups are being mixed into the metaphorical salad, they too preserve much of their own identity. There is Black Power, Chicano Power; Project Pole; Kiss Me, I'm Italian (or Irish, or Ukrainian, or . . .). Celebrations of Italian holidays multiply, as do those of Slovaks, Germans, the followers of St. Patrick, and others. Simpson proudly tells others that his family's name used to be Szymczak. Cassius Clay reaches back to a part of Africa to become Muhammad Ali.

Books get written about the salad bowl—some of them excellent. Nathan Glazer and Daniel Patrick Moynihan, whose names indicate that they represent two different ingredients in the American salad, published in 1963 *Beyond the Melting Pot: The Negroes, Puerto Ricans, Jews, Italians, and Irish of New York City,* which quickly went through seven printings and then a second edition, in 1970.

Peter Schrag, in *The Decline of the Wasp* (1971), argued that the old Anglo-Saxon core of America was vanishing:

> The center has begun to disappear, and the action originates at the periphery. Jews and Negroes, Catholics and immigrants: Mailer and Roth, Malamud and Bellow, Ellison and Baldwin; Harold Cruse and John A. Williams; Edward Teller and Henry Kissinger; Hans Morgenthau and Wernher von Braun; Ralph Nader and Cesar Chavez; Bruno Bettelheim and Erik Erikson; John Rock and Jonas Salk; Daniel Berrigan and Philip Berrigan; Paul Goodman and Herbert Marcuse; Abbie Hoffman and Julius Hoffman; Eldridge Cleaver and Malcolm X and Martin Luther King. The 1969 Pulitzer Prize for nonfiction was divided between a Jew from Brooklyn (Mailer) and a French immigrant (René Dubos) and the prize for fiction awarded to an American Indian (Scott Momaday). The targets of the big taunt of the late sixties were Mrs. Robinson, the uptight suburban housewife of *The Graduate* and the Simon and Garfunkel song, and the Middle American square who played golf every weekend, voted Republican and regarded his children as the carriers of his unfulfilled corporate ambitions.

The Rise of the Unmeltable Ethnics (1973), by Michael Novak, opened with these quotations:

> We consistently have fallen for the old melting-pot concepts. But there *never* was a melting pot; there is not *now* a melting pot; there never will be a melting pot; and if there were, it would be such a tasteless soup that we would have to go back and start all over! —Black civil rights leader Bayard Rustin.

> The melting pot was essentially an Anglo-Saxon effort to rub out the past of others. —Novelist James T. Farrell.

> Ethnicity as a something larger than self, making the self a bridge to the past, is very important. . . . Culturally the ethnic groups are now the richest and most interesting. —Critic Alfred Kazin.

Novak treated especially the Italians, Jews, Slavs, and other white ethnics, particularly from southern and eastern Europe. He declared flatly, "There is no such thing as *homo Americanus,*" no "common culture," even though there is an "*appearance* of sameness." Americans have "mainly internal" differences, which derive chiefly from their various ethnic inheritances. "New magazines concerned with ethnicity are springing up," Novak told us; "new ethnic museums and archives, new ethnic curricula, are under way."

In 1977 appeared an excellent comprehensive survey by Maxine Seller, *To Seek America: A History of Ethnic Life in the United States.* "In the 1970's," she said, "the melting pot was being replaced by the idea of cultural pluralism as the key to an understanding of American society." She treated historically such topics as ethnic ghettos, the roles of immigrant women, adult education and other education, and the ethnic press, theater, and literature. Commenting on the children of those who immigrated early in the century, she referred to their names: "Symbolic of Americanization was the changing of many family names: Hershkovitz became Hersh, Bodinski became Boden, Rugero became Rogers. Edmund Sixtus Marciszewski became Ed Muskie."

Looking at the new life-styles of the young in the 1970s, one ethnic parent said, "I feel like a chicken that has hatched a duck's egg." But, Seller observed, although superficialities in life-styles could not be passed on by parents to their children,

> What they could and did pass on . . . were values and priorities, ways of expressing (or not expressing) emotion, subtle preferences, and unconscious practices that affected the texture of life in the home, on the job, and in the neighborhood. Ethnic patterns brought from the old country as "cultural baggage" survived in America if they were useful to the younger generation.

Seller mentioned as examples the close ties within Italian families, the child-centeredness of many Jewish families, the choice of jobs as illustrated by the Greek, Jewish, and Oriental predilection for small business, and widespread Mexican hostility toward other Mexicans who advanced into the middle or upper middle class.

One of the biggest objections to the melting-pot metaphor, I believe, is that already quoted from Irish James T. Farrell: "an Anglo-Saxon effort to rub out the past of others." The English Americans, in on the ground floor and more numerous and powerful than the Irish and the Germans who came in the nineteenth century, ran the schools and most other social institutions and enforced or tried to enforce or at least encourage the same conformities within the immigrant groups that they themselves chose to live with. Later the Irish and the Germans, who had been thus molded, joined those of Anglo-Saxon descent in trying to cram or lead southern and eastern Europeans into the same mold. And almost everybody tried to induce blacks to act like whites, Latinos to act like people from farther north.

Bayard Rustin strikes at the second major weakness of the melting-pot philosophy when he says that it would result in "tasteless soup." If we all had the same interests, likes, dislikes, urges, hair color, skin color, emotional reactions—what a dully predictable world we would live in! We would in effect all be named Smith, but without the variations that now differentiate one Smith from another.

The chief objection to the salad-bowl metaphor—although I think it is closer to reality than that of the melting pot—is that the partial separation it implies can be misinterpreted as an endorsement of complete separation. It then becomes a third metaphor—the compartmented box: blacks in this compartment, Jews in that, Poles in that, Chinese off in that corner, Italians on this side, Spanish speakers here, WASPs there. The problem then would be, as Maxine Seller phrases it, "a dangerous upsurge of tribalism that would destroy the unifying bonds of a common American culture."

Divisiveness, even separation, could result if Americans in general started thinking more largely than we do now in terms of "we" and "they." Canada illustrates the danger in its split between French and English, with recurrent threats of secession by the French, and a sometimes intense dislike or even hatred between representatives of the two groups. Another parallel is in Belgium, with its often rancorous disagreements between Flemings and Walloons. And in the Balkans the Serbs, Croats, Slovenes, Slovaks, Albanians, Bulgarians, Greeks, Romanians, and a few other ethnic or subethnic groups have been lacking in unity through most of history, clashing at a border, warring, overrunning territory, seldom able to make or keep agreements among themselves, seldom able to band together to oppose a common enemy.

Maybe Balkanization could not happen here, but consider this passage from Seller about experiences we have already had:

> Affirmative action programs helped some with Spanish surnames, but it could be argued that these same programs worked against people with Italian, Slavic, or Jewish surnames. Covertly and overtly, ethnic groups continued to battle one another in many areas of American life. Polish and Italian Catholics still complained that the Irish shut them out of positions of influence in the American Catholic Church. Southern and Eastern European groups fought the Irish on the one hand and blacks and Puerto Ricans on the other for control of unions, jobs, neighborhoods, and political machines. Ethnic communities battled one another, and nonethnics as well, for control of lucrative underworld activities such as gambling, prostitution, and drug distribution.

Each year we have a few race riots, large or small, in our cities. Small skirmishes are much more frequent: Puerto Ricans vs. blacks or whites, Cubans against anyone who represents an "establishment" that they think is neglecting them, black neighborhood gangs against white gangs—the newspapers tell many such stories, but residents of some areas can tell many more that are never reported in print.

While still rather unorganized, the ethnic or racial groups cause only relatively small problems. But if strong, militant leaders of a group ever emerge, the consequences could become very serious. They almost became so in the sixties, when there actually was talk of separation, of a separate black nation. What may happen in the future—the near future—when those with Spanish surnames are more numerous than the blacks? Just as Quebec has strongly threatened to secede and become a separate French-speaking nation, it is at least possible that Spanish speakers in the United States may seek some sort of special identity, and that many blacks may renew their own search.

A more likely threat than a split into two or three or more nations is a deterioration into the sort of compartment dwelling that exists in India, which is fragmented a hundred ways by language, religion, other beliefs, economic status, color, even by names. If we should become an India, our power to act as a nation, our ability to agree on laws to enforce them, our strength to build physically and intellectually as we have in the past, our unified defense against outside aggression—all these may be endangered.

As a nation we have accomplished as much as we have because through much of our history we have remembered and followed the slogan "E pluribus unum," even to the extent of imprinting it on the coins we handle daily. We have been and are *one* nation derived from *many* backgrounds. To continue as a world leader, to continue even to exist as a nation, we must still follow that slogan.

My study of American surnames has led me inevitably into considerable reading about the many lands from which the names have come, and into other reading about what bearers of the multitudinous names have accomplished once they were in a place where they could use their varied talents fully. Although in this book I could give no more than a few examples of what representatives of some of the groups have accomplished and contributed, my study has brought me increased respect, admiration, and affection for every group that has come here. Regardless of previous location or condition, color or religious faith, each has done something to improve the lives of the rest of us.

Our one-nation-from-many, our *unum,* our union has worked, most of the time, because in general certain conditions have existed. For it to continue working, similar conditions, I believe, must be maintained in the future.

1. *A common language.* Millions of immigrants got off the boats knowing no more than a few words of English or none at all. They or if not they, their children, set out immediately to learn the language that was most commonly spoken here. They did not ask for special schools or other special help in doing so. They learned English, good or bad, on the street, on the job, in classrooms where almost everybody else already spoke English, from the neighbors, in whatever circumstances they found themselves. (Today they also have

television, a powerful tool for learning a language.) Those millions of immigrants and immigrants' children, one way or another, did learn English—some painfully, some joyfully, some more successfully than others.

But such learning by more recent comers is now threatened. With all good intentions, the federal government, abetted by some groups of teachers, has mandated that schools offer instruction in students' own languages. If a school district has within its boundaries twenty or more students with similar language backgrounds, the district is obligated to offer that instruction or face the loss of federal funds. A sure result, government protestations to the contrary, is a reduced opportunity to learn and use English.

As Henry Catto, chairman of Washington Communications Corporation and a former ambassador to El Salvador, explained in *Newsweek,* ". . . students now have the *right* to be taught not only in Chinese or in Spanish, but also in Aleut, Navajo, Apache, Japanese, Yiddish, Russian, Tagalog, or any of 60-odd additional tongues." Catto foresees catastrophic results:

> By the end of the next decade it is entirely possible that the United States will once again confront the fateful choice it faced in 1860: schism or civil war. The cause this time will be language, and the crisis will have resulted in no small measure from government policy.

A large proportion of America's past successes in science, in manufacturing, in commerce, in peace and in war might not have occurred if communication among Americans had been made difficult by substantial language barriers. A common language is essential if successes are to continue.

2. *Education.* In *The Promised Land* (1912) Mary Antin, a Russian Jew who came here as a child, wrote of her father:

> [Education] was the one thing that he was able to promise us when he sent for us; surer, safer than bread or butter. . . . Father himself conducted us to school [on our first day]. He would not have delegated that mission to the President of the United States. He had awaited the day with impatience equal to mine, and the

visions he saw as he hurried us over the sun-flecked pavement transcended all my dreams. . . . No application made, no questions asked, no examinations, rulings, exclusions; no machinations, no fees. The doors stood open for every one of us.

The Reverend Jesse Jackson is a leader of the many blacks who share the visions of Mary Antin's father. And in New York City and Miami and Phoenix and San Diego and Chicago I have heard Puerto Rican, Cuban, and Mexican leaders talk about similar visions. "Your future is determined right here," they tell the children they see in crowded gymnasiums or auditoriums. "Stay in school. Learn in school. *Spend* your time, don't *kill* it."

America needs those young people. But it needs them educated. Not just to read and write. Not just to excel in basketball or in playing the guitar. They need to be *educated,* as Mary Antin was, to know the past, to understand some of the possibilities of the future.

3. *The work ethic.* It is fashionable in some quarters today to pooh-pooh the work ethic that most immigrants (and natives, too) once accepted unquestioningly. But now some natives and some newly arrived Americans-to-be regard the United States as a place for easy handouts, a place where others must and will support them.

Parasitism, however, is a disease. It weakens the host, but the parasite is even worse off, for it can never be more than a parasite.

My German-Danish-Finnish grandfather could be stern. He used to say, "Dem dot von't vork don't eat."

4. *Respect for one's own heritage.* A few pages back I quoted Louis Adamic's Mr. Kobotchnik, who said, "I came from the Carpathian mountains. If that's not the best place to come from, I'm sorry, I can't help it, but that's where I come from, so my name is Kobotchnik."

Every place is the best place to come from, Mr. Kobotchnik. Every place on the only earth we have. The Carpathian Mountains, which include parts of Czechoslovakia, Poland, Hungary, Romania, and the Soviet Union, is the best place, for their people grow up amidst rugged beauty, they learn to enjoy and to create music, some of them write poetry, they work with soil and with oil wells and in factories, they share with the rest of the world the joys and the frustrations of childhood, of love, of parenting, they dream dreams. They know what a blue-collar housewife interviewed by Studs Terkel meant when she said, "What I'm beginning to understand is there's a human possibility. That's where all the excitement is. If you can be part of that, you're aware and alive. It's not a dream, it's possible."

An adobe village in Mexico can be the best place to come from, and so can Madrid or London or Paris or Algiers or Djakarta or a rice paddy in China, a *padi* in Malaysia.

Heritages differ, but who can say that one is superior to another? Most of us have both heroes and horse thieves somewhere in our backgrounds. Most of us, too, have hard-working men and women back there, and tough and tender ones, and many flowers that blushed unseen, maybe a mute Milton, more than likely a heart or two or a dozen hearts "pregnant with celestial fire," as Thomas Gray put it a couple of hundred years ago.

5. *Acceptance.* Although there have been obvious lapses, Americans' record for acceptance of others has been pretty good. In our salad bowl we permit lettuce, endive, or cabbage, an array of other vegetables, fish, fowl, or ham, apples, pears, pineapple, raisins, or nuts, dressings with names like French, Italian, Greek, Russian—all somewhat stirred together, but each usually still distinguishable if we look hard enough.

A pretty good record. But not *very* good. The term "changing neighborhood" usually implies a lack of acceptance. *They* are coming in, so *we* will move out (and probably that's what *they* want us to do). The Puerto Ricans live where the blacks lived where the Jews or Italians lived where the Irish lived where the Germans lived where the English built the first houses two centuries ago—unless it was somebody else.

Carl Ross, in *The Finn Factor,* gives an example in what happened in a Brooklyn neighborhood in 1977. The same kind of sequence has happened often and in many places.

From the waterfront up the hill from the subway line were the tokens of a new community, a new immigration—store fronts announcing "Se Hablan Español," "Se Venden Ropa," or "Hierramentos," instead of "Rautakauppa," as the hardware store in old "Finntown" on Eighth Avenue announced.

My friend, who had come to America as a child of five nearly a decade before I was born, talked of the passing of the Finnish community with sadness, and of the feeling among the local Finns that the new immigrants from Puerto Rico were intruders whom it was necessary to flee. But she knew that the flight meant the end of a community, of a cultural entity that would not again be reconstructed anywhere else. And that is in urban America the dilemma of the old ethnic communities: to remain or disperse.

Or perhaps: to remain, to go, or to mingle. To go implies rejection: "I won't live next door to someone like *that!* Those people [Check all that apply] are dirty, are foreigners, are dirty foreigners, have too many kids, won't work, aren't our kind, would rather be with their own kind, probably steal anything that's not nailed down, don't talk American like we do, have got funny names."

Acceptance of names is often symbolic of broader acceptance. Again, Americans' record is pretty good. True, we've punished some people for having "wrong" names: laughed at them, talked about having to sneeze their names, called them "Wop" because of final vowels or "Bohunk" because of other endings, sometimes by mistake told Scottish McNeal that no Irish need apply, sometimes denied a job to Polish Spodobalski (which means ‹pleasant and agreeable›) until he changed his name to something we liked.

But in general we've accepted people's names without much fuss. They're here—1,286,556 names—getting stirred around more and more in our big salad bowl. And maybe that's a pretty good sign.

MAJOR SOURCES

Onomastics

Anyone working on American surnames must have ready access to two books by Elsdon C. Smith: *New Dictionary of American Family Names* (New York: Harper & Row, 1973), an alphabetical listing of perhaps 20,000 names, indicating for each the country or countries of probable origin and one or more definitions; and *American Surnames* (Philadelphia: Chilton Book Company, 1969), which discusses and generously illustrates patronyms and the three other major varieties of surnames.

Much less inclusive is L. G. Pine's *The Story of Surnames* (Newton Abbot, England: David & Charles, 1969). Intended for young readers is Eloise Lambert and Mario Pei's *Our Names: Where They Came From and What They Mean* (New York: Lothrop, Lee, and Shepard, 1960). One of England's leading onomatists, C. L'Estrange Ewen, published in England in 1931 his scholarly *A History of Surnames in the British Isles,* which was reprinted in Baltimore in 1968 by the Genealogical Publishing Company. That company has also reprinted several hundred other relevant book-length works, such as lists of early German, Irish, or other settlers in American colonies and states.

Numerous short articles on American surnames from foreign countries have been published in *Names,* the quarterly journal of the American Names Society. Several books on surnames from a specific national or ethnic heritage have also been published. I found especially useful Benzion C. Kaganoff's *A Dictionary of Jewish Names and Their History* (New York: Schocken Books, 1977).

Statistics

Once in about a decade the U.S. Social Security Administration compiles and mimeographs an edition of *Distribution of Surnames in the Social Security Number File*. It is from the latest available (1974) edition of this that I obtained information about the relative commonness of American family names. The booklet lists in numerical and alphabetical order all of the 3,169 surnames registered with the SSA by 10,000 or more persons each. It has two weaknesses: (1) It gives only the first six letters of a name, so that GRIFFIn and GRIFFIth and GRIFFIths, for instance, cannot be separated; and (2) it includes people now dead who were once on SSA rolls, and it cannot include young children and others, such as illegal aliens, who have no Social Security numbers.

Statistics on population and immigration are found in the many volumes of U.S. census reports and are summarized in the annual *Statistical Abstract of the United States*.

In 1932 the American Council of Learned Societies reprinted a study issued a year earlier by the American Historical Association. Reprinted again in 1969 by the Genealogical Publishing Company, this is the definitive *Surnames in the United States Census of 1790,* a statistical analysis of our first census. The U.S. Government Printing Office in 1909 issued the analytical *A Century of Population Growth (1790–1890),* also reprinted, in 1970, by the Genealogical Publishing Company.

General American History

Books on American social history that pay considerable attention to immigration and immigrants include the following, all of which are both scholarly and readable:

Boorstin, Daniel J., *The Americans* (New York: Vintage Books, 3 vols., 1958, 1965, 1974).

Degler, Carl N., *Out of Our Past: The Forces That Shaped Modern America* (New York: Harper & Row, 1970).

Furnas, J. C., *The Americans: A Social History, 1587–1914* (New York: Capricorn Books, 2 vols., 1969).

Handlin, Oscar, *The Americans* (Boston: Little, Brown, 1963). (Several other books by Professor Handlin also pertain to immigration and early settlers.)

Wright, Louis B., *The Cultural Life of the American Colonies, 1607–1763* (New York: Harper & Row, 1957).

The Annals of America (Chicago: Encyclopaedia Britannica, 1968–1977), upon which I frequently drew, consists of 20 volumes of reprints of historic documents, speeches, articles, and other significant materials.

History of American Immigration

I found particularly helpful two books: Maldwyn Jones's *American Immigration* (Chicago: University of Chicago Press, 1960), and, for an account of what happened to immigrants after they arrived, Maxine Seller's *To Seek America: A History of Ethnic Life in the United States* (New York: Jerome S. Ozer, 1977).

Louis Adamic's *From Many Lands* (New York: Harper, 1939) and his *A Nation of Nations* (New York: Harper, 1944) are delightfully anecdotal. Two co-authored books of which Leonard Dinnerstein is the senior author are *Uncertain Americans* (New York: Oxford University Press, 1977) and *Natives and Strangers* (New York: Oxford University Press, 1979). A personalized account by a rather recent immigrant is Ted Morgan's *On Becoming American* (Boston: Houghton Mifflin, 1978). Concerned mainly with the pre-World War II flood of distinguished refugees from Europe is Laura Fermi's *Illustrious Immigrants* (Chicago: University of Chicago Press, 1968); the author's husband, atomic physicist Enrico Fermi, was one of those immigrants, and she knew personally many of the others. Addressed to the young reader is Eleanor Tripp's *To America* (New York: Harcourt, Brace, & World, 1969); I bought my own copy of this and several other books on immigration at the base of the Statue of Liberty. In a now-old book, *In the Shadow of Liberty,* Edward Corsi delightfully recounted the history of Ellis Island (New York: Macmillan Co., 1935). Thomas C. Wheeler's *The Immigrant*

Experience (New York: Dial Press, 1971) is a collection descriptively subtitled *The Anguish of Becoming American.*

Some writers are especially interested in what is happening to second- or third-generation Americans. These include Nathan Glazer and Daniel P. Moynihan, *Beyond the Melting Pot: The Negroes, Puerto Ricans, Jews, Italians, and Irish of New York City* (Cambridge: M.I.T. Press, 1963; second ed., 1970); Michael Novak, *The Rise of the Unmeltable Ethnics* (New York: Macmillan Publishing Co., Inc., 1973), who concentrates on Greeks, Italians, and Poles and other Slavs; and Peter Schrag, *The Decline of the Wasp* (New York: Simon and Schuster, 1971), whose thesis is that the center of power in America is shifting from White Anglo-Saxon Protestants to Jews and to "Negro revolutionaries, Irish-Catholic politicians, respectable *mafiosi.*"

Specific National and Ethnic Groups

Readers interested in following the American lives of a specific national or ethnic group may find much information in a series of many volumes, most of them entitled *The ____ in America,* published by Oceana Press, Dobbs Ferry, New York. Each book is a chronological and condensed but sometimes anecdotal listing that shows historical highlights in each group's attempt to become Americanized. From this series I used the volumes on the following groups:

Blacks	(by Irving J. Sloan, 1968)
Chicanos	(Richard A. Garcia, 1977)
Czechs	(Vera Laska, 1978)
Dutch	(Pamela and J. W. Smit, 1972)
Estonians	(Jaan Pennar, 1975)
Japanese	(Masako Herman, 1974)
Lithuanians	(Algirdas M. Budreckis, 1976)
Portuguese	(Manoel Cardozo, 1976)
Romanians	(Vladimir Wertsman, 1975)
Scandinavians	(Howard B. Furer, 1972)

Other books on specific groups include these:

ARABS

Aswad, Barbara, ed., *Arabic Speaking Communities in American Cities* (New York: Center for Migration Studies, 1974).

Elkholy, Abdo A., *The Arab Moslems in the United States* (New Haven: College and University Press, 1966).

Hitti, Philip K., *The Syrian in America* (New York: George H. Doran, 1924).

BLACKS

Puckett, Newbell Niles, collector, and Heller, Murray, ed., *Black Names in America: Origins and Usage* (Boston: G. K. Hall, 1975).

CHINESE

Potter, George, *In the Golden Door* (Westport, Conn.: Greenwood Press, 1960).

Tow, J. S., *The Real Chinese in America* (New York: Academy Press, 1923).

DUTCH

The Dutch in America, 1609–1974 (Boston, G. K. Hall, 1975).

FINNS

Jallkanen, Ralph J., *The Finns in North America* (Hancock, Mich.: Michigan State Press for Suomi College, 1969).

Ross, Carl, *The Finn Factor* (New York Mills, Minn.: Parta Printers, 1977).

GERMANS

Pittinger, Lucy, *The Germans in Colonial Times* (Philadelphia: J. B. Lippincott, 1901).

GREEKS

Burgess, Thomas, *Greeks in America* (Boston: Sherman, French, 1913).

HUNGARIANS

Lengyel, Emil, *The Land and People of Hungary* (Philadelphia: J. B. Lippincott, 1965).

IRISH

Fallows, Marjorie R., *Irish Americans* (Englewood Cliffs, N.J.: Prentice-Hall, 1979).

ITALIANS

Schiavo, Giovanni, *The Italians in America Before the Revolution* (New York: Vigo Press, 1976).

Moquin, Wayne, ed., *A Documentary History of the Italian Americans* (New York: Praeger, 1974).

JAPANESE

Ichihashi, Yamato, *Japanese in the United States* (Stanford: Stanford University Press, 1932).

Montero, Darrel, *Japanese Americans* (Boulder: Westview Press, 1980).

JEWS

Schoener, Allon, ed., *Portal to America: The Lower East Side, 1870–1925* (New York: Holt, Rinehart, and Winston, 1967).

KOREANS

Kim, Warren Y., *Koreans in America* (Seoul, Korea, 1971).

NORWEGIANS

Blegen, Theodore C., *Norwegian Migration to America* (Northfield, Minn.: Norwegian American Historical Assn., 1931).

POLES

Polzin, Theresita, *The Polish Americans: Whence and Whither* (Pulaski, Wis.: Franciscan Publishers, 1972).

PORTUGUESE

Wolforth, Sandra, *The Portuguese in America* (San Francisco: R & E Research Associates, 1978).

PUERTO RICANS

Fitzpatrick, Joseph P., *Puerto Rican Americans* (Englewood Cliffs, N.J.: Prentice-Hall, 1971).

RUSSIANS

Davis, Jerome, *The Russian Immigrant* (New York: Macmillan Co., 1922).

Manning, Clarence A., *Russian Influence in Early America* (New York: Library Publishers, 1953).

SCOTCH-IRISH

Leyburn, James G., *The Scotch-Irish: A Social History* (Chapel Hill: University of North Carolina Press, 1962).

SOUTH SLAVS

Prpic, George J., *South Slavic Immigration to America* (Boston: Twayne Publishers, 1978).

SPANISH

Gorden, Raymond L., *Spanish Personal Names* (Antioch, Ohio: Antioch College, 1968, mimeographed).

SWISS

Swiss-American Historical Society, *Prominent Americans of Swiss Origin* (New York: John White & Co., 1932).

——— *The Swiss in the United States* (Madison, Wis.: Swiss-American Historical Society, 1940).

UKRAINIANS

Halich, Wasyl, *Ukrainians in the United States.* (Chicago: University of Chicago Press, 1937).

WELSH

Hartmann, Edward G., *Americans from Wales* (Boston: Christopher Publishing House, 1967).

YUGOSLAVS

Govorchin, Gerald G., *Americans from Yugoslavia* (Gainesville, Fla.: University of Florida Press, 1961).

Lovrich, Frank M., *The Social System of a Rural Yugoslav-American Community* (San Francisco: R & E Research Associates, 1971).

INDEX OF NAMES

Parentheses are used to save space in showing some alternative spellings. Thus Com(p)stock means Comstock and Compstock. Abram(ic) (ovich) (ovitz) (owitz) represents five spellings.